POEMS

BY RUDOLPH RAY PORCHE

RUDOLPH PORCHE

NEWMAN SPRINGS PUBLISHING
320 Broad Street
Red Bank, NJ 07701

First originally published by Newman Springs Publishing 2021

ISBN 978-1-63692-402-1 (Paperback)
ISBN 978-1-63692-403-8 (Digital)

Printed in the United States of America

A TREE

There's so many wonderful things about a tree,
That's beneficial for more than me and thee.
They remove carbon dioxide from the atmosphere,
Then emit oxygen, which we value so dear.
Without oxygen, animals could not survive here.
In a tree, birds and squirrels may build their nest.
Off the ground, their locations serves them best.
A shady spot on a hot summer day feels good.
A variety of trees provide fruit, nuts, and sap for food.
Many have beautiful flowers and provide firewood.
Magnolias, crepe myrtle, cherry, and pear, to name a few,
Adorn the lawns, streets, and many an avenue.
Pines, maples, and rubber trees, produce a valuable sap.
These trees, an industrious person may tap.
Other things we harvest from many a tree,
Coconuts, dates, coffee, syrup, and much tea.
A tree provides lumber for construction timber,
Furniture and charcoal for good barbeque ember.
In olden days, wooden ships that sailed the seas
Were made from the finest wood of available trees.
Hardwoods, like mahogany, oak, and teak,
Luxury boat builders and craftsmen seek.
Wood from trees were used to cook and heat,
Instead of electricity, gas, coal, or peat.
Useful and a beautiful sight, many will rightly agree,
Is a forest of many trees, as far as one can see.

—December 21, 2019

A BURDEN

I don't want to be a burden at all,
But that's what I will be if I fall.
So very careful I try to be, you see,
Winter, Spring, Summer and the Fall.

No longer can I run or play ball,
Nor do I take daily walks in the Mall.
I use my "walker" to walk down the hall.

When the phone rings, no matter who does call,
I don't rush to answer, but neither do I stall,
But I won't answer it if I have to crawl.

Too many "crank calls" I get anyhow,
Or it's for money, I'm not a "cash cow."
I know that many people need more than "chow,"
And I've donated to legitimate causes then and now.
Many are "bogus," tho to seem true, they swear and vow.

Some callers are persistent, they have a lot of gall.
If I could catch them, I'd punch 'em in the "eyeball."
I could reach things a lot better if I were tall,
But I'm told not to use a stool, y'all.

—April 5, 2020, 1:00 a.m.

A CHILL OR A COLD

Catch a chill, catch a cold,
Is an old wives' tale, I'm told.
It's true still, especially if you're old.
Precaution is best, even if you're bold.

To avoid sneezing and wheezing,
When the air is damp and freezing,
Be advised, wear a hat and a coat,
Aboard a boat, ashore or afloat.

Keeping your feet warm and dry,
Could prevent a cold, if you try.
Who wants the sniffles and a runny nose,
With watery eyes? No one I suppose.

By using good ole common sense,
One may avoid misery and an unwanted expense.
Prevention is surely better than the cure,
Certainly better on the purse, I'm quite sure.

Be smart, do your part, be wise,
Take precautions before you get watery eyes.

A COLD PLACE

The winters are very severe, very harsh,
The plains look like a frozen marsh.
Breaths freeze in the cold air,
Frosty, very frosty becomes all hair.

Surviving in winter is a chore,
Everyone works harder than ever before.
If feed gets much too low,
Fewer cattle will survive.
Shelter from the cold, they know,
Will keep more of them alive.

Everywhere, blankets and blankets of snow,
Where can the cattle really go?
Frozen solid becomes the creek,
When 'tis water the cattle seek.

The house stays cozy and warm,
There's enough firewood already cut.
Here they're safe and free from harm,
Their abode is merely adobe,
But it's much better than a hut.

The cast iron stove is great,
Many meals cooked they ate.
In it a fire is always burning,

A kettle sitting on top,
Has water that is always hot.
If coffee or tea they're yearning,
They can brew it nonstop.

Every year "cold hazards" they face,
Yet they tolerate such a cold place.
In winter they move at a slower pace,
But they move and they move with grace.

—October 20, 2001

A COP

He's a good respectable cop,
A veteran of the police force.
Beer or liquor, he touches nary a drop.
Crime, he is committed to stop,
By "community watch" which he does endorse.
He wonders why so many people misbehave,
Acting as tho they were raised in a cave.
Why, everywhere there's a "crime wave."

Fighting crime comes at a high cost.
Too much money is wasted, just lost.
The costly "war on drugs"
In many sectors is being fought.
Today, 'tis not only the thugs,
People of all walk, are sought and caught.
Perhaps 'tis the neighbor next door,
"Shooting up," "snorting" or smoking "pot."
Experimenting, "just for kicks," they explore,
Is it more or less, than a few decades before?
Perhaps more but less, he thinks not.

During his many days on "the street,"
Many, many "characters" he did meet.
Never was there a dull moment on his beat,
Steadfastly, he always took the "heat."
He is very professional, very discreet.
He nabbed thieves stealing cars or robbing a shop,
Thugs mugging someone, running from a cop.

Drunks or drug addicts "taking a hit,"
Revelers drinking, not knowing when to quit.
Even youngsters swiping a soda pop.

Now that he's a detective,
Can he be much more effective?
Is he privy to bigger things that matter?
Is he savvy enough to head up the ladder?
He'll be involved in more homicides,
That seems to be coming from all sides.
Every day, somewhere, someone dies,
Of natural causes, are murdered or suicides.

Victims are of different races, gender and ages.
Their obits show up on the news pages.
To solve so many crimes is quite a chore,
Possibly harder than any job he's held before.
His family, he tries not to ignore,
As for the force, he's "true blue" to the core.
He's tough, thorough, dedicated and pure,
Confident and reliable, of his ability he's sure.
Challenges he welcomes and is ready to meet.
He's a good cop, who's hard to beat.
An ideal lawman you're happy to greet,
When you meet him on the street.

—August 6, 2001

A DATE

She did not decline,
His generous offer to dine.
He appeared to be gentle and kind,
And a good man is still hard to find.
That the wine was fine,
Was true, it was simply divine.
Delicious too, was the sumptuous meal,
Warm inside, it made her feel.
The more she ate and ate,
The more she did contemplate.
Would they have a debate?
Later, she and her date?
Would he keep her out late?
Would he continue to be nice?
Or would he resort to some vice?
Would she, or could she, remain a lady,
Or would she succumb to something shady?
Their conversation went a bit slow,
So they agreed to go to a show.
'Twas their first date, they didn't know,
But each wondered how it would go.
They enjoyed the show,
And as it neared the end,
She realized and turned all aglow,
Her honor, she did not have to defend.
He took her home and then she knew,
No longer would she be lonely or blue.
More dates, they would certainly make,
For each other's sake.

—December 17, 2000

A DIABETIC

He's a diabetic,
He's no longer athletic,
He's not very energetic,
'Tis so, so pathetic.

He won't take anyone's advice.
He is playing with loaded dice.
"Check your sugar," he's been told,
"If you desire to grow old."
Being very macho, lo and behold,
He ignores signs and clues, hot or cold.

Never did he or anyone check his feet,
Whether it was rain or shine, snow or sleet.
A blister got infected, wouldn't heal,
Feeling no pain, he didn't squeal.
Given advice he always did scoff,
'Till finally they cut his leg off.

He has totally ignored his diet,
Prefers to eat everything in sight.
Now he is barely able to see,
If not careful, he can run into a tree.

Before long his kidneys did fail,
Remedies tried were to no avail.
They put him on a dialysis machine,

Two or three times each week.
Now he's grumpy and at times, obscene.
'Tis evident that he is very weak.

How long can he last this way?
How much pain can he bear each day?
'Tis very unlikely that he'll get better,
Even if he follows "orders" to the letter.
He waited too long, too late.
It's plain what is his fate.

—September 1, 2001

A FISH

Have you ever made a wish?
Where you could be a fish?
Day and night, swim and swim,
Go anywhere, just on a whim.

Travel with many in a school,
Around reefs, in a lagoon or large pool.
With clear water and food for all,
Just swim, swim and have a ball.

Not a sardine nor a mullet,
Who is apt to end up in one's gullet.
But a swordfish or a big shark,
Big enough to go anywhere and park.
Be it daylight, be it dark.

Be a goldfish, inside a pond outside,
Underneath a shady tree, with plants inside.
Pond lilies displayed with pride,
With other plants providing cover, to hide.

An aquarium, is that okay?
Just swim; gaze at onlookers, who stay,
While food is handed out each day,
But confined in a definite way.

Perhaps a big gar in a bayou,
With much food to swallow, not chew.
No fish is ever large enough to avoid man,
Who'll catch and eat anything he can.

—June 4, 2000

A GREAT FEELING

'Tis great to be alive,
Not to have to arise at five,
To be able to enjoy a weekend drive,
Still be able to actually drive.

As a Senior Citizen, I realize,
To stay alive, is to strive,
To get my body to stabilize,
Not let unwanted changes metabolize.

Modern medicine should be praised,
So much is done today, I'm amazed.
Operations where recovery once was slow,
That usually took a week or more,
Have been simplified, I know.
Recovery now is a day or so,
And patients are less sore.

Today my activities are less,
'Tis not because I need more rest.
I'm less mobile, in fact, I'm a mess.
To detect deficiencies, I take a test,
To repair damages, I do my best.

The many years ago,
That I did actually smoke,
Could easily have, you know,
Caused me to have a stroke.

Doctors detected blockages,
And immediately planned a cure,
Preventing a heart attack, I'm sure.

After my next procedure, I surmise,
That I must necessarily, exercise.
Losing weight, my doctor did emphasize,
Would, my poor health, vitalize.
While decreasing my large size.

—October 5, 2000

A HUMAN'S LIFE

Birth is the act of being born,
It is the phase when we exit the womb.
After many births, a mother may feel tired and worn.
Death is the end of life, the end of all earthly strife.
After death, bodies are buried or placed in a tomb.
Some may be cremated or buried at sea,
Nowadays it's a matter of choice, you see.
Between birth and death is our life span,
This is true of every child, woman, and every man.
We're all born to die, that's true, no lie.
'Tis a certainty that we cannot deny.
Big and small, short and tall, death claims us all.
How long we live, may depend on a lot,
Genes, greens, beans we eat, or diseases we've got.
We freeze to death when too cold, die in fires too hot.
Because of wars, we're bombed or shot,
Or killed by terrorists with an evil plot.
Tornadoes, earthquakes, mudslides, take their toll, I'm told,
Sad to say, on the very young and very old.
Misuse and abuse of drugs, alcohol, tobacco and such,
Accidents, suicides, homicides are way too much.
Plane crashes, shipwrecks, train wrecks, kill a lot, too.
Wild animals, bees, mosquitoes, kill more than a few.
To avoid disasters, people don't know what to do.
Birth, a divine event, a miracle to behold,
Is held in awe, by many, the young and the old.
Sadly, some infants at birth, do die,
I don't deny that some people wonder, why?
Whatever the reason, 'tis enough to make a body cry.

—February 1, 2013

A JOURNEY

We hoist our sails,
Preparing to sail very far away.
O'er horizons afar,
Guided by a distant star.

When prevalent winds prevail,
We'll have an easy day.
Perhaps using a single sail,
To sail into some small, quiet bay.

When winds are calm and still,
And a beach we would assail,
We couldn't see the nearest hill,
We may try and try, to no avail.

Too much wind, such as gales,
Could do damage, tear our sails.
The waves could really toss us about,
No one would hear us cry out.

With luck, we'll reach our journey's end,
Succeed in finishing a trip.
'Tis pleasant, traveling with a friend,
Especially one, that gives me no lip.

—November 23, 1999

A SIGN OF OLD AGE

Mirror, Mirror, I need to know,
Are you a friend or a foe?
What I see in this reflection,
Is it true, or is it a deception?
Has something altered the reception,
That affects my brain and my perception?

My skin, my poor blotched, aged skin.
Scaly, stretched and everywhere it's thin.
Can it be affected outside and within,
Above and below, my chin and my shin,
By what I've done or where I've been?

The idea, this simple notion,
Applying this or that cream or lotion,
Appears to be temporary, at best.
'Tis not a matter of a simple test,
Or Mother Nature doing this in jest.
I must be aging, like all the rest,

Like an oldster in a "nursing home,"
Who is referred to as a "guest,"
But ofttimes may be treated as a pest.
In jest, by an old friend, I was told,
You better have plenty of gold,
So during the golden years, be bold,
Try to fight the heat and the cold.
Be at ease, try not to burn up or freeze.

—December 6, 2010

A TV KISS

Watching a couple on TV kiss,
I thought, "My goodness, what's this?"
He inhaled her upper lip, is this bliss?
Then her lower lip, not a spot did he miss.

Their lips made a smacking, slurping sound,
Without de-lipping, they rolled around on the ground.
This kiss was long, too long, methinks,
'Tis not romantic, in fact, it stinks.

He released her lips then licked her face,
Then her neck, her ears, what a disgrace.
Surely young people don't consider this fun,
Many, I bet, would "hightail it," run.

Kissing on TV is seldom just a peck.
It's usually a "gyration of sorts," by heck.
Women kiss a man and lick a chestful of hair,
'Tis doubtful that there's any romance there.

On TV, few women appear to be pure or demure.
Decadence is portrayed "for ratings," I'm sure.
The appearance of vulgarity seems to be everywhere.
Tho slutty images they project, they just don't care.

'Tis all about money, that's what seems to count,
Anything, anyone, anywhere, some people will mount.
When watching a movie, it's viewer beware,
Point of fact, movie attendance creates this nightmare.

—September 3, 2001

20

ABUSED

Abused infants, of all colors and races,
Pay a very dear price, it does seem.
No matter if they're naughty or nice,
Their punishment, at times, is too extreme,
Broken ribs, cracked skulls or bashed-in faces.

Toddlers beaten and violently shaken,
From their parents are often taken.
Instead of parents assuring they're protected,
The youngsters, by their parents, are neglected.
An abused child's mind may be forever affected.

Out of anger, a child may easily get maimed,
Drugs and excessive drinking is oft claimed,
When in a courtroom the parents are shamed.
When placed in someone's care or trust,
A child's safety and well-being is a must.
A serious violation of that trust may be a crime,
The perpetrator could and should serve time.

When the child gets a bit older,
The abuser may also become bolder.
With a glib tongue he may entice,
The child into some vices, by being extra nice.

The abuser may be a person of high standing,
In the community or even a religious sect,
A teacher or coach that's very demanding,
Or too often, a parent that's much less than perfect.

A child, out of adoration or maybe, fear,
May do anything for people they hold dear.
Abusers, be they sick or just plain mean,
Or, do evil just to be amused,
When caught and if they don't "come clean,"
Must be judged carefully, and if need be, excused,
Since many are also falsely accused.

—August 21, 2001

ACHES, ACHES

Many bones, many muscles, ache and ache,
Is the cause, the medicines that I take?
Is it the bones that years ago did break?
Could it be because I eat cookies and cake,
Fry foods instead of broil or bake?

Perhaps I eat too many substitutes that are fake.
Instead of fish from a river or lake.
Are these some of the errors that I make?
Must I diet for my health's sake,
And more often use the hoe and rake?

Should I replace Corn Flakes with Bran Flakes,
Rib eye steaks with some type of fish cakes?
Earlier in the morning should I awake,
Start to exercise before work at daybreak?

Doubt and confusion may cause me to shake.
Luckily, I'm not in a canoe in the middle of a lake.
I'm at home where good food or drink I can partake.
I think I'll take a break before I make a mistake.

—2016

ACTIVITIES

South Louisiana, my stomping ground,
Has much to offer, I've found.
No mountains, but lots of greenery,
In all directions, witness beautiful scenery.
Bayous, lakes and many a stream,
With a variety of seafood, they teem.
Woodlands with an abundance of wildlife,
'Tis truly "a Sportsman's Paradise."
Many places are available to fish,
Salt water or fresh water, whenever you wish.
Oysters, crabs, crawfish, when in season,
Limits on all are within reason.
Hunting is permitted a certain time of the year,
Seasons are for rabbit, squirrel, alligator, bear and deer.
Quail, turkey, dove, and waterfowls of many types,
Including, rails, geese, ducks, coots, and snipes.
Bird Watchers, too, can have a ball,
During winter, spring, summer and fall.
Many bird species visiting have landed,
Some are caught, measured, weighted and banded.
"Swamp Tours" are available, easy to find,
Spot denizens of the prehistoric kind.
In winter, see the "Duck Hunter's" blind,
In the marsh, lake or rice fields, if they've a mind.
Water Sports are many, too,
Besides fishing, many ski or ride their "skidoo,"
Sail the large lakes and many bays,
On beaches, swim and enjoy the sun's rays.

There are parks to picnic or ride a bike,
On trails some ride "horseback" or hike.
Take a "Mississippi River Boat" ride if you like,
On the levee, let the boy fly his kite.
It can get very hot during our summer,
Our winters are usually mild.
Stormy days can be a bummer,
When turbulent weather gets too wild.
Yes, here there is much you can do,
Yes, we have Mardi Gras and its hullabaloo.
Yes, we have the French Quarter, where anything goes,
Yes, we have New Orleans and its woes.
I live, and prefer, the North Shore, not the City,
But then, I'm a Country Boy, at heart.
Our entire area could be cleaner, 'tis a pity,
It would take everybody, to do his or her part.

—September 10, 2000

AGING 2001

'Tis no great fun,
To get old, tired and weak,
To know I'll never again run,
My knees always hurt and squeak.

My hips also cause pain,
So does my back, again and again.
When fifty yards I walk,
I'm too out of breath to talk.

A dry, hacking cough, I can't shake,
No matter what I do or take.
'Tis my penalty, my doctor does proclaim,
Since in So. La. I choose to remain.

Medicine for diabetes and cholesterol,
For my prostate and blood pressure, too.
These I take daily for health control,
Like my doctor has told me to do.

My teeth are now causing me trouble.
On my gums, infection has caused a bubble.
A "root canal" is now needed.
Is my dentist to be believed and heeded?

My big toe has a spur,
Causing some pain to occur.
A Podiatrist I now consult,
Hoping to get a positive result.

As I said, "Aging is no great fun,"
But what can you do, in the long run?
You take all kinds of test,
Hope and pray for the best.

—December 11, 2001

AILMENT

For his ailment,
Is there a cure?
He's ever so silent.
Is he very insecure?

He's constantly in pain,
Of that I'm quite sure.
Yet, his demeanor does remain,
Gentle and his intentions are pure.

Like other Seniors I know,
He's not ever "on the go."
He stays home a lot, alone,
It's quiet, peaceful, when all are gone.

He goes to bed,
Very late, nearly every night.
Many thoughts are in his head,
As he watches TV and write.

He arises late in the morn,
E'en if awaken early by the phone.
Falling asleep again is easy,
It's restful and breathing is less wheezy.

—January 26, 2000

AL AND RUBY

That you're both still on your feet,
That you can still dance "to the beat,"
That you've been married half a century is a feat,
That, as young folks say today, "is very neat."
'Tis true, believe it or not,
Fifty years ago you two tied the knot.
Ruby, you found in Al,
Not only a great lover, but also a pal.
Al, with Ruby you also did find,
A great love, a wife that was devoted and kind.
You each found a loyal mate,
Perhaps you sensed this on your first date.
If some sorrow and hardship was to be your fate,
You would share, to each other, you could relate.
Ills and woes didn't keep you down, at any rate.
Soon you had children and they number six,
You managed, problems, if any, you did fix.
Few times, at each other, perhaps you did shout.
Marriage, after a while, you did find out,
Has its ups and down, good and bad.
Weary days, dreary days, days when you're sad or glad.
Time went by, it really flew,
Grandchildren arrived as the family really grew.
There were many happy times, you all knew,
That family, togetherness, loyalty, was nothing new.
Tending to the Elderly in a Nursing Home,
Ruby was busy while Al did (on the job) roam.
On return trips to Alaska and later Singapore,

The family went together, no matter how hard the chore.
Both retired, you now have more time for ease,
Yet, ills and woes, still persist, come like a breeze.
You do the right thing to stay trim and fit,
Though you may have an ache, you have your wit.
Today is a day for celebration,
For fifty years of joy and some tribulation,
With little, if any, condemnation.
So, without any qualm or reservation,
Without adulation or indignation,
We wish you both a day of jubilation.
Happy Anniversary!
We love you, Phyllis and Ray.

ALL IS NOT WELL

As you can tell, all is not well,
Looks like it won't be for quite a spell.
My hair is too long, you might say "shaggy,"
But then my pants may be considered "baggy."

This COVID-19 pandemic is terrible, obscene,
Being "self-quarantined" we shouldn't make a scene.
My toenails are in need of a pedicure,
If and when the Salons will open, I'm not sure.

Presently, Barbershops, Salons and such are closed,
Two more weeks of "stay at home" is proposed.
People are still dying at an alarming rate,
Some wonder, "Will I be next? What's my fate?"

Boredom may be worse than having a bad cold,
Not only for the young, but also for the old.
The temptation to disobey orders is great,
But be aware, if you dare, even one mistake,
May cause you misery, that you cannot shake.

—May 1, 2020

ALMOST ALONE

We're both in the house,
Yet, at times, I feel quite alone.
She's in another room, quiet as a mouse,
Using the computer or the phone.

The computer can become an addiction,
Playing games can be an affliction.
Hours are spent on the "chat line."
Peacefully chatting, 'tis OK, fine.

Times I think, "I'll be darn,"
I yawn, 'tis already three in the morn.
When will she ever give up?
Will she remain "online" 'till dawn, sunup?

Other times, she sits and knit.
Starts an afghan, then won't quit.
One hundred plus hours to complete,
Says 'tis therapeutic, hard to beat.

I think and let my mind wander and roam,
Then I may decide to write a poem.
Perhaps they're silly, make little sense,
Perhaps they're truthful, with little consequence.
Then again, it may be just pretense.

—August 23, 1999

ALMS

On the street corner, with open palms,
Begging each passerby for alms.
Is he really in desperate need,
Or collecting money for greed or misdeed?

Many able and healthy people beg,
Faking disabilities, blindness to bad leg.
They depend on sympathetic people to give,
Find that "begging is easy money" a way to live.

Parents teach children to beg today,
At a supermarket and at Walmart, they beg away.
They beg for trips, special events or such,
Uniforms, etc., it is all too, too, much.

Begging is easy money, so why work,
This is what is taught, so many people shirk.
Some at street intersections wave a can,
Pestering motorists, begging or making a demand.

Some have a sign, "Will work for food,"
They do accept cash, that's understood.
Do they ever get asked to work at all,
Or was an unwillingness to work, their downfall?

In dire need, I'm sure many people are.
They seek and find aid, near and far.
On a street corner, they need not be.
Abuses in begging, has toughened many like me.

Being approached and accosted at every turn,
Is harassment, gives me a slow burn.
Seems everybody wants a bit of my cash,
An outright gift, for hash,
Or to increase their stash?

—November 5, 1999

ALONE

Alone in the large crowd,
I could scream out loud.
Why am I here, anyway?
How did I come this way?

I don't seem to remember a thing,
Who I am or what I did bring.
Yet, here I am, but why?
Oh, oh, I'm about to cry.

What's this bump on my head?
Was I mugged, today?
Was I just left for dead,
Or was I hurt some other way?

My name, my name, what can it be?
There's no sign of any ID.
Nary a thing was left on me,
No wallet, no watch, not even, a key.

'Tis funny that I feel no pain,
Oh my, my mind is feeling numb.
My head, where had it lain?
From where, oh where, did I come?

—March, 6, 1999

AMATEUR COOK

He was an amateur cook,
Who seldom went by the book.
If a recipe, he'd just read,
It was jotted mentally, in his head.

Onions and peppers, he did sauté,
For the omelet, he cooked his way.
The fish, freshly caught, he'd fillet,
Then fry or poach it, that very same day.

Potatoes, dug fresh out of the soil,
He would peel and then parboil.
Then he'd mash them and patties make,
Before placing them into the oven to bake.

On special days, he'd make a gumbo,
With shrimp, oysters and with a crab or so.
Rice was cooked in a special pot,
That cooked it, turned itself off, kept it hot.

Barbeque was his forte.
He usually did it on Saturday or Sunday.
Chicken, steak, ribs of beef or pork,
So tender, you could cut them with a fork.

Jambalaya, he cooked real good,
It is one of my favorite food.
He was also great cooking red beans and rice.
It was very nice, even with little spice.

—November 24, 1999

AMID THE CROWD

Dressed "to the nines" in his Sunday suit,
Camera focused, doing fine, ready to shoot.
When lo and behold, the urge to poot,
Overpowered, the nervous, poor old coot.
What to do? The question was moot.

"Let 'er Rip, don't give a hoot,"
Did he hear a voice, or did it say "scoot"?
With the poot, to his chagrin, did he feel poop?
He glanced and saw a grinning couple on the stoop.
Was the cause, a "dip" he'd eaten with scoops?

Did more poop come as he uttered "oops"?
With each click and camera flash flicker,
He suddenly became sick, then sicker.
To assess the damage, he felt he must leave.
But how? He had no trick up his sleeve.

With embarrassment and amid a maddening crowd,
His thoughts were chagrin and dread.
Was it odoriferous and did it spread?
Without hesitation, he quietly slipped away,
To locate a "Men's Room," he made his way.
The "poop" he found, to his surprise,
Was small and odorless, not as he did surmise.

—March 5, 2013

AN ASSET

In a strange Café I sat,
The waitress came over in two seconds flat.
Looking up, I'd caught her eye,
As she was approaching by.

With a smile she said, "Hi, hon."
Already her heart I'd won?
Taking my order, she was very sweet,
I thought, "I really must be discreet."

Then I heard at the table next,
She repeated, "Hi, honey" without pretext.
Watching as from table to table she went,
Her energy was endless, never spent.

Again and again, "Hi, honey" she repeated,
Now I felt a tiny bit cheated.
Was she really a real big flirt,
Sashaying around, moving her skirt?

Then I began to realize,
She was a waitress, "much on the go."
Every man felt she was his prize.
She was so nice, e'en to people she did not know.

Upon leaving, I left a nice tip.
She'd been very congenial, not flip.
I thought, for that Café, I do attest,
A waitress like her, is an important asset.

—October 4, 1999

ANIMALS 2001

A squirrel scampered around a tree.
For winter, he was getting prepared.
Gathering nuts he was busy as a bee.
Going from tree to tree, he dared.
The acorns were large and plentiful.
His harvest would be good and bountiful.

He competed with others, mainly the deer.
They ate many acorns year after year.
Tirelessly he gathered his share.
Very well, this winter, he'd fare.

By the tree line, pressing their luck,
Appeared a doe and fawn and then a buck.
With the hunting season open for deer,
A shot might ring out, loud and clear.

In the meadow, covered with dew,
Was spotted a ram with his favorite ewe.
Many animals may have been yet asleep,
Not so, this small flock of sheep.

The goats, acting spry and frisky,
Didn't realize that their location was risky.
A hunter, still groggy and half asleep,
May not distinguish between deer, goats, and sheep.

Suddenly, along the fence line,
Came a long line of cattle.
Everything appeared to be really fine,
But was the bellowing bull seeking a battle?
The horses paid him no mind.
They'd dealt before with his noisy kind.
They grazed and grazed, ignoring the rest.
Grazing was what they enjoyed best.

—November 26, 2001

MORE ANIMALS

Lions are usually proud beasts,
Each member of the "pride."
Together they may enjoys feasts,
Once the big male steps aside.

Apes come together as a group,
Form a unit, called a "troop."
Organized, they're not a rowdy band,
But move about orderly, through their land.

Wolves, too, form a group, a "pack."
Together they live and socialize.
United, well planned, they attack,
Game for food, their skills they utilize.

Do birds go by an internal clock,
As they migrate, in a "flock"?
Do they experience any fright,
During their flight, especially, at night?

Does any fish get really smart,
As they swim together in a "school"?
Is it when they decide to part,
They get hooked, like a fool?

—August 21, 1999

ANOTHER PROBLEM

'Tis Saturday, 5:00 o'clock in the morn,
I can't go to sleep e'en tho I'm tired and worn.
A cough with phlegm, I cannot seem to shake,
No matter what I gargle with or cough drops I take.
Thursday night, for a while, I couldn't catch my breath,
For a second, I thought that it might cause my death.

Friday, I felt a little better most of the day.
I hoped the chicken noodle soup would chase the cough away.
But nay, I'm coughing with phlegm, what can I say?
I've gargled with saltwater and with Chloroseptic,
Taken cough drops, drank hot tea and apple cider, it's hectic.
Yesterday, I thought I'd found the cure,
Now it's Saturday and I am *not so sure.*

If I survive tonight, I'll see what tomorrow will bring.
Perhaps in a day or so I will beat this thing.
'Tis Sunday and I don't feel any better.
I'll see my doctor Tuesday and follow his orders to the letter.
An X-ray showed fluid in my lungs and around my heart.
Now I feel as though I'm coming apart.

In the hospital for a spell, liquid Lasix made me well.
Home with oxygen and Nebulizer, what's to tell?
Nurses and therapists visited me again and again.
Treatments and exercises were done with little pain.
Following instructions, will I have much to gain?
Taking everything day by day is how I remain.

—January 26, 2019

ANOTHER BARBEQUE

The weekend barbeque,
Is something many love to do.
Grilling hot dogs, hamburgers or steak,
Are choices that many do make.
Chicken is also meat many choose.
No matter which, you can't lose.

When a friend is eager and willing,
To do the "chilling and the grilling,"
Don't deny him of this pleasure.
He may want to "show off" his treasure.
Perhaps he bought a fancy barbeque pit,
That he wants to test, see if it's a hit,
With his family, neighbor and friend.
Is this the beginning of a new trend?

In midsummer 'tis much too hot,
To barbeque outside, even by the pool,
Unless 'tis a breezy, shady spot,
That is fairly nice and cool.
Sometimes the heat is hard to bear,
Even tho that "great taste" is there.

The spring and in the fall,
Some consider the best time of all,
To "grill and chill" and eat outdoor,
With pleasure, as their parents did before.
Today, many, many things go onto the grill,

43

Many meats and different kinds of fish,
Vegetables too, many varieties, if they wish.
Shrimp and crab, may complete a dish.
Any of this, on the grill, may just fill the bill.
Grilling, somehow, give many a big thrill.
Charcoal grill or gas grill,
Which is the best to use?
For the taste, one kind some refuse.
For many others, either fits the bill.
No matter which they favor,
Grilled foods, many people do savor.
Most who barbeque, it seems, are men.
Women don't seem eager for this to end,
Nor do they want to reverse the trend.
Women prefer their air-conditioned kitchen.
When praising the men, do they just pretend?

—August 12, 2001

ANOTHER DAY

Another day of pain and sorrow,
Much like yesterday and I suspect, tomorrow.
Sleeping a greater part of the day,
Awake, very little she has to say.

Medicine scheduled every six hours or so,
More when necessary, when she's "gung ho."
Too often bewildered, dazed or confused,
Seems no way to keep her amused.

Her taste buds must be impaired,
Little appetite for anything prepared.
Water with ice, she does drink a lot,
But only when ice, the water has got.

Not recognizing things or someone is sad.
Memory loss is very, very bad.
Chair to sofa, sofa to chair,
Wee baby steps, eventually gets her there.
With some mobility, she desires to go everywhere.

Boredom is a problem, of course,
But in her condition, is there any recourse?

—October 27, 2013

ANOTHER DREAM

I dreamed and dreamed as I slept and slept,
In my dream I wept and wept.
Because the "spring in my step,"
Was replaced by the "fall of my arches."
No matter what I tried, I was very inept.
No longer was I able to go on marches.

My overworked, tired old heart,
Was it causing me to fall apart?
My brain was drained and had gone awry.
Perhaps, this was making me cry.
Suddenly I felt that I was too young to die.
What was happening and why? Indeed why?

Because of hysteria, I suddenly awoken,
Relieved I was that nothing was broken.
Asleep again, dreaming in a very deep sleep,
I was a teen, driving over hills very steep.

The weather was hazard, sleeting and sleeting.
Warned to be careful, my childhood was fleeting.
It would last only a few short years.
But immaturity, I was told, can last forever.
It's expressed daily, sans shame, fear or tears.
Rainy or cold, drive carefully in such weather.

Now you are bold and you've been told,
Take heed if you wish to grow old.

—retyped February 25, 2020

ANOTHER SAD LAD

The sad lad, the poor dear,
Had a tired, weary look on his face.
Just like some of his peers,
His wish is to venture into space.

With Sci-Fi, he's fascinated.
He reads all the available books on the subject.
Movies about space, to him, are never outdated,
To discuss these topics, they never do object.

Computers are neat, really okay,
Especially the games he can play all day.
Comic books, too, have great appeal.
Superheroes deal harshly, with killers who steal.

Now, on the matter concerning school,
Some subjects, he finds not too cool.
Math is difficult, he feels like a fool.
Perhaps, he doesn't use the proper tool.

History, is it necessary to know,
About events, that occurred eons ago?
English, he can understand the need,
For communication, to travel, and to read.

An education, he knows he needs to get,
If he plans to amount to anything.
The discipline needed, he's not acquired yet.
As he matures, what will the future bring?

—January 30, 2000

ART

The beauty in art that we see,
May differ between you and me.
What's pleasing for one's eye,
May be meaningless to another guy.

Art appreciation is taught in school.
Discussions are held in class.
In a museum, you won't be the fool,
If this course, you do pass.

Most people, simply like what they like.
They think their taste are as good as any.
To them, others can go fly a kite.
They feel like their knowledge, is simply uncanny.

Art may be expressed in many ways,
Some form may be short, other takes days.
A painting, a sculpture, is a type of art form.
Nothing has to be usual or the norm.

People do strange things,
They say, for the sake of art.
It's justified, no shame, to them, it brings,
So they all play their role, act their part.

—September 23, 1999

AT THE FAIR

At the annual country fair,
Just about everyone goes there.
'Tis amusement many seek to find,
In many things, but of a different kind.
Livestock is viewed at a steady pace,
By young and old, each gender and of each race.
'Tis the expression on their face,
That gratifies the ones with animals in place.
Farm equipment is usually on display,
Tractors, mowers, and pumps used to spray.
Trailers used to haul animals around,
Plows, discs, and tillers to work the ground.
On display there's usually lots of food.
Ribbons honor the best and the very good.
See varieties of pickles and jarred fruit.
Observe vegetables, legumes, and edible roots.
Enjoy crafts of many sorts, made by hand.
Are all made by the proud people of the land?
Children run, yell, and scamper about,
Occasionally, at them, their parents shout,
Teenagers find a chance to "pair off,"
Where few will laugh at them and scoff.
On the midway and fairway,
Are many rides and games to play.
For young swains 'tis the Ferris wheel,
That they think is a heck of a deal.
They take their date for a ride,
Swing and shake the seat to make her squeal.

Her affection, does she reveal,
When she hugs him tightly to her side?
Then he swells with pride.
Other rides may be more daring,
But ignored by the wiser and more caring.
Merry-go-rounds please the younger set,
Even the older, if romantic they get.
At night, if there is a stage,
A "big name" star may put on a show.
One that's very popular, the current rage,
Will entice the whole county to go.
Very popular too, is the rodeo.

AT THE PARK

'Twas a beautiful afternoon,
Part of a pleasant and enjoyable day.
The baby was having her way
Playing, it was the First of June.

In the Park, atop a platform high,
Then sliding down a chute.
With a smile and a sigh,
She was so happy, so very cute.

Not wanting to stop,
Not even to enjoy a snowball.
From here to there she'd run and hop,
Never fearing that she might fall.

For this tireless tot,
Who is two months shy of two,
E'en tho 'twas kinda hot,
She kept on doing what she wanted to do.

Finally she admitted to a pal she knew,
That she, in her diaper, had made poo-poo.
That put an end to her fun,
To the house, for a change, we had to run.

At the house, she was still spry,
Just playful, she did not cry.
Before her bath, she was fed,
But lo, she refused to go to bed.

So we sang, played with her game,
Until finally, her Mom and Dad came.

—June 1, 1999

ATHLETE

Tall and slim, he's fast on his feet,
Played soccer in summers past.
He excels in track, during a meet.
How long, will this, enthusiasm last?

In football, he's a running back,
But feels that weight, he does lack.
In Junior High, many players weigh more,
Than two hundred fifty pounds.
They hit, you're bound to get sore.

Big guys, make him run really fast,
He doesn't look back, but races toward the goal.
If they tackle him, he'll try to last,
To finish the game, but he must be bold.

He knows bones, at times, do break,
Playing contact sports like this.
Does he play, for his parents' sake,
Or fear that too many good times he'd miss?

He doesn't look like the rugged type,
But looks do deceive, they say.
Without much "fanfare or hype,"
He was "first string" every time they did play.

—November 8, 1999

BACK THEN

As young parents we knew,
Every family living on the avenue.
Neighbors casually dropped in often,
For a cup of coffee or two.
A game of bridge, every now and then,
Was entertainment for more than a few.

Minor problems occurred at schools,
Usually because someone disobeyed the rules.
'Twas nothing like the problems schools face today,
That is dreadful and fearful, I dare say.

Security at school, a major issue now,
Wasn't a problem, students were safer, somehow.
Few, if any students, drove a car.
Parking areas were of very limited space.
Now acres and acres, too much land, by far,
Are costing taxpayers, it's a waste and a disgrace.

Buses are provided, but all don't ride.
Nor do many use bicycles, it may hurt their pride.
Neighborhood schools did work best.
This I do believe and to that I would attest.

Bigger is not better, I don't believe.
In smaller schools, it's easier to achieve.
Neighborhood schools had better control.
There was no need for a "safety patrol,"
Except to guide "young ones" across the street.
The grounds and classrooms were kept clean and neat.

—March 2, 2008

BARRED BARD

The unhappy, drunken bard,
From many places he was barred.
He was drinking much "too hard."
E'en tho he was considered a "card,"
Many also dubbed him "a tub of lard."

Like a member of a "motley band,"
Who, many places, was also banned.
Depressed, he couldn't understand,
Who would make such a demand.

He thought of a particular morning,
About a small town he'd seen in mourning.
They grieved for a lost soul,
Who had once been a native of Seoul.
He'd been a trusted hardworking miner,
Who had come here when still a minor.
He'd been barred from more than one place.
Because of his face, color or race?

The bard longed for wide-open spaces,
He'd get away, from many, many faces.
To be free like an eagle in her aerie,
High in a treetop where it's very airy.

He planned to go out, hunt deer.
He decided to go on his ole "John Deere."
He told his "honey," the sweet dear,
He'd return soon, not to fear.

The hunt was a big success.
It relieved him of much stress.
He was home and sober he would stay,
Better he'd feel, facing each day.

—October 6, 2001

BE AWARE OF THE RAMP

There's a ramp in Slidell,
Where some drivers don't fare well.
Many take a nasty spill,
When, too fast they go, as some will.
They experience anything but a thrill.

It's clearly posted with a sign,
For slow speeds, was the design.
Going too fast, some can't make
The turn, though they apply their brake.

Tankers especially, seem prone to flip,
As they try to go around,
At much too fast a clip.
Suddenly 'tis crash,
If they're able, away they dash,
After the tankers hits the ground.

Drivers may be killed,
After their vehicle has "spilled."
'Tis a shame, don't they know,
That "20 MPH" means, "SLOW"?

Some, however, seem never to learn,
If you ignore signs, you may burn.
'Tis sad, but so true.
Just what can you or I do?

Speed bumps may cause a lot of cussing,
Cause much discussing and fussing.
But, better to be mad, turn beet red,
Than to flip, be maimed or wind up dead.

—October 7, 2000

BEANS

One of my favorite dish,
Is the plain old "bean."
Whichever one that I wish,
Be it white, red, black or green.

Beans, I love to eat with rice.
Also great, is a "bean soup."
With sausage, beans go nice,
With chicken, too, fresh from the coop.

Even cold, beans taste good,
In a salad, too.
They are considered a healthy food,
So, they are also good for you.

Red beans and rice,
Its popularity is seen,
And at a decent, low price,
Down south, in New Orleans.

'Tis not a myth, but true,
Beans are very nutritious, too.
I find the taste great, also,
But then, I'm just an ordinary Joe!

—August 25, 1999

BEAUTY

Beauty is everywhere for me to see,
Flora, fauna and much humanity.
Flowers, flowering vines and trees.
Blue birds, red birds, woodpeckers and chickadees.

Squirrels, possums, coons and loons.
Ducks, geese, swans and other fowls,
Are attractive as are coyotes and wolves that howls.
Humanity, I'm concerned about.
Many people are lovely, some are not.

We don't communicate as well as we could,
Or be kind to each other the way we should.
I wonder how my progeny will be.
In the future, I hope it'll be peace and harmony.

But crime is rampant and vandalism is "out of hand."
Many teens are in gangs, with older members they band.
Jails are overcrowded, "bursting at the seams."
Is "early release" the answer, are there other means?

Dogs and cats are great when they behave,
But much love and affection they crave.
Love and affection carries a lot of weight,
When it's freely given before it's too late.

—February 29, 2020, 9:00 a.m.

BEFORE MY
MEMORY GOES

While my memory is still intact,
I shall record what may be a simple fact.
All the medicine I take every day,
May be causing my memory to fade away.

Although I sleep eight hours or more,
Three or four hours after I'm awake,
I'm drowsy, droopy and I fall asleep and snore.
I surmise it's caused by the medicine I take.

To quit taking the medicine may be unwise.
That doctors prescribe more is no surprise.
It's getting where I can't think clearly anymore.
All I know, my joints ache and my muscles are sore.

When I get up I can hardly walk,
My throat has phlegm, it's hard to talk,
So, instead of sitting around and gawk,

I try to read and read, but I just doze and doze.
That's how it'll be from now on, I suppose,
Unless drastic changes occur, who knows?
Like they say, "That's how the wind blows."

Cicero said, "The life given us by Nature is short,
But the memory of a life well spent is eternal."

—July 6, 2016

BEST OF THE WEST

He could hardly do a thing,
Didn't play a fiddle, guitar or sing.
About little he could brag,
Out on the range he knew would be a drag.
From the East, he'd come West,
Promised his Dad he'd do his best.
He was the family friend's guest,
Thought he would be there for a rest.
He envisioned a quiet, peaceful summer,
Hoping it wouldn't turn out to be a bummer.

On a horse he was a bit uneasy.
Riding him made him very queasy.
He preferred the new four-wheeler,
They'd just received from the dealer.
He'd never ridden a horse before.
He'd practice, then practice more,
Help out with any chore.
Past summers he'd spent at the seashore.
Out West, he'd try and do his best,
So that he could hang out with the rest.

He got to help at roundup time,
Heard stories about rustling being a crime.
"Few are stolen, the market is less demanding,"
Cowpokes said as they did the branding.
He didn't see any guns ablazing,

Only saw lots of cattle agrazing.
Had the entire West really become tame?
Was "shootin'" only reserved for game?

The open country he began to really enjoy.
About most things he was no longer coy.
Now in his prime, he'd take more time,
To spend in the West and be with the Best.

—October 3, 2001

BETTER DAYS

He was a true Gent.
Reminiscence of a loyal Knight,
Many, many days he had spent,
Not seeking nor running from a fight.

Men admired his style.
The ladies adored his smile.
A hero, he was considered by many.
In a way, 'twas all very uncanny.

Growing up on a farm,
He concerned himself little about charm.
Hard work he never has feared.
'Twas the way that he was reared.

He left the farm when merely twenty.
Soon, misery and harm he'd seen aplenty.
City folks were no less friendly, no less gritty,
But chivalry seemed lost, 'twas a pity.

The populace seemed more wary.
A stranger's burden, would they not carry?
Could he possibly change their ways?
Would his deeds be worthy of praise?
His hope was for much better days.

He gave of himself and treated all others,
As though they were his sisters and brothers.
He helped the elderly and the needy,
Whether rich or poor or ugly and seedy.
He did it not for personal gain or wealth.
It just made him happy and he enjoyed good health.

—November 18, 2001

BIG COUNTRY

Across the great expanse,
Which stretches far and wide,
They really dare to take a chance,
When horses, so fast, they ride.

Neighbors are distant and very few.
They labor and toil just as we do.
Maybe they're friendly, maybe not,
But each other is all that they've got.

As beautiful a scenery, is there,
As 'twas ever meant to be.
In all directions, just everywhere,
Just as far, as the eye can see.

Craggy hills and mountain sides,
Where many a wild creature abides.
Many streams flow their own way,
Except when beavers decide to stay.

Beautiful, yet, big and harsh,
But different than our lowly flatland,
With many a bog and marsh,
Is this country, so big and so grand.

In the valley there's a misty hue,
Beneath a sky, that is so blue.
Wildflowers cover the ground.
What peace, nowhere is there a sound.

—January 9, 2000

BISCUITS

The big round biscuit,
Was flaky with a buttery taste.
'Twas much better than a Triscuit,
So he ate two in great haste.
Quickly he reached for another.
"Wait a second," said his Mother.
"Others, too, are ready to eat."
Sheepishly, he retracted in defeat.

He proceeded to eat some grits,
Mixed with fried eggs, what a deal.
To eat bacon he removed his mitts,
Using both hands to eat the meal.
His Mother refilled the biscuit dish,
With more biscuits, to his delight.
Three more fulfilled his wish,
With fig preserves, 'twas just right.

His Mother, he did so please,
Glad he was back and that she was able,
To cook and serve them at the table,
See them all content, not ill at ease.

'Twas for her biscuits he'd had a yen.
'Twas so long ago he didn't say when.
He remembered eating a lot of "hard tack,"
That some called "biscuits" some time back.
He'd tasted biscuits like she did bake.

They looked the same but were hard to eat.
Some were flaky and thin, crumbled like cake.
His Mother's biscuits just couldn't be beat.

—September 6, 2001

BLOOD

"Blood is thicker than water."
Is this true, as ofttimes said?
Surely, 'tis how it oughta
Be, by jove, if we use our head.

Who would forsake, a son or daughter,
Or their dear Mom or Dad?
It would be like taking a lamb to slaughter.
It would make many very, very sad.

People usually favor their kin,
When it comes to jobs and such.
Nepotism should be considered a sin,
But lo, it's around much, much too much.

Yes, water is not as thick as blood.
Deny a relative and your name becomes mud.
The same ole saying still goes,
It's "who" that counts, not "what" one knows.

Helping relatives could be a good thing,
Only if it remains proper and legal.
But to "dole out favors" like a king,
May be unethical and not at all regal.

"Blood is thicker" now consider the spouse,
Spouse comes first, or you're a louse.
But then, are not you and spouse as one?
If so, then "blood" again has won.

—September 10, 1999

BLUEBIRD

The Bluebird was late.
She was on a quest,
Searching for a mate,
To help her, build her nest.

Atop a lone fence post,
The box looked very old.
To her, 'twas the utmost.
It was the best along the road.

The inside was very clean,
The best, the bird had seen.
Nary a twig nor straw,
Pleased, she was, at what she saw.

A mate, she soon did find.
They were of the same mind.
A nest, they worked on together,
Preparing, for the spring weather.

In the spring,
Her eggs, she began to lay.
This was, "her thing,"
Laying about one egg a day.

Soon the nest,
Had eggs, numbering five.
She'd done her very best,
Now she would sit, sit and sit,
'Till all the chicks did exit
Every last shell, alive.

—February 10, 1999

BLUE HOUSE

The blue ginger bread house,
On top of a distant hill,
For a decade was unoccupied and still,
Except for a rat and a mouse.

Clothes in the closet was neat.
Food in the pantry, no one did eat.
Knickknacks all over the shelf,
A broken doll, in a corner by itself.

A wedding dress inside a chest,
Neatly packed, looking its best.
It was like new, not torn.
Had it been proudly worn,
Some long, long ago day?
No one was left around to say.

The furniture was still all there,
Linens and towels in their place.
A brush that once combed hair,
Dishes in cabinet, silverware in a case.

Family records, all intact,
Was the end of this family, a fact?
It's sad and hard to contemplate,
Just what was really their fate?

—September 12, 2001

77

BOLD ONES

To live where 'tis so cold,
Takes someone stout of heart and bold.
'Tis big country, that's for sure,
The air is cold, crisp and pure.

Neighbors are very far apart.
They keep busy tending to their own.
Perhaps from the very first start,
Newcomers may feel lonely and groan.

Big game is bountiful there.
Antelope, deer and elk roam everywhere.
Residents hunt to stock up their larder,
With great meat, before times get harder.

Cattle graze in the wide-open spaces,
But grass is sparse in many places.
Several acres may only support one cow,
Yet, they are fat, as corn-fed, somehow.

No doubt 'tis a tough and hard life,
For the husband, with children, and a wife.
It can be good tho, with some strife.
Quite, peaceful and where gossip is not rife.

—December 27, 1999

BOTTLE

The bottle was his best friend.
He nursed every drop to the very end.
Earlier, he never drank on the job,
But off duty, he became a slob.

On the weekends, he often withdrew,
Into his bedroom to stay.
There, he'd remain, he knew,
To drink and drink all of the day.

His wife was at a loss,
Concerned about her hubby.
Weekdays, he didn't act the boss,
Could be gentle, get very chubby.

The situation did get much worse.
Eventually, they did get a divorce.
Each went their separate way.
I'm sad, when I think about it today.

It got bad, with the bottle.
When on the road, he'd race full throttle.
Of many dangers, he was unaware,
Or perhaps, he just didn't care.

Drinking, part of him it did rob.
Before long, he did lose his job.
He left the state, went away.
His whereabouts are unknown, to this day.

—September 27, 1999

BOUDIN

Boudin, a type of sausage that's nice,
A yummy blend of pork, rice and spice.
A zesty taste at an affordable price.
As a meal, boudin and red beans may suffice.

An octogenarian, I've enjoyed boudin all my life,
As do my family, so did my late wife.
Fond memories of days long ago,
When visiting Lafayette, to the Corner Pantry we'd go,
Specifically to buy boudin from Mr. Arceneaux.

Two five-pound boxes he'd wrap "to go."
Then he'd heat two links for my wife and me,
As "lagniappe" for us to eat en route, you see.
His "gift" he'd say, for our patronage in the past.
His was a long friendship that certainly did last.

After Mr. and Mrs. Arceneaux were gone,
Their son ran the "Corner Pantry" alone.
Until this very day, when boudin I eat,
I think of the Arceneauxs and their special treat.

How they were thoughtful, generous and always sweet.
They were the essence of Cajuns you want to meet.
For me, boudin is here to stay.
In fact, I ate and thoroughly enjoyed some today!

—April 10, 2014

BRASH COED

The brash, sassy, new college coed,
By an escort, to her dormitory, was led.
Her room was unkempt, all messed up,
With paper plates and paper cups.

The impetuous, saucy, impudent, lass,
Was renowned for her brashness.
Much studying, she'd need to pass.
Famous also, she was for her crassness.

Pleased that she was "well-endowed,"
The lass had a plan, she'd figured how,
To circumvent the "brass," here and now.
She would "do her thing," as far as the law allowed.
To her roommate, she asked aloud,
"Can you honestly, answer me now?
Am I not beautiful, do I stand out in a crowd,
Or do I look like a little ole ordinary cow?"

The lass, in class, did display,
Her "talents," in a subtle, provocative way.
A young professor, she teased to please,
Counting on her beauty to "carry" her with ease.
Her roommate, a true beauty, with class,
Was surprised and really taken aback.
She felt it her duty to tell the brash lass,
She had beauty, but "class," she surely did lack.

In time, the lass came to realize,
That her gifted beauty, would win her no prize.
She'd have to mature, buckle down,
Study hard, just like all the rest,
If she expected to last, stay around,
And be able to pass every given test.

—September 8, 2000

BREAK THE FAST

Every so often, every now and then,
I find myself busy as a barnyard hen.
Then for a quick breakfast, I may take,
A delicious and nutritious Glucerna Shake.

To replace a meal, it's also a very good deal,
Also for a quick snack, when snacks you lack.
Other shakes like Boost and Ensure,
Works well too, you can be sure.

For breakfast I like to switch about,
Fix meals that are easy and fast, with good taste.
Like toast with peanut butter, jam and banana,
Very easily made in haste.

Cold cereal with fruit I eat a lot.
Hot cereal, I'll microwave or cook in a pot.
"Egg omelets" and bacon, I microwave,
Or just use skillets I've got.

"Eggs blindfolded" or "eggs in the hole,"
I cook in a frying pan, like I was told.
To cook another way, I'm not that bold.
It's "old-fashioned" and I'm old.

My son cooks breakfast when he's around.
He's apt to try any new recipe he's found.
Pancakes and waffles he cooks very well,
But it's the "egg omelets" where he does excel.

—May 6, 2020

BREAKFAST

Breakfast, usually the first meal of the day,
Should be enough to start you on your way.
Buttered biscuits, a fried egg, ham, and grits,
Could be as good as any breakfast at the Ritz.

A scrambled egg, sausage, "tater tots" and jam on toast,
Should satisfy the hunger and appetite of most.
Poached egg, mixed fruit, and "cream of wheat,"
For a light breakfast may be hard to beat.

A plain bagel with cream cheese and a bowl of oatmeal,
As a first meal for some may be ideal.
Whole wheat toast, bacon, and grits with shrimp,
When you serve yourself, don't be frugal or skimp.

With almond milk, the cereal that I eat and like,
Is cheerios with fiber one and a banana, it's light.
With much delight, thrice a week, I enjoy every bite.
Every now and then, I eat waffles or pancakes,
With maple syrup, they're both very easy to make,
And not very long at all does it take.

The above may be served with coffee, cow's milk or tea.
Nowadays, none of these three does appeal to me.
I most likely will drink a fruit juice instead.
My "taste buds" changed, maybe it's all in my head.

—Wednesday, November 13, 2019

BUFFETS

Buffets are generally very nice,
Most of the people will agree.
Especially when the price,
Is "two for one" or better yet, "free."
Casinos, along the Gulf Coast,
Offer these specials, the most.
Many "Seniors" are ofttimes seen there.
They seem to come from everywhere.
Many people drive, many come by bus.
Popular meals are a very "big draw."
The slogan "Leave the driving to us"
Is accepted, by many a "Maw Maw and Paw Paw."
The people, the people, "sakes alive,"
Lines form before and after five.
Special nights, from far away, many drive.
They crowd in, like "bees to the hive."
Again, I say, the buffets are great,
But really, is any food worth a two-hour wait?
Two hours? Maybe I exaggerate,
But, long waits, long lines, are not for me,
Even if the cost is "half price or free."

—August 1, 1999

BUFFETS

At an "all you can eat buffet,"
People eat more than usual that day,
But, 'tis not because of what they pay.
If they eat more than they need,
Is that considered to be greed?
Is that inherent in the seed,
Of a particular and distinct breed?

A sign reads "All you can eat Catfish,"
'Tis great, for ones who relish that dish.
This may be the answer to their wish.
So, they overeat and overstuff,
Until they've had more than enough.

When people really exceed their need,
Perhaps it can be considered greed.
Yes, yes indeed, yes indeed.
To just fulfill the need,
how many of us do heed?

Many tend to "Supersize,"
When they "load up" with their eyes.
With no one to supervise or criticize,
Eating may become a culinary exercise.

—April 2011

BUGGY DAZE

Muggy, buggy, days of summer,
At times, can be a real bummer.
Beautiful summer days,
Can turn into a summer daze.

Bugs, bugs, can be seen everywhere.
They get into your eyes, mouth, ears and hair.
Venture out, only if you dare.
Many bugs tend to swarm,
When the weather is muggy and warm.

Conditions for mosquitoes are just right.
You may feel them day and night.
They come buzzing around only to bite.
Flies of all kind will bite, too,
Aggravate the daylights out of you.

Chiggers and ticks are "diggers" I dread.
They bite and bury their head.
This causes a terrible itch,
When scratched, makes a sore which,
May get infected, put you to bed.

Hornets, wasps and stinging bees,
May nest in the ground or around trees.
They inject venom when they sting.
Swelling occurs from the sting of these.
So, if allergic, repellent you should bring.

Pesky gnats, a certain time of the year,
Appear around the face, the neck, behind the ear.
Very small, they're hard to see,
Are bothersome and bite like the flea.

—May 23, 2000

BULLETS

Firing bullets into the air,
Just isn't right, just isn't fair.
'Tis a dumb way, if you care,
To celebrate, the New Year anywhere.

Yet some, I'm sure will dare,
To defy, the law here and there.
They may later, scratch their hair,
As they go off to jail somewhere.

Falling bullets maim and kill,
Innocents reveling or standing still.
They're unaware that danger lurks,
Because, of gun-firing, careless jerks.

Be smart, be safe, and stay alive.
Avoid large crowds celebrating outside.
It gets dark shortly after five.
Remain indoors instead of a "joyride."

Head for cover around midnight,
That's the time fireworks, they ignite.
Watch everything on TV, out of sight,
Be around later to enjoy the night-light,
And start the New Year right.

—December 27, 1999

BUTT AND GUT NURSE

She is known as the Butt and Gut Nurse.
During colonoscopies she does assist.
To become a nurse was a challenge she couldn't resist.
Some other jobs she may consider to be worse.
That they do save lives, she does insist.

Early cancer detection she does advise,
Is very important and a "word to the wise."
During the procedure they do sedate,
The patient, to ensure that they feel no pain.
Polyps seen, they can very easily eradicate,
All of them, right then, again and again.

Saving lives is her aim and her goal.
This may be done by treating the heart and soul.
She considers this her duty and does her job.
After the procedure, most people are relieved and glad.
Few, if any, are unhappy, may weep and sob.
That many do not heed her advice is truly sad.
It could be fatal, that's really bad.

—August 22, 2018

CABBAGE

Cabbage, with their round head,
Are available in green or in red.
Prepared in many a different way,
It is delicious, good on any day.

For a salad, fix a slaw.
It's tasty, made with cabbage that is raw.
Cabbage can go into a soup or two,
May be filling and low cal too.

Stuffed cabbage, cabbage wrapped around meat,
'Tis hearty and very good to eat.
Smothered cabbage is also fine,
A very great dish, when you dine.

Corned beef and cabbage, a good choice,
Many chose it in years past.
People would sing, dance and rejoice,
As long as all the full bellies did last.

Sauerkraut and pork, a great cabbage dish,
That we eat at home as oft as we wish.
Cabbage is used also in Chinese food,
Fixed just right and very, very good.

—November 16, 1999

CAGED BIRD

Does a bird in a cage,
Ever go into a rage,
When a cat comes near,
No matter his size or age?

Does a bird flutter with fear,
Tho the cage is quite strong,
Front, sides and rear?
Does he fear something is wrong,
That he is not safe in here,
From the cat or others? Dear, dear.

In a cage the canary sings,
Sometimes all the day long.
Is it because of the joy he brings,
Or that he's very proud of his song?

A pair of pretty parakeets,
Enjoy various kinds of treats.
If one does learn to talk,
He can become "cock of the walk."

Lovely "lovebirds" are a cute pair.
Inside a cage, they go nowhere.
Are they content to just "bill and coo"?
With or without consent, 'tis all they do.

Some caged finches lead a good life.
Their cage, a large room, is a hit.
On other birds eggs they readily sit.
Is it their pleasure or is it their strife?

Many parrots love to talk.
To anyone, seldom do they balk.
They mimic words and sound,
Whistle when dogs come around.

Inside cages they squawk and squawk,
While at passersby they gawk.
Caged, they're safe from any hawk.

—September 8, 2001

CAN YOU BELIEVE?

Today, one shouldn't pay too much heed,
To everything they do, see or read.
Apparently civility, oath or creed,
Does satisfy the great, great need,
Of some newsperson's greed, yes greed.

Money, seeking more money, they are bold.
Some follow the flock, like sheep in the fold.
Entertainment seems to be their goal.
To achieve this, they will ruin one's soul.

"Ratings" to them, is pure gold.
While many truths they may withhold.
Either way, they hope the public is sold,
On what they spew, they are very bold.

Sad meets bad, or is it mad?
From the stage they engage or enrage.
No matter, the gender, color or age.

—2017

CANADA TRIP

We once took a northern trip.
'Twas very late in the year.
By Van, not by plane or ship,
To hunt for the black bear and the deer.
The trip was somewhat uneventful.
For a week, 'twas not too long.
The sights, they were very beautiful.
Odors of the firs and pines were strong.
We crossed into Canada with ease.
The populace seemed eager to please.
Our lodgings were plain, but neat,
Very comfortable, and much to eat.
Walking through the North wood,
Was a chore, tedious and tough.
Fallen, rotten trees made it rough,
But we hunted the best way we could.
Two deer were brought in the first night.
At camp, they made a pretty sight.
We'd seen one or two more that day.
Through the thicket, they'd gotten away.
Returning to camp the next day,
"Someone stole a deer," we heard the cook say.
We notified the Canadian RCMP.
They then took proper measures, you see.
The "deer nappers" were caught with dispatch.
They were told to make restitution, natch.
No one bagged a black bear,
No more deer either, but we didn't care.

On our return we drove straight through,
Stopping only for gas, eats and brew.
By each taking a turn to drive,
We were not too tired, safe and alive.
The trip was a pleasurable one.
The scenery was a delight at best.
After all was said and done,
We deemed the trip a very big success.

—April 10, 1999

CANCER

Dreadful words we hate to hear,
"Your tumor is malignant, my dear."
Stunned, you think, "What do I have to fear?
Is the end of my life, my demise, near?"
Options, I'm told, are very clear.

Surgery is out, so too, is radiation.
Chemotherapy may be my only salvation.
"Stage 3, non-small cell cancer," news I did dread.
Refusing "chemo," I will probably wind up dead.
Confined to my left lung the cancer had not spread.

The radiation doctor assured me he could shrink it.
Low dose radiation I took for a 6 week duration.
The tumor did shrink, as predicted, after radiation.
Can you imagine, just think of my elation.

Now, I thought, I may live a while longer.
Perhaps my body will get a bit healthier and stronger.
The way things really happen, how they are,
I consider myself very lucky, so far.

My kidneys, I'm now very concerned about.
Slowly, but surely, they're about to give out.
My GFR number is a low seventeen,
If it gets much lower, I will likely exit my earthly scene.
The latest news is, "that the cancer cells are all dead."
I'm in slightly better shape now to "look ahead."

—February 2019

CANDY JAR

On the bar is a box of cigars and a candy jar.
They are not too near nor are they too far.
Too often, to this jar I'm drawn.
The cigar I leave alone, the sweet tooth is my own.

Candy is handy when sweets I desire.
Chocolate with coconuts or with nuts I admire.
Peppermints and other mints also are very fine.
Snickers, Mars Bars and many others I won't define,
Are tasty and satisfy me after I dine.

The jar on the bar, doesn't stay full very long.
Others love candy and know where the jar does belong.
Every girl and it seems every boy,
Pick candy that's so handy from the jar.
Perhaps a Hershey Bar or an Almond Joy,
They may choose "for later to enjoy,"
While they cruise around town in the car.

Thanks to the Host with the Most, by far,
With the cigars and the candy jar on the bar.

—July 8, 2016

CARDINALS

In an azalea bush, the cardinals build their nest.
To raise their young, they do their very best.
Occasionally, they fly to a tree nearby,
But seem to keep an eye on their nest and the sky.

They're beautiful birds, especially the male.
Admired by many, he's handsome from head to tail.
His crimson body is truly a deep red,
With a little black around his beak and lower head.

Somehow, there seems to be fewer now than years ago.
Did many perish? If no, where did they go?
Birds in general, seem to disappear.
There are fewer around year after year.

Many species I no longer see,
Blackbirds, bluebirds, purple martins and quails,
Others too. What happened, where did we fail?
I hope that there will always be,
Cardinals around for all to see.
They are very beautiful, perched in a tree.

—December 5, 2018, 10:30 p.m.

CATFISH

Many locals' favorite type of fish,
Is the abundant scaleless, whiskered catfish.
Fried or broiled, it's a very tasty dish.
Or cooked in other ways, if you wish.

It's people's choice, cooked fillets or whole.
In "all you can eat specials" they have a role.
Lots of catfish are raised in a pond,
Fed high protein food, of them people are fond.

On the banks of a bayou, with line on a bamboo pole,
Using any kind of bait, or at a favorite fishing hole,
Catfishing is relaxing and good for the soul.
In rivers, bayous and canals, stretching a "trout line."
For hooking catfish, usually works just fine.

Using "hoop nets" in those same waterways,
Is a great way to trap catfish and better it pays.
In the Mississippi River, "hoop nets" may be found,
That catch catfish weighing up to one hundred pounds.

Catfish may also be bought that is imported.
It's a fish, that makes a dish, that's easily afforded.

—Monday, November 11, 2019, 3:40 p.m.

CELL PHONES

A cell phone is now common gear,
Seems everyone has one by his ear.
On the street, inside buildings and inside the car,
They telephone, whether near or far.
Away from the house, but not very long,
You'd think something went wrong.
Driving, they call "on the go."
They can't wait ten minutes or so.

'Tis a special night, all is fine,
You and yours just begin to dine.
Luckily, you got a special table,
There's no TV; they're not on cable.
Behind, you suddenly hear "squawking,"
On a cell phone, a diner is talking.
It's impossible not to overhear,
Every word that is said, he's so near.

Glancing about, you see he's not alone.
Three others are also using their phone.
Privacy, they don't worry about.
Every so often, one does shout.
You notice, out on the street,
Adults and teens are chatting away.
Seems that everyone you meet,
Always have a thing or two to say.

They have cell phones to "keep in touch."
Some talk and talk but don't say much.
'Tis everyone, sweethearts, sister and brother,
Spouses checking on each other.

Cell phones are useful tools.
They prove their worth every day.
But lo, too many fools,
Use them more for fun and play?

—October 8, 2001

CHAIR TRAVEL

How wonderful 'tis today,
That I can explore,
Worlds that are very far away,
Without ever going out my door.
On television, I can see places,
And people of many different races.
By taping, I may set my on pace,
Pause, if I wish to study a face.
TV with the large screen,
Better displays a beautiful scene.
Pictures are so lifelike, so clear.
'Tis like you're there, real near,
Especially with the sounds you hear.
Grand Palaces, you can tour,
While at home, safe and secure.
Visiting many in a single day,
In a comfortable, relaxing way.
Some distant and intriguing land,
May seem enticing, appear grand.
Beaches, with pure white sand,
Beckon, seem to pull you by the hand.
Want to see Ancient Rome,
Without ever having to leave home?
Play a tape that shows it all,
The times of Caesar, up 'til last fall.
Read a book, if you prefer some "quiet,"
On history, geography, or about a diet.
Perhaps, a novel about Romance,

About Lovers who met by chance.
Topic on the past, present and future,
Are available, pick what suits you.
Religion, UFOs, Magic, Truth or Fiction,
It's all there, in some form of diction.
On the Internet, you may go worldwide,
For information, games of fun, or as a guide.
Make friends, the whole world over,
Chat, do research, watch Rover roll in the clover.
There's much out there today,
That the young and the old can do,
Without having to go away,
Yet, do what really pleases you!

—March 5, 1999

CHANGES

My skin, my poor skin, is so very thin,
All over my arms, face and chin.
White is my hair, that once was fair,
Each eye, at times, feel very dry,
No need to cry, but I wonder why.

My face, is ofttimes, very red.
'Tis Rosacea or Psoriasis, that I dread.
My neck disappeared as I grew older.
My head now rests atop my shoulder.

As big as my chest, is now my waist,
Blame foods I like best, none goes to waste.
Painful is my back, legs, and knees,
At times, my side, too, when I sneeze.
My hands weakened, too weak to squeeze,
To open jars, etc. that once I did with ease.

Changes, changes, though slowly they came,
If they continue, I fear I may go lame.
That, I fear, would be worse than a shame.
Perhaps I am entirely and solely to blame,
I'm at my wit's end, tired of this game.

—December 20, 2012

CHEATER

He was a downright cheat.
A real glib-tongued, dead beat.
He talked his way thru schools,
Treated others as tho they were fools.
He cheated on every test,
Instead of studying, to do his best.
He thought he was better than the rest.
By and by, he became a petty thief.
Stealing lunch money, causing grief.
In his late teens, he got mean,
He stole and stole, got away clean.
Avoiding the cops, leaving the scene.
Stealing autos became his style.
He was getting rich in a short while.
He was a conniver, cunning and sly.
He really knew how to cheat and lie.
It mattered not who he cheated and why,
The amount, perhaps insignificant, he got by,
Solely on his wits, he did rely.
He did make many a deal,
Pretending to make an "honest buy."
All the while he aimed to steal,
By not paying, just lie, lie, and lie.
Always some excuse he did make,
Tho what he'd say was a lie, a fake.
Without hesitation, he'd take and take,
Always just for him, for Pete's sake.
His conscience bothers him not.
He can finagle from you, all you've got.

—August 7, 2001

CHILD ON THE SWING

The child on the swing,
Appeared sullen, depressed and glum,
Not wanting, nor doing anything,
Refusing a drink, candy and gum.

'Tis sad to see a child that way.
What can you do or say?
Should you interfere or not?
That's the question, that I've got.

Many will advise, say no,
Better to look away and go.
It pains your heart, though,
Seeing a child with so much woe.

You observe, from a distant seat,
Making sure to remain discreet.
The child, after a while, begins to play,
With another child, in a friendly way.

You wonder, was it his mood,
That caused him to sulk and brood?
Relieved, you go your own way,
'Twas no need to meddle, this day.

—August 11, 1999

CHILLING AND GRILLING

For many men, chilling and grilling,
Is a weekend ritual that is thrilling.
Oh yes, the food is delicious and filling.
To do this, many men are able and willing.

Barbeque while sipping a brew or two,
Sadly, is what too many men may do.
The self-proclaimed "grill master,"
Thinks he's the best even if not faster.
He's just better than the rest.

Chicken, sausage, hamburger or steak,
Most prefer to grill, not fry or bake.
Ribs and vegetables on the grill,
Can be tasty, even fit the bill.

Corn with the husk, cook very well,
On the grill, as anyone can tell.
Shish kebab and garlic bread,
Grill well, too, while many are fed.

—typed February 17, 2020

CHRISTMAS 1996

What a wonderful, lovely day, Christmas 1996,
Everybody was happy and gay, nothing to assemble or fix.
The food was great, we ate and ate,
Turkey cooked to perfection, all you could eat,
Stuffing, dressing, confection, and some other meat.

The weather was nice, a day we did really enjoy,
Presents aplenty, from watches to spice,
Stockings with goodies and more than one toy,
Enough presents to satisfy every girl and every boy.

"Trivia Pursuit," a game that was played by a few.
Others who didn't want to do the same,
Did whatever they wanted to do.
The day was one of harmony and love,
For this we thank the "Son and the Lord" above.

Yes, Christmas 1996, a very great day,
We'll remember for many years to come.
No unhappiness, did any one display,
But gratitude by all, much surprise by some.

We missed the ones absent, each had their reason,
To be away during this holiday season.

—December 1996

CIGARETTES

Cigarettes, cigarettes, cigarettes,
If they haven't killed you yet,
They'll help you become broke,
Each time you take that puff of smoke.

The price paid today is very high.
Yet, many only shrug and sigh.
Oblivious that they may die,
They continue to smoke, smoke and buy.

Warnings, warnings, on every pack,
Say that smoking may affect your health.
Perhaps some warnings, they do lack,
About how they may affect your wealth.

Tobacco affects many others, too,
Who don't smoke, but dip or chew.
Secondhand smoke, what does it do,
Irritate, bother or terribly offend you?

Tobacco users have their rights, don't they?
Most establishments oblige them in some way.
Smoking areas are posted in many places today,
While more ban smoking, more every day,
Many nonsmokers are having their say.

Yet, amid all the hype, about all this,
Somehow, something does seem to be amiss.
To tax, and tax this product more and more,
Seems unjust, unfair, as many have said before.

—May 11, 2000

CLAUDIA

On weekends you mow my lawn,
Usually after you've mowed your own.
A hat covers your head so that your face won't burn,
While you drive your mower, a "zero turn."
Like a pro, you handle the machine fast or slow,
To and fro, forward, backwards, any way you want it go.
Enjoying this task, you seem to glow.
How much this means to me, you may never know.
Two acres you cut in a very short time.
Trimming around trees, you can turn on a dime.
You perspire, your cheeks may turn red and shine.
That you proposed to do this for me was divine.
I'm at a loss how to thank you enough.
For me to do this every week would be tough.
I thank you, Claudia, from the bottom of my heart.
I'll be grateful to you until this life I depart.
When we sit and chat, you make my day.
Happy Birthday, Claudia, Happy Birthday.
Your neighbor and dear friend, Ray!

—November 2, 2018

CLOUDS

They were beautiful, snowy white,
With a background that was azure blue.
'Twas really a wonderful, pleasing sight,
Changing shapes the way that they do.

Lying on my back, I gazed at the cloud,
Watching as it slowly moved away.
Near a window, away from the crowd,
I enjoyed the view this particular day.

Suddenly, within my line of view,
A new cloud did appear.
An ominous gray, then a darker hue,
I thought, "'Twill rain, I fear."

Dark, the sky suddenly did turn,
Swift enough to cause me concern.
A sign of rain, or even a storm,
Hopefully, it won't cause damage or harm.

What luck!! The clouds drifted away.
The rain didn't come today.
Clear skies and a very bright sun,
Reappeared, I'm thrilled, ready for some fun.

—May 3, 1999

COFFEE OR TEA

I take my coffee, sweet and black.
Some drink tea that's green.
I may drink two cups, back to back.
The amount I once drank was obscene.

Coffee with caffeine, some can't tolerate,
Especially in the evening, late.
Anytime, any kind, I drink mine.
In fact, many times, it's just divine.

I buy my coffee, roasted and ground.
Any place, I seldom "shop around."
I compare prices more so than brand.
Brewed right, to me, they all taste grand.

Seldom do I ever drink tea.
Somehow, tea is just not for me.
Like coffee, my tea must be sweet.
Otherwise, it's definitely not a treat.

But then, perhaps I'm an oddball,
Since I eat no doughnuts at all.
Never, ever, do I drink,
Coffee, nor tea in bed.
'Tis unnecessary, I think.
It could eventually "go to my head."

My "sweets" I prefer "in the flesh,"
Or perhaps in fruit, when it's fresh.

—October 7, 2000

COMICS

Many Comedians are still around,
But more are of the racy type, I've found.
Their kind of humor I find,
Is mostly very ugly and unkind.

Clean-cut jokes are now very few.
Gone are many clean Comics we knew.
Popular ones today prefer to spew,
Foul language, lewd remarks, too.

The crude and rude words they spout,
The rude things they anxiously talk about,
Temps many people to shout,
"What makes them think they have clout?"

Four-letter words, they put to use,
So often, to the point of abuse.
If shock, some people display,
They're tickled, it's made their day.

Morally, they don't seem to care,
If the very young hear, and are aware.
They pick up and repeat anywhere,
This garbage they pass as "fun fare."

Amazingly, their audience is big,
So they continue to dig and dig,
All the dirt that they possibly can,
On all, or any rich or famous man.

—September 28, 1999

COMMISSIONER

It's her first day, her first election,
That she worked at the Poll.
There was one, only one selection,
Voters voted on, listed on the Roll.

To no one's surprise, few came.
She thought, "What a shame.
Is it fair to take my pay,
When I did so little, today?"

All day, 'twas sit and wait, wait and sit,
Did she think, "Should I quit?"
I hope the thought ne'er crossed her mind.
To voters, she was polite and kind.

Next election, she may be proud,
Having to handle a much larger crowd.
All day, she'll be busy as a bee.
'Twill be quite different, she'll see.

Today, I hope she does not,
Form the wrong impression.
Today is slow and boring, yet,
She should not, must not,
Go into any kind of depression.
Other days will be busier, you bet.

Just wait until the 7th of November,
After working at Presidential Election.
She may need to rest thru December,
To get back into the swing, regain perfection.

—October 7, 2000

COMPETITORS

Why do we seem to compete,
With some people, whenever we meet?
Will it make our life more complete,
To strive for "that important seat"?
Siblings may ofttimes vie,
For their Mother's "love and affection."
They may say "that they'll die
If things don't come in their direction."
Chicks compete in the nest,
For the morsels that they ingest.
Some get bigger than the rest,
Because, "they always win the contest."
Kittens, too, act this way.
Their Mothers seemingly cares not.
The smallest seem to have no say,
Gets less than what the others got.
Wolves compete to lead the pack.
Dogs do much the same.
Discipline, they don't lack.
All seem to understand the "game."
People compete in "daily life."
They struggle to do their best.
It's a good feeling, worth the strife,
To know that you're a "notch above the rest."
Athletes compete for "the gold."
Yachtsmen compete for "the cup."
Skiers compete in the cold.
Surfers compete whenever "the surf is up."

Racers try hard to win the race.
Others may be pleased to "just save face."
Many strive to "get ahead,"
And "failure" is their biggest "dread."

—July 10, 1999

COMPUTER BOY

The computer was his joy.
'Twas like another toy.
Games on it, he did play,
Many times, most every day.

Sometimes it's used as a tool,
To do "homework" for school.
There is information galore,
About many things, and much more.

He enjoys the "Internet."
Many things there, he can get.
He can "chat" with someone,
Or "surf the net," just for fun.

He's able to obtain "news and weather,"
Or speak to a girl named, "Heather."
From friends and family, he gets "e-mail."
He may identify words, without fail.

He can easily write,
A letter, a poem, or such.
Incorrect words, the computer will "highlight."
A feature he likes, very much.

Personal cards, he can create,
For most any occasion or date.
Serious, funny or in between,
With more than one, available scene.

There seems to be something
Out there for everyone.
For work, or just plain fun.
Be aware, the time is near,
If it's not already here,
When computers will be,
A required piece of gear,
For a student to complete his
Final, "High School Year."

—February 19, 1999

CONVICTS

Convicts, in the days of yore,
Were never pampered at all.
Like many in jails before,
Most lived with "chain and ball."

Hard labor was the order of the day.
Mercy was very seldom shown.
Guards had their say and their way.
The "workday" began before dawn.

Living conditions oft were crude.
Life was miserable and hard.
Politeness, was out, everyone was rude.
Pastime was perhaps a game of cards.

Few, if any, attempt was made to reform,
Convicts, no matter what the verdicts.
Some labored on a penal farm.
Few, however, escaped some form of harm.

Things have changed a bit, today.
Convicts are now allowed time to play.
They even get to watch TV, you see,
Attend school, work towards a degree.

—September 2, 1999

COOL OK, COLD NAY NAY

Cold weather is upon us again,
Just after we got over the rain.
But how long will Jack Frost remain?

Wednesday we expect to see our first freeze.
I hope I don't catch a cold and sneeze.
By staying indoors, I avoid the slightest breeze.
My late mate is not home to hug and squeeze.

Now that she's gone, life is more of a struggle.
Being alone, I miss the warmth of a good snuggle.
Although her feet were usually cold as ice,
When she touched my warm feet, it was nice.

Now when it's cold, my feet also get cold.
Is this because I've gotten cold and old?
That I dislike cold weather I've not denied,
No matter in which abode that I abide.

It seems only oldsters are on my side.
Bu lo, we oldsters no longer preside.
Sometimes the situation is not what we desired.
That's OK, we're mostly tired and retired.
We're content, that for peace, we've tried.
We'll keep doing or best, hoping all are satisfied.

—Saturday, November 9, 2019, 10:00 p.m.

COOL WEATHER

Soon it will come around,
A complete change, in the weather.
Already leaves are falling to the ground,
So start to unpack the sweater.

Before long, a jacket will be better,
Perhaps one of very fine leather.
Parkas lined with extra fine feather,
Will be better for icy cold weather.

Changes will soon be here.
Pleasant fall weather, we will cheer.
'Twill not last too long, I fear,
So check up on good winter gear.

Cool weather I enjoy a lot,
And feel safe with a flu shot.
But when very cold weather I've got,
I stay indoors where 'tis nice and hot.
'Tis better for me, like it or not.

Next to the "rebirths" in the spring,
The natural beauty in the fall,
Changes in color in the trees and all,
Is a beautiful setting y'all,
Creating a more picturesque thing.

—October 4, 1999

CORN PICKING

We would get up around four,
Down a breakfast of grits, eggs, and more.
By five we'd be out the door,
As we'd done many mornings before.
'Twas best early in the morn,
To be in the field to break the corn,
Before the sun got very hot.
The mules and we got too hot to trot.

Two mules pulled the wagon slow.
While we walked along each a row,
Into the wagon ears of corn we'd throw,
Until it filled and homeward we'd go.
Hastily it was unloaded into the barn,
Every single ear of corn, by hand.
By then we'd be tired and worn,
Like most farmers who work the land.

The corn was ripe and dry.
It needed harvesting and we'd try.
Bad weather, pests and crows,
Could do damage, who knows?
The corn in the field that we found,
Would have to last the winter and beyond.
Every ear of corn was vital to us,
So we gathered it with very little fuss.

Some corn we always did shell,
To feed chickens, and other fouls well.
The fouls we raised after they did hatch,
Were fed corn we had, not chicken scratch.
Some were fed milk before "being dressed."
A better taste was what many expressed.
Pigs were fed corn and slop,
But corn and milk before we went chop, chop.
Feed and food we had aplenty,
But for money we were "hard-pressed."
In fact, at times, we didn't have any.
Yet, I don't remember us being very depressed.

—October 2, 2001

COUNTRY FARM

The hare got caught in the snare,
Just as the bear left his lair.
The hare and the bear were an odd pair.
They were seen together most everywhere.
The cock, atop the shop, did crow.
'Twas sunup, he wanted all to know.
The fox eyed the hen inside the pen.
He'd seen her behind the ox, near his den.
The lamb, everywhere, followed the ewe.
She was her provider, protector, she knew.
If she and the ewe got into a stew,
The ram would help them, out of a jam, 'twas true.
The frisky little pig, dancing a jig,
Must have thought his was big,
As he toyed with the big hog near the bog,
Resting by a log, out of sight of the dog.
The large white, snowy goose,
Impressive, once he was loose,
Gave chase, with haste, to the bear cub,
Who was rooting around for some grub.
The very agile cat,
Waited and waited, then caught the rat.
With patience, he'd sat and sat.
Then in a flash, that was that.
The cow, too, was up by now,
Waiting for the milkmaid.
The lass, would pass somehow,
Through the menagerie, she said.

The horse, the goat and the steer,
Meandered, but stayed clear,
Of the milkmaid, out of fear,
Or respect for the lass, the dear.

—August 20, 1999

COUNTRY WIFE

Unlike the country wife of yore,
Many things, today's country wife,
Just doesn't do anymore.
Her family, she does not ignore,
Despite changes in her way of life.
Milking cows is no longer her chore.
Milk and eggs, she gets from the store.
Feeding chickens, was such a bore,
As was slopping the sow and the boar.
Boucheries, we don't hear of anymore,
Lard is passé, unhealthy, to the core.
Churning butter is no longer her job,
Nor is shucking corn, for "corn on the cob."
Beans and peas, she doesn't shell herself.
At the store, she gets them right off the shelf.
She may have a small garden plot,
With vegetables, greens, herbs, and the lot.
Tomatoes and cucumbers, the least some have got.
Some grow peppers, both mild and hot.
No gingham or any homemade dress,
She wears "store bought" like the rest.
Seeking the latest fashions, is her quest.
She strives to look her best.
Her workload reduced, she's under less stress.
No longer is she under any duress.
No matter what she plans to do,
She's no longer awakened by a "cock-a-doodle-do."
Ole country style living is now in the past.

Modern technologies have made the changes fast.
Different, is today's country wife,
She's well educated, much, much, more liberated.
Very modern, she lives a different life,
Than the wife of "yesteryear," who was much underrated.

—August 15, 2000

COWPOKES

Cowpokes ate their grub,
If they washed, 'twas a light scrub.
All day long in a dusty trail,
Then to the chuck wagon they'd hightail.
'Twas usual for the cowpoke,
To "roll his own" and enjoy a smoke.

Night meal was a large juicy steak,
With beans and perhaps, bread.
This would do until daybreak,
When they'd awaken with a clear head.
Breakfast might be steak with egg.
There was plenty, no need to beg.

In the saddle very long hours,
Many days went without baths or showers.
Driving cattle was their job, their aim.
Getting the job done was their claim.
Over hills, plains, across river and stream.
Successful ones gained much fame.

From a "cattle town" trains would take,
The cattle to cities far and wide,
Where people enjoyed beef, a steak,
And into leather became the hide.
Cattle drives ended years and years ago.
This way must have been much too slow.
Trailer trucks haul many cattle today.
It's been that way for many a day.

Slaughterhouses today are few.
Killing and skinning few butchers do.
Big companies process beef after slaughter,
Shipping beef by the half or the quarter.

—September 13, 2001

CRAWFISH

The crawfish, a main Cajun dish,
Is served in Louisiana quite a lot.
They satisfy, many in Texas who wish,
To add to their recipes of the Mex-Tex, they've got.

Crawfish grown in California now,
Wind up in Louisiana restaurants somehow.
They are shipped during Louisiana's off-season.
Few Californians eat them, is the reason.

My brother, in Colorado today,
With his family, celebrated his birthday.
He ate his favorite, crawfish etouffee.
Crawfish from his ranch pond, he did say.

Crawfish from China, we still get,
Tho the price is now very high, you bet.
The increase in tariff, did the trick,
The price more than doubled, real quick,
'Tis enough to make me sick.

Peeled and frozen, crawfish does last.
It's been done a lot in the past.
Delicious crawfish are served in many ways,
Plentiful, in season, which can last many days.

—September 19, 1999

CROCODILE

The croc is a menacing creature.
Powerful jaws are his main feature.
With his powerful tail he can also,
Break the legs of game or foe.

Crocs are their young ones' savior,
Carrying their babies inside their mouth.
Once thought 'twas cannibalistic behavior,
'Tis protective instinct, without a doubt.

Crocs, like gators, are now farm raised,
Commercially, for their skin and meat.
The taste of their meat, highly praised,
The quality of their skin is hard to beat.

A croc is a reptile,
Who has, for eons, been around.
In Africa, in and around the Nile,
In Australia too, they abound.

If you launch at a dock,
The small flatboat that you've got,
You may be in for a shock,
If suddenly you meet with a croc.

Don't delay, be on your way,
Don't feed nor harass,
If a croc you see that day,
And near him you happen to pass.

—September 3, 1999

CRUDE ONES

Seemingly from nowhere, they crawl,
On walls, graffito, they scrawl.
Then onto a lounge chair, they sprawl,
As tho nothing has happened, what gall.

Public and private property they debase,
Each and every time they deface,
Buildings, bridges, or any place,
That's visible, in any case.

Some may even get a thrill,
Shooting signs, etc., at will.
Going up or down a hill,
A stray bullet may even kill.

Such actions are mean, ugly and crude,
Just as some talk is profane and rude.
You don't have to be a prude,
Nor act like the ignorant and lewd.

Damage done, who will pay?
The cost, who will defray?
The public, you and I, I say,
Will pay, in some form, some way.

—November, 28, 1999

CRUISE

While you sail upon the seas,
Enjoying the soft, willowy breeze,
Wishing all the while that I were there,
I'll be comfortable, in my easy chair.

'Tis not just a notion,
That the motion of the ocean,
Can make one very, very sick,
And can happen very, very quick.

When you see within your view,
O'er the waters clear and azure blue,
The sandy beaches that beckon you,
Your thoughts may be, "What, what to do?"

Go ashore on a tropical isle,
See the sights or shop a while?
You may opt to just beguile
Your time, in your own style.

Aboard ship 'tis ofttimes told,
The spread of food is a sight to behold.
Food to satisfy the young and the old,
Feast upon feast, the least, as flavors unfold.

I wish all of you a very pleasant trip,
While ashore and aboard ship.
Remember tho, everything in moderation,
Except sun lotion, take the sun into consideration.
Bon Voyage, Bon voyage, vous avec le courage.

You leave on Mother's Day,
Enjoy, have it your way!

—May 12, 2000

CRUISE AT SEA, NOT FOR ME

To take a cruise, I care not.
Again, I refuse, whilst my comfy abode I've got.
From my easy chair, TV entertains me a lot.
To me, 'tis fair, ease and comfort is what I care about.
Frills and thrills, eats and eats, cold or hot,
Tempt me little since my maneuverability is shot.
Cruising at sea, you see, is not for me,
Just to overeat and a few isles to see.
All this costs, 'tis definitely not for free.
But, with me, many I'm sure, may disagree.
Yes, hordes sail with joy and glee,
To celebrate onshore and far out at sea.
Food and entertainment may seem to be free,
Once you're aboard and have prepaid your fee.
What do most do on a cruise?
Party, party, eat, eat, and perhaps abuse booze.
Then perhaps, occasionally take a snooze.
On an isle, they may stop and shop,
"Local color," many merrily take in.
Another isle, is their next hop.
They do things all over again.
So, if a cruise is right for thee,
Take it, enjoy it, with blessings from me.
But don't pressure me, let me be.
I won't be another "old man at sea."

—April 2011

CUTE MUTE

The sad young lad was so cute.
Could he talk, was he a mute?
Inside this room at the head of the stairs,
He sat and sat, his eyes just blank stares.
Was he aware that someone was there?
Perhaps he just didn't really care.

Had he been scared or traumatized,
Forced to do something uncivilized?
Had he been given an awful beating?
Was he caught lying or cheating?
Why did he not say a thing?
Inside his head, did a bell ring?

Pitiful he did seem.
His doleful eyes had no gleam.
As he stared, did he also dream?
Alone in this little room,
Did he foresee just gloom and doom?

Had he ever had any moral support,
From family, friends or any sort?
Had he engaged in any kind of sport?
His silence was deafening, he didn't cry.
Doctors and nurses had all wondered why.
What dark secret did he really hide,
That his mind clams shut and keeps inside?

Perhaps someday it will all come out.
He may wake up one day and begin to shout.
He may cry and then he may not,
The truth, which is what it's all about.

—August 20, 2001

DADDY

There he lies in his bed,
No strength to even lift his head.
He seems fragile, looks so frail,
Too weak, at times, to moan and wail.
He doesn't drink and we all fret.
Is it because, his bed, he doesn't want to wet?
But why does he not also eat,
Almost nothing, no vegetables, no meat?
Weeks ago, in a dehydrated state,
He was hospitalized, given fluid thru the vein.
Things went bad, my brother did relate.
He yanked out the IV, created a scene.
He told the MD, "At home I want to go.
I don't want to die in this hospital bed.
I want to be home with my wife and kids, instead."
"You may die," said the MD, "this I want you to know."
Now, days in bed he has lain,
With little to drink and less to eat.
Remedies have been mostly in vain,
Yet, he rebounds, seems he won't be beat.
Spurts of strength he may at times display,
Mostly at night, seldom during the day.
Most times he seems lucid, may even smile,
Yet, he goes into a tantrum, once in a while.
His sons and daughters are devoted to him.
They cater to his needs, his every whim.
Some are with him daily, day in and day out.
They listen for his "whisper," he cannot shout.

144

It's tough, just stop and think,
To depend entirely on another,
For everything, be it bath, food or drink.
And the loss of modesty, Oh brother!
I commend my siblings, they do their best.
Several have their "hands more full" than the rest.
Yet, each seem ready to do what they can.
Some grandkids, too, deserve a mighty big hand.
Everyone's daily routine is now broken,
But no complaints are heard, few words are spoken.
What lies ahead? the question for many.
Decisions will be made with minds that are canny.
In his condition, will he reach ninety-eight?
Could be, who knows his fate?
Others have expired, much to our surprise,
Yet, some are tougher than we realize.

DANCING 2001

Many do call it "dancing,"
Yet, all I see is jumping and prancing.
The ones who "keep in step,"
Are said to be really "hep."

The "two steps" some still do.
For some, 'tis all they ever knew.
The "polka" I see no more.
It's done much less, I guess, than before.
"Ballroom" dancing is seldom seen,
In ballrooms, or even the TV screen.
Musicals, with "fancy dancing" on TV,
Are old, very old, I agree.
Movies with the "flamingo and tango,"
Were also made a long time ago.

When did you last see anyone "jitterbug"?
Now some just shuffle around and hug.
Some oldsters still know "the twist."
They'll dance "the twist" if you insist.
The "Charleston" and "tap dancing,"
Were once popular, the rage.
Are they now performed on any stage?
How often do you see an "Irish Jig"?
Now 'tis "innovative dancing," you dig?
Teenagers "Bop the Bunny Hop" at the "Hop,"
They go and go, don't know when to stop.

Some "Square Dancers" form a club.
They make appearances to entertain.
They don't dance for cash or any grub,
But for the pleasure and joy all gain.
"Line dancing" is popular today.
No partner is necessary to dance away.
You dance with "others" that way.
The "leader" or the "tempo" leads the "sway."
'Tis a popular way to exercise,
While having fun, as one may surmise.

—October 29, 2001

DANS LA COUR

Le velain chien a manage toute le pain,
Un chien qui vout a rein.
La chienne est la avec un chaine,
Elle apres dormir dessous une chene.

La tortue, pauve bete, est perdu,
Elle chercher pour des carotte cru.
Elle fait pas tros bien.
Ye vas la lache dumaine,
Ou dans la semaine prochaine.

Le chat et la chatte, et dans la cour,
Il sont apres courir pour attraper la poule.
La poule ca cache dans la cabane.
Le chat a courir dans le champ de canne.

Le fermier et sa jeune femme,
Comprendre pas comment sa s'est passe,
Eux vas comprendre peut-etre jamais.

—December 28, 2019

DAUGHTERS

What is a daughter worth?
How do we really measure?
With goats, sheep, pigs or a plot of earth,
Or perhaps, with some modern-day treasure?

Within the past few years,
I've seen a daughter's worth displayed.
By my sisters, the dears,
So often, in many, many ways.

When Parents need 24-hour care,
'Tis usually the daughters that are there,
Cooking, washing, changing daily wears,
Cleaning house and kitchen wares.

Staying bedside throughout the night,
Listening for the slightest demand.
Obeying any wish a parent might
Make and treat them with a delicate hand.

Yes, I've seen what a daughter is worth,
Very often, again and again.
I've treasured my only one, since her birth,
And now I wish we'd had ten.

—March 24, 1999

DAVID TVEIT, MD

A doctor that I admire is David Tveit.
He's very knowledgeable and does things right.
The women on his staff are pleasant and bright.
They're efficient, kind and very polite.
When Doctor Tveit is not available, his cohort I see.
He, too, is also wise and very good to me.
I'm very grateful and happy to be,
In the care of such people, yes siree!
My life is literally in their capable hands.
It's comforting to know they do their best to understand,
What's happening in my body and what it demands.
When people do their best, you can't ask for more.
Whatever the outcome, whatever is in store.
Perhaps Mother Nature is keeping score.
So, if you're ailing 'cause your kidneys are failing,
Take my advice, see Dr. Tveit once or twice.
I think you'll agree with me, he's the one to see.
You'll find that he can help thee, I guarantee.
I'm his "patient" patient.

—October 6, 2019

DEAR MARY

Mary Dear, don't be contrary nor live in fear.
When around people, just don't get too near,
No closer than six feet, I hear.
No need to be afraid, lose hope or despair.
Spend more time in your "lounge chair."

When you go outdoors to do a chore,
Or have to shop at a shop or any store,
Heed the warnings given, you know the score.
Be wise, improvise and do less, not more.

Things you care to do and do dare, just prepare.
When outdoors, no matter the chore or the task,
Be sure to cover your mouth with a mask.
This coronavirus thing is very, very bad,
One of the worst that we've ever had.

So little that we know about this thing,
Except a lot of misery and woe it does bring.
But if we remain calm and do as experts say,
We may get to live yet another day.

Again, Mary Dear, be wise and don't despair,
But be aware of COVID-19 that's in the air.
The best of luck to you!

—April 8, 2020, 10:00 a.m.

DEAR DEER

His daughter, the sweet dear,
Spotted the small feeding deer.
Eating tree leaves without fear,
Of her although she was near.

Thinking how great, how grand,
She fully extended her small hand.
In an effort to become a friend,
She knew that much would depend,
On keeping intruders off her land.

Their land had many, many deer.
She'd observed them year after year.
She admired their beauty and charm,
Was determined to keep them from harm.
She posted signs saying "No Trespass."
The deer, she wanted no one to harass.

Ofttimes in the early dawn,
A doe would appear with her fawn.
Some days she'd have more luck,
Does and fawns appeared with a buck.
In the clearing, first appeared the doe,
After the "all clear," the buck did go.

Eventually, some deer were almost tame.
As she meandered, near her they came.
She even gave some a name.

She hoped they'd eat out of her hand.
Toward that goal, she planned and planned.
Trying to get them to appear "on demand,"
She may get them, somehow, to understand,
That life for them and her, will be grand.

—August 28, 2001

DEATH

Death comes to us all.
'Tis sad but, oh so true.
When to someone dear, it does befall,
It deeply pains us, me and you.

Death comes to us all.
We're told time and time again.
The sorrow is there, when one "answers the call,"
The grief, the tears, we cannot refrain.

Death comes to us all.
When is it our time? We cannot foretell.
For many it's a tragedy, a big downfall,
For some a relief, from a living hell.

Death comes to us all.
Too soon, occurring at times, the same place.
Its visit, ofttimes, we try to stall,
E'en tho the inevitable, stares us in the face.

Death comes to us all.
Yes, we'll all have our turn someday.
Hopefully it'll come peacefully, summer or fall,
When we expire and are taken away.

Death comes to us all.
'Tis our fate, our final destiny.
It happens to all creatures, big and small,
Without prejudice, it is pure equality!

—June 16, 1997

DEER, OH DEAR

Not fully awake, as I did stretch and yawn,
In my front yard, my attention was drawn.
It was very early, one very frosty morn.
Like magic, two deer did appear.

Beautiful they looked that chilly dawn,
A lovely Doe and her newborn Fawn,
Right there in my front lawn.

She was seen a few times before,
Under the streetlight on the corner of my yard.
My neighbor saw her from her front door.
A few times at night, "she seemed on her guard."

Since "Katrina," back to Nature my field has gone.
This attracts wildlife, so the deer are not alone.
Possums, Coons, and other quadrupeds freely roam.
Many Critters, in the field, find a home.

Much wildlife today struggle to stay alive,
Their habitat is disappearing, it's hard to survive.
Subdivision after subdivision suddenly do appear,
Where forests were, this happens year after year.

Wildlife have fewer and fewer places to go.
Will many wild ones disappear? It does seem so.

—April 4, 2020, 10:00 a.m.

DERELICT

Who is this "bag lady" on the roadside?
Every day, she sits, waits for a ride.
Truckers willingly give her a lift.
She hops in and away they shift.

Has she fallen off the "ugly tree,"
Hit each and every branch?
Is she searching for a "husband-to-be,"
That owns, some kind of a ranch?

What has happened to this lady?
Was she once a "beauty queen?"
Was she involved in something shady?
Was she making "every scene"?

It has faded, her beautiful glow.
What happened, will we ever know?
Once a bright and "free spirit,"
We see something now, but don't like it.

Her "good looks" are really gone.
Her diet took her to "skin and bone."
She's no longer a "queen on her throne,"
But a derelict melted "like an ice cream cone."

How does someone become such a wreck,
    Not caring about a thing, by heck?
No longer does anything seem to matter,
No cooking, no messing with any batter.

—September 19, 2020

DIETING

Over and over we've been told,
The adverse effect of eating too much fat.
Yet, many eat fat, are they being bold?
They've lost weight, are proud of that.

We're also warned about the egg yolk.
Eating too many, causes strokes.
Again and again we're told 'tis no joke,
No more than three or four per week, folks.

Other doctors say it isn't so.
Eating fat is the way to go.
Fat, they say is not at fault,
But cut out the sugar and the salt.

Now I'm confused, I do admit.
I need to lose a lot of weight.
Whatever I do is a miss and hit,
What I eat, and I mean eat, I hate.

I try to eat according to the "pyramid,"
As prescribed by the American Heart Association.
Yet, I must do wrong, tho naught is hid,
I'm not losing weight and am still on medication.

It seems to be a losing fight,
For me, for others, who share my plight.
On a strict diet, we lose a little then gain a lot.
Over and again, frustration is all we've got.

—October 8, 1999

DIMPLES

She had just one dimple.
It was prominent on her cheek.
He teased her, 'twas simple,
When he met her once a week.

His dimple was on his chin,
Like a renowned movie star.
He too, was teased now and then,
Because of his dimple, and his scar.

Dimples were not oft seen,
Among neither their friends nor their peers.
They considered them cute, not obscene,
Proud they'd been of them all these years.

Dimples were the reason that they had met.
They were brought together as a joke.
Strong feelings immediately, both did get,
When, to each other, they first spoke.

Shy and bashful, they were in their teens,
Not because of a dimple, but pimples galore.
Neither had frequently made the scenes.
They laughed at how they'd endured the sneers.
Married, they've been happy for years.
Their dimple, they each simply adore.

—September 11, 2001

DISHWASHER

The dishwasher washes each dish,
To be sure it is clean.
This may be done however we wish,
By human hands, or an easier way, the machine.

The dishwasher machine, many utilize,
Because, one may easily surmise,
'Tis the best way to sterilize,
Dishes, pots, pans and silverware,
Without any damage or compromise,
To hands, no scalding, no wear and tear.

Dishes rinsed right away,
Immediately, after use, each day,
Will be easier to clean,
Whether using hands or machine.

Pasta, eggs, berries and such,
When dried on a dish, pan or fork,
May be much, much too much,
For some machine to do its work.

A fork with dried-on rice,
Is a "turnoff," not very nice.
When served with a dish, utensil or pan,
That has any dried-on, leftover food,
Usually will, any diner, woman or man,
Be the cause of their sour mood.

The remedy to prevent this,
Is simply to scrape and rinse.
It does make a lot of sense.
Not a dish, pot or utensil should one miss.

To be served on a plate that is not clean,
Is disgusting, almost obscene.
Whether it's a café or fancy place,
Whether 'tis cheap or too high a price,
Apologies usually do not suffice.
Unclean utensils or dishes, is a disgrace.
It simply cannot be tolerated, in any case,
No matter what is said, "to save face."

—August 11, 2001

DISTRACTION

Drinking hot coffee while they drive,
Is why some people are no longer alive.
While drinking, keep thinking, it's the spill,
That causes the risk, that usually will kill.

To wipe the mess, you take your eyes off the road.
As you may guess, in a flash you may crash,
Destroying you and all of your load.

Hot soup can be just as bad.
You need 3 hands for wheel, bowl and spoon.
But you only have 2 hands and that's sad.
A scalded lap may cause a wreck, too soon.

Fried chicken, hamburgers, chili, and tacos,
May be poor choices while driving, who knows?
Sloppy Joes or barbecued foods that drips,
Are dangerous and risky, could spoil many trips.

Jelly and cream-filled donuts or ice cream in cones,
If they mess your shirt, it may rattle your bones.
Supersized drinks with flimsy cups and tops,
If they're hyper-caffeinated, you may soon see cops.

Most dangerous of all, is eating and using a cell phone.
The distraction when making the call, after all,
May cause a wreck and POOF, you're gone!
If they had a mate, 'tis too late, the mate is now alone.

—Monday, November 4, 2019, 8:20 p.m.

DOGS IN NEED

Post Katrina, many dogs in need,
Included every size, color and breed.
Many rescuers, with undue speed,
Answered the call, yes indeed.

Dogs full of anxiety, fright and fight,
Were truly a very pitiful sight.
Many rescued were flown to many a site,
Where they were received with much delight,
Cared for and loved after a long flight.

To the North, East and to the West,
Wherever it was considered best.
Locating the dog's owners was a chore.
Luckily, the Internet helped, more and more.

Good homes were often provided,
For the "unclaimed and/or the undecided."
Many owners were probably lost.
Katrina had caused such a tremendous cost.

Each survivor was thankful for his or her life.
But today, many still endure much strife.
Full recovery is not nearly complete,
As evidenced by many, many a street.

—November 8, 2007

DOUBTS

While my health declines in my waning years,
I find that I have more doubts than fears.
"Fear of Dying," I don't think that I possess.
Apparently, dying is just another process.

'Tis not dying I dread, but the thought of pain.
Often I hear this, it's a sad, sad refrain.
But I have wondered about that again and again.
Worrying about dying, there is really nothing to gain.

"Living" is one thing, "Existing" is another.
"Living" is exciting, "Existing" is barely living, Brother.
With doubts, such as these, will meds put me at ease?
Do some Pharmacies really charge what they please?
Do doctors try to appease,
Knowing that long waits make us ill at ease?

Are some medications making us obese?
Will some of my pains ever go away, ever cease?
We endure and hope doctors will cure our disease.
These words (not mine) I believe without a doubt:
"When the mind suffers, the body cries out."

—June 6, 2016

DREAMING

Dreaming, I was aloft,
In a cloud, pure white and soft.
The view down below,
Was of places, covered with snow.

One house stood above all.
'Twas some distance from the mall.
On the computer, the wife was "online,"
While at the mall, many were "in line."

Resting on the cloud up high,
I was relieved, gave a sigh.
Christmas was drawing nigh,
Presents, we still must buy.

To place an order, 'tis late,
Standing in line, we really hate.
So we'll make it simple, be brash,
This time, give good ole cash.

I awoke, but stayed in bed,
Tossed and turned, shook my head.
I thought, "Shopping can be a chore.
Should I again fall asleep, dream some more?"

—December 16, 1999

DREAMS, DREAMS

In my solitude I sit and I write,
About things crude, rude, wrong or right.
Is the world so filled with blight,
That the haze impairs my view, my sight?

Though I try hard, with all my might,
It seems my dreams aren't always bright.
No matter how often I dream, night after night,
Many scenes are about courage or fright.

Like slaying a dragon as a medieval knight.
Then claiming honors with pure delight.
In other dreams I reach a new height,
That fills me with fear that I cannot fight.

Suddenly, I soar like an eagle in full flight,
So high that the Earth is out of sight.
On a planet that is sunshiny and bright,
With beautiful landscapes, a very special site.

There's no night, it's always daylight,
But not enough breeze to fly a kite.
As I ponder and analyze my plight,
My mind is muddy, I realize things aren't right.

Am I being tested or bested, out of spite,
Because I drank a Coke instead of a Sprite,
Or some other silly kind of trite,
That was important, yet I considered slight?
Would a shinning bright Knight, suddenly, me smite?
I woke up, it was past midnight.

—November 8, 2007

DREAMS

I dreamt as I slept and slept.
In my dream, I wept and wept,
Because the spring in my step,
Was replaced by the fall of my arches.
No longer was I able, nor adept,
To continue my work or go on any marches.
My poor, overworked, tired old heart,
Was it causing me to fall apart?
My brain was drained, had gone awry.
Perhaps this was causing me to cry.
Suddenly, I felt that I was too young to die.
What was happening and why? Indeed why?
Because of hysteria, I suddenly awoke.
Relieved I was, that nothing broke.
Asleep again, dreaming while in a deep sleep,
I was in my teens, driving over hills very steep.
The weather was hazardous, sleeting and sleeting.
I was warned to be careful, my childhood was fleeting.
And was reminded, it lasts only a few short years.
But immaturity, I was told, can last forever.
This is expressed daily, without shame, fear or tears.
So be smart, drive carefully in such weather.
Now you are bold, but remember, you've been told.
Take heed, watch your speed, if you wish to grow old.
Again I awoke, reached for a coke, but I was too cold.
So instead, I slowly dragged myself out of bed,
Washed my face and tried to clear my head.

—August 30, 2013

DRINKING

In College, many have a yearning,
To smoke and taste the pleasure of a drink.
Though it is a place of "higher learning,"
Few will stop and really think.

Some may drink for pleasure and fun,
Makes them feel more at ease.
Some drink with "new friends they've won,"
The "in crowd" they want to appease.

Some drink occasionally, rather mildly.
Some drink excessively and wildly.
Some drink almost nothing but beer,
Perhaps, a six-pack a day, just for cheer.

Hopeless ones, drink to "drown their sorrow."
They've "irrigated them," they find on the morrow.
'Tis very sad and very bad.
Hardly, are they ever very glad.

Some can't "hold their liquor."
A few drinks and they are very woozy.
They get a buzz, this way a lot quicker,
But then, they're not very choosy.

Some drink, drive and then are caught.
For some, a real lesson they're taught.
Some don't learn, get in harm's way,
Then are "put away" for a "very long stay."

—September 17, 1999

DRIZZLE

Drizzle, drizzle, all the day,
Puts my mood, in a dreary way.
Not able to work outside,
Retired, should I leave my bedside?

Reading my paper takes a while.
Little news good, more seems vile.
Disasters are occurring worldwide,
Few safe places, nowhere to hide.

With "idle hands" 'tis true,
The mind wanders, "What to do?"
Meanwhile, listening to the rain,
Today, little progress, little gain.

'Tis a good time,
To telephone a friend or two,
Call some relatives, spend the dime,
Exchange ideas and points of view.

Be generous with yourself,
Rest, while you have the chance.
Watch your back, reaching for that shelf,
Always maintain a proper stance.

Remember, after the rain,
The chores will still remain.
But tomorrow is another day,
To do things, once the rain has gone away.

—September 2, 1999

DRY, DRY

It falls from my head.
Embarrassed, I see it did spread.
Dried old skin that's dead,
'Tis dandruff, a sight I dread.

On my shirt that's blue,
It tends to look like snow.
Tho I shampoo, shampoo and shampoo,
It's always there, just won't go.

Trying to prevent these flakes,
I've even used baby oil.
All my attempts are just mistakes.
Thinking about it makes my blood boil.

'Tis not too noticeable on my head,
Since my hair is now all white.
But on my shoulders and my sheets in bed,
'Tis not a very pleasant sight.

I notice dried skin, on either side
Of, my very prominent nose.
'Tis unsightly, very hard to hide,
Also gets sore, as you might suppose.

Yes, my skin gets very dry and flaky,
In the crease, of my double chin,
Other spots get dry and become achy.
Is it because I'm fat and not thin?

Is this another penalty we must pay,
For simply, getting older?
'Tis not pleasant, I dare say,
'Tis as bad as being colder and colder.

—March 8, 1999

DURING A CRISIS

During the coronavirus crisis, how a man does behave,
May determine whether he is a Knight or a Knave.
A Knight deserving to be called "Sir,"
Surely should be honest, truthful and pure,
That many men may qualify today, I'm not so sure.

Honesty is a trait that many do lack.
That's a shame, today no one has your back.
Once a man's word was good as gold,
But today, it's hard to trust the young or the old.

The "love of money," sad to say,
Is very prevalent, seen everywhere today.
Yet first responders and caretakers are heroes and sheroes,
But in the populace are also many weirdos.

After hearing about many sad tales,
It's evident that common sense does not always prevail.
Many people tend to do things their way,
Regardless of what authorities may do or say.

That they endanger the lives of others matters not.
Again, 'tis good common sense they haven't got.
Some may just be a simple lout.

—May 7, 2020

DWELLING PLACE

Places where we choose to dwell,
Depends if we do or don't fare well.
Rich or poor, it matters not.
What we can afford, is what we've got.
Indians on the Plains lived in a Tepee,
Roaming, seemingly, happy and free.
Eskimos lived in their Igloo,
Roaming freely and apparently happy, too.
Wooden houses with a roof of tin,
Is what many people lived in.
Houses of brick, a choice that many make,
Looks good, even if it's fake.
Dwellings of marble with a roof of slate,
Is ideal, if love abounds instead of hate.
Castles and Chateaus seem so romantic,
But tales of horror depict some residents as frantic.
Many live long in a meager abode,
As do many in a beautiful manor or estate.
But many in a "nursing home" live by their code,
When their destiny is sealed by fate.
Most "nursing home residents" have no choice.
Constant care they really do need.
Many seem unhappy, have little to rejoice.
They're lonely, feel neglected and are miserable, indeed.
Just imagine having to wait,
After the "urge," a half hour to urinate.
Unable to do anything on your own,
But wait, suffer, and groan and groan.

Why is this? Whom do you ask?
Do "aids" receive too little pay for too hard a task?
Nurses also complain, some after many years resign.
No benefits, understaffed, is this all by some design?
Wheelchair bound and in dire pain,
In an emergency they're transported to the doctor's domain.
Appointments mean very little, they just remain,
Perhaps two or more hours before they are seen.
Family members, at a loss, just sigh and sigh,
They feel so helpless that they could and do cry.
'Tis terrible to see a loved one suffer this way.
They hope and pray for a much better day.

—June 20, 2000

EASTER 2016

Easter came and fast it went,
The day was great, a wonderful event.
Sumptuous was the feast on the table,
Most of the family came, ones that were able.

Indoor games were played in the afternoon.
Rains stopped, so Logan and I played outside soon.
GI Joe on a parachute was tossed up high,
It thrilled Logan to see him float from the sky.

Soon it was time to eat one more.
Time elapsed, life resumed as before.
Eric and Regina were wonderful hosts.
Others did their part, most could boast.

Delicious food was plentiful, all had their fill.
Everyone served themselves and ate at will.
The youngsters had their Easter Egg Hunt, too.
Easter 2016 was a Happy Day, no one was blue.

EASTER 2020

This Easter, unlike many Easters before,
Many Churches have closed their door.
This is happening all over, yes, worldwide,
Because of COVID-19, so many people have died.

Masses for the masses, in many an empty church was spoken.
Obeying the orders, no laws were broken.
Many Church Services are being held "online."
For lots of Worshipers, that works fine.
The message given is still divine.

Worldwide, people were told to "stay at home."
Bad is the CORONAVIRUS pandemic, so don't roam.
Another reason not to stray today,
We're under a "tornado watch," a storm is headed our way.
From 2 p.m. to 10 p.m. we've been told "beware,"
Strong winds and possibly tornadoes will fill the air.

Statistics on COVID-19 as of yesterday were:
Worldwide, 108,770 deaths out of 1,779,099 cases;
USA, 20,577 deaths out of 532,879 cases;
LOUISIANA, 806 deaths out of 20,014 cases.
This includes all peoples of different faiths and races.

—April 12, 2020, 2:00 p.m.

EATING

Babies are at peace and rest,
When they nurse on Mother's breast.
Weaned and still a small tot,
Many will eat whatever they've got.

But somehow along the way,
A child begins to have her say.
Certain foods a child may not eat.
To some its vegetables, to others meat.

When a child becomes the age of two,
Some Mothers know not what to do.
The child is now very picky
About food, thinks some of it is icky.

Now five and beginning school,
The child's eating habits includes junk food.
Chips, burgers and fries are "cool."
Other unhealthy choices are not good.

Children seem to get their way.
Many frequent "fast foods" day after day.
Their parents must dislike to cook.
Nutrition means little, open your eyes, look.

Manners too, are gone somehow,
From "family restaurants" everywhere.
People don't remove their cap or hat.
The young, the old, many do that.

Good habits, good manners, what a shame.
Is it the kids or parents that are to blame?
"Good manners," I heard at some earlier date,
"Is to eat the last bean and pea in your plate."

—June 21, 1999

ELF ON THE SHELF

The wily, old Elf on the shelf,
Was elusive and adept at shielding himself.
Some in the building were aware,
That he frequently visited there.

An old housekeeper, a noted shrew,
Never discussed what she knew.
Perhaps 'twas because her favorite brew,
Was "special tea," she hid from the crew.

Occasionally, when the cold wind blew,
Bedlam prevailed and things were askew.
From the shelf, the Elf withdrew,
To sneak a nip of the shrew's brew.

Mysterious, weird, uncanny, and awry,
Were happenings in this house that many knew.
'Twas puzzling, no matter how hard they did try.
No one knew why, somebody seemed to cry.
It did upset more than a few.
To remedy the situation, what could they do?

Perhaps the situation would clear up by itself,
Without interference from the old Elf on the shelf.
Did he mysteriously appear from nowhere,
Just to scare the old shrew who seemed to be everywhere?

—November 6, 2012

ENTERTAINER

He was not at the top of his class,
All the while he attended school.
Hardly considered as being crass,
He certainly was not a fool.

Always pursuing his dream,
Nothing, would he let block his way.
Though it was not always "peaches and cream,"
He fought his battles, day by day.

Lacking the metals, silver and gold,
He had an abundance of "brass."
The "people" he said, as he often told,
Their curiosity, would form them into a mass.

To be a man of society and culture,
Was his goal, his great desire.
His crude ways hampered his future,
He needed "polish" to cool his fire.

To the middle class, he did appeal.
He was considered a genius, not crazy.
Everything he did was with ardor and zeal.
Never, ever, would he be considered lazy.

Eventually, he did attain his goal,
Made and lost millions, gained worldwide fame.
Considered a "master entertainer" by young and old,
Forever in history, will remain his name.

—September 13, 1999

EVA LOU

What was it that did compel,
Her to cross the street?
Looking back, 'tis hard to tell.
'Twas Pat, she planned to meet.

Was she attracted to the machine shop?
It was only a skip and a hop.
Did she seek a tug or a propeller,
Or a hug, from a certain fellow?

She attended a strict, private school,
Was a good student, certainly no fool.
Her hormones, did they begin to rage,
Compelling her to act this way, at her age?

Whenever, whatever, something did work.
Never a duty did she ever shirk.
Discussions begun always did end,
For fifty-four years, she's had a husband
And a very dear friend!

—RRP, a friend

EVERY TWEET, NOT A TREAT

Facelifts and many other enhancements, too,
Are up to individuals, what they want to do.
Do most women invest in their breast,
For medical reasons, or simply to look their best?

Whatever the reason, it is theirs alone,
To "naysayers," I say, "Be gone."
This is nobody's business, you see,
So everyone should just let them be.

Too many people seem to meddle,
In other's affair, for smut to peddle.
"Facebook," as many now well know,
May reveal more than some want to show.

If you care, pay attention, you better beware,
Be concerned and consider what you share.
It may be used against you, even if you dare,
To contradict someone who doesn't care,

About anyone's feelings or are not discreet,
Concerning events or people they meet,
Even as they stroll up and down the street.
But then, for people nosy and very upbeat,
They may consider these things "a treat."

To some "oldsters" and there's many of us,
Invasion of privacy can cause us to fuss.
We feel like, "Who can you trust?"
We say, "Every Tweet is not a Treat."

—August 1, 2013

EVILDOERS

Evildoers, are they not everywhere?
Many, many people they do scare.
Is their goal, to intimate or inflict pain,
Even if they have very little to gain?
They succeed in creating fear,
For many, that we may hold dear.
Some are fanatics, we often hear.
They brainwash people of all ages,
Quoting verses from many pages.
Do they indoctrinate by stages?
Some are looked upon as a Prophet.
Too many "scam" people for a profit.
People that hope and have a desire,
To escape God's wrath and hell's fire.
Told to believe, yearn, and learn,
That if they can't discern, they'll burn.
Evildoers insist on having their way.
When "bucked" they may maim or even slay,
Anyone, in their "fold," who disobey.
They claim and practice "their" religion,
Insist all members made their own decision,
Joined and remain at their own volition.
"Evil," 'tis said, will be overcome by "good."
For some, that's not yet understood.
Evil comes in so many forms.
Many, many people it does harm.
It promotes hatred in one way or another,
Tears apart families, brother against brother.

190

Over religion, color, idealism or race,
Fighting over differences, is it not a disgrace?
Life would be far less cruel,
If we all obeyed the "Golden Rule":
"Do unto others as you would have them do unto you."
Is this not really true?
Yet, can we keep "turning the other cheek" and pretend?
There comes a time when you must "defend."

—October 12, 2001

EX-GI JOE

A once proud veteran of a foreign war,
Awarded a Purple Heart and a Silver Star.
He eagerly displays his medals and his scar,
The many times he frequents a bar.
Since he lost his family, house and car.

While in the military, orders he could take.
Tough decisions, he didn't have to make.
Food and shelter were generally provided.
He obeyed orders without question, once decided.
When discharged he was at a loss.
For the first time, he had no boss.

He found no job with much appeal.
His conscience wouldn't let him steal.
But it took money for drinks and a meal.
Begging seemed a quicker and better way.
It became easier and easier every day.

He did hesitate at the first start,
But soon realized that people had a "big heart."
With their money, they generously did part.
With his relatives and friends now all gone,
Emaciated, in poor health, merely skin and bone,
He spends his days mostly all alone.
The nights under the stars and the moon,
He wishes his end would come soon.

Homeless, with no place to go,
Nothing left but his medals to show,
Just another body languidly on skid row.
How low can one go, really how low?
Sadly, denizens on skid row know, they know.
Poor Joe, poor, poor, ex-GI Joe.

—July 27, 2007

EXOTIC ISLE

Did you ever yearn to be,
On an Exotic Isle,
In a far and distant sea,
If even for a "short while"?
A place where time "stood still,"
Where you can "do your thing" at will.
Where everyone "sets their own pace,"
No competition for "space or place."
Where friendliness is the key,
For total "peace and harmony."
Where there is no sign of greed,
But sharing, where there is a need.
Plentiful food in plants and tree,
Bountiful fish in a "deep blue sea."
Beautiful scenery for all to see,
White sandy beaches, clean and free.
Where games played, are simple and fun,
Enjoyed by both sexes, by virtually everyone.
Where dancing is usually an expression, a relief,
Of "gratitude, thankfulness and also grief."
Where everyone you meet,
With a broad smile, you they greet.
Where life is "simple and plain,"
But joyful, just the same.

—July 10, 1999

EX-SMOKER

For forty years I did smoke,
Usually, over three packs a day.
I was addicted in the worst way.
Luckily, I didn't get a stroke.
I quit "cold turkey" as I spoke,
"I quit, that's it, 'tis New Year's Day."

For forty years of torment, I apologize,
Truly, I just didn't realize,
I was so foolish and unwise,
How smoke irritates and aggravates,
Some people, especially their eyes.
I was such an ingrate.

What a shame, during my "prime time,"
I smoked; when I asked, "Do you mind?"
Most all said no, they were so kind.
An occasional "I do" someone might chime.

After sixteen years "smoke free,"
Will I ever know the damage done to me?
Doubts and fears, year after year,
Wondering if my lungs are clear.

Many ex-smokers today get almost rabid,
When a smoker lit and next to them sits.
Furiously, they denounce "his habit."
Outraged, they may go into fits.

Many years, did I cause much grief.
Was smoking, for me, that much relief?
I never considered smoking as an intrusion.
Most of my peers smoked, without confusion.
The pleasure, we professed, was an illusion.

I'm seventy-one, to everyone, this is my advice,
    "Never, don't ever, start to smoke.
If you do you'll get addicted, pay the price.
That would be a great pity, that's no joke."

—September 14, 2000

FIRE

Fire is very useful for one and all.
It keeps us warm in the winter and the fall.
Used wisely for cooking, it's an aid for every wife,
But raging out of control, it destroys property and life.

When a building is on fire,
Firemen work to snuff out the flame.
Then the Fire Marshall's main desire,
Is to determine how it started and who is to blame.

Without fire, most of us would remain in the dark.
But, much damage can be caused by "just a spark."
For heating and cooking, it became a big hit,
But, after camping, be sure no fire remains lit.

During forest fires, carelessness is too often the reason,
Especially during a drought, a very dry season.
Treated with respect, fire can be good for our health,
Can be lifesaving, but too often can cause death.

Fires demand a lot, a tremendous amount of respect.
Certain safety rules one should never, never neglect.
One false move and it may be your neck, by heck!
The rest of your life, you'd be a wreck.

—October 9, 2010

FAIL TO FEAR

When gainful employment you seek,
Be much more bold than meek.
Dress appropriately, be clean and neat,
Shave the beard from face, chin, and cheek.

Be positive, don't even think defeat.
Be concise and polite, not crude nor rude.
Do your best to be in a good mood.
To gain respect and latitude,
Put gratitude in your attitude.

For an interview, don't worry nor dread.
Try to remain focused and think ahead.
As someone once so aptly said,
"Don't fear to fail, but fail to fear."
Although you may be nervous and queasy,
Just don't give up too easy.
Do your best to pass any test.

—March 11, 2009

FAILING AND AILING

If he did inhale a pail of ale,
It would land him in jail, without fail.
Though it's true that he knew,
He had an addiction for the brew,
He overindulged, had more than a few.

As a hobo, he'd ridden the rails,
Slept in barns, on hay, bales and bales.
Walked and plodded o'er hill and dale,
With his trusted dog, an Airedale.

Occasionally, the dog caught a rabbit or quail.
Too often they ate bread, dry and stale,
With soup handed to them in a pail.
Finding shelter from sun, rain, and hail,
Proved to be difficult, too often they did fail.

Now feeble, very often he ails.
With weak lungs, it's difficult to inhale.
Though he doesn't cry, moan or wail,
He dreams of watching pods of whales,
From the deck of majestic ships he sails,
Across oceans from China to Wales.

—October 9, 2011

FAIS-DODO

Saturdays, they are sure to go
To the party, to the "Fais-deaux-deaux."
Thibodeaux, Gros, Breaux and Boudreaux,
Each may have his "Cherie" in tow.

They dance, dance and dance,
All day and probably all night long.
To eat and drink, they don't miss a chance,
While they enjoy each and every song.

Many friends they see and meet,
As they amble, chat, drink and eat.
None are strangers here in this land.
All know the members of the Cajun Band.

Weekdays, everyone toils and toils,
Working steadily, working very hard.
Many days they enjoy crawfish boils.
Many nights, 'tis "booray" a game of cards.

Boudin, cracklings, and hog's head cheese,
For most, is sure to please.
Jambalaya, gumbo, and crawfish etouffee,
Is sure to complete everyone's day.

—June 4, 2000

FAMILY

My children and grandchildren are dear to me,
I'm proud and love my family and progeny.
Grateful am I, for my wife and the children she bore,
Although after four, she didn't want more.

Nieces and nephews, I have aplenty.
Together, my wife and I have very many.
Loving them was always my goal,
As was Phyllis, God rest her soul.

A great family is more precious than gold.
You realize this more and more, as you get old.
In our youth, did we express this less?
Perhaps we were not bold or just plain cold.
Interest may have been lacking, 'tis anybody's guess.

Life is short and families should stick together,
No matter how calm or stormy the weather.
If all families did, things may be much better.

—Friday, October 18, 2019

FARMER OR SHRIMPER

'Twas a violent, raging storm,
That gave him cause for alarm.
He'd come straight from the farm.
No one had twisted his arm,
But he knew not the potential for harm.
'Twas his first trip out to sea,
To shrimp, make big money, you see.
High hopes now suddenly turned into fear,
More and more, as the storm drew ever so near.
The sea was really getting rough.
He was suddenly queasy the going was tough.
Waves were now very, very high.
Would he live through this, would he die?
Survival was now his main concern,
What, if anything, was he going to learn?
He wondered, would they remain afloat?
He held on for dear life inside the boat.
Oh, to be back on the farm, he did yearn.
Eventually, the storm had passed,
'Twas a nightmare while it did last.
He wanted to head for the shore, and fast.
They checked the nets and the mast.
The skipper decided the nets they would cast.
He expressed concern, did not agree, He'd had his fill
of the sea. Back on the farm he wanted to be
As soon as possible, was his plea.

—November 16, 2000

FAST-FOOD MOOD

The "home-cooked meal"
Is becoming very rare.
Too many a "big deal"
Looms here and there.

Chicken, hamburgers, pizza and tacos,
Available most anywhere one goes.
Other "quick meals," too,
Are seen on many a "daily menu."

That "tots," before the age of two,
Can recognize many a big sign,
Like the "big arch," the way they do.
'Tis not by chance, but by design.

"French Fries," they learn real quick
To say, perhaps along with "coke."
Allowing a child to eat 'til they get sick,
Some parents laugh, but 'tis no joke.

Parents who allow the very young,
To choose most all of their "eats"
May, later on feel like they were stung,
By "high health bills" caused by "treats."

Look around, what do you see?
"Eateries," some plain and some very fancy.
In a small town, they may number a score,
A larger town, perhaps, many, many more.

Who supports these "eating places"?
Parents and children, with happy faces,
Tell the whole story.
Since "vegetables" are not a child's favorite food,
'Tis glory, glory, glory,
When "fast food" is for the brood.

Mom too, enjoys this a lot.
No cooking, means not cleaning a pot.
Perhaps she works "full-time,"
Like it or not.
Music to her ears, are the words, "takeout."

—March 1, 1999

FIFTY YEARS

Fifty years we've been wed,
That long, we've shared a bed.
Fifty years we've stayed together,
Through fair and stormy weather.
Many things, we discuss and disagree,
But, each other's faults we always see.
We argue about petty things,
Yet, appreciate the happiness some bring.
Our children are all full-grown,
Have long ago, from our home been gone.
Our children have their own children away from home.
They "flew the coop," away they've flown.
Fifty years we've "kept our head,"
Although, many tears have been shed.
Fifty years, 'twas not always easy,
To keep the wheels turning, keep them greasy.
Fifty years, do we have to celebrate?
In order to remain happy with our mate?
Traveling, traveling, is not really great,
When one dislikes it, so what's our fate?
Fifty years, must we renew each vow,
E'en tho 'twas done right at the beginning?
Seems to be redundant, somehow.
Do you renew and renew, is there no ending?
Fifty years, fifty years, my dear.
It went by swiftly, but have no fear.
We'll just "play it by ear,"
Stay close to each other, very near.

Without celebration nor any kind of fete,
We'll do fairly well just don't you fret.
Upcoming years may be the best years yet.
We'll survive, be alive, and enjoy many a "tête-à-tête."

—April 30, 2000

FISH FRY

Every year, 'tis his wish,
To catch and fry a lot of fish.
He invites his "High School Class"
Most everyone attend, very few pass.

It's the Class of 1943,
56 years ago and they're great to see.
Most are very lively and spry,
Each and every Girl and Guy.

Other friends are invited, too.
Collectively, 'tis quite a crew.
Many "chip in" and "give a hand."
Beside food, they provide a band.

The fried fish is tops on the menu.
The food, the eats, is always great,
Including chili, that someone does create.
The variety of desserts is delicious, too.

Classmates mingle gleefully, reminisce.
They chat about that and this.
Eating ends and they begin to dance,
To old tunes, with mates or "free lance."

—August 10, 1999

FLAPDOODLE

Too many Jackanapes, today abound.
In government, many, many are found.
Perhaps, what sticks in my craw, a very big flaw,
Is that too many are degreed in law.

Lawmakers and lawbreakers may have a common bond.
Perhaps it's greed, much evidence has been found.
Shenanigans and backroom deals abound.
Seems that some people run everything into the ground.

The "blame game" many, many seem to play.
That is how some spend most of their day.
Very little is done, although much they have to say.
Such is the "lot" of many Politicos, today.
Their only interest seems to be "to have their own way."

Louts and the drivel that they spout,
Seldom is just talk, but they usually shout,
No matter what the subject is about.
Instead of many good deeds to tout,
'Tis gossip that they prefer to flout.
Flapdoodle, yes flapdoodle, is their game,
They practice it over and over, without shame.
Spin and more spin, comes from within.
It is unethical, if not a sin.
Yet, who is really to blame?

FLIGHT TO UNITE

Was it out of fright,
That they hugged real tight,
Embraced with all their might?
He was her "shining Knight."
They had suddenly seen the light.

If anyone spoke "out of spite,"
They'd tell them to "go fly a kite,"
With much "gusto and delight."
Wouldn't that be bright?

Wedding expenses seemed out of sight.
No one they feared, knew their plight.
After much discussion, but no fight,
They felt they would do right,
By eloping that very night.
So they took a "flight to unite."

—August 2010

FLIRT

When she donned her red skirt,
Magically, she became a flirt.
Wearing an open-front silk shirt,
She attracted men and ofttimes a squirt.

Red shoes complimented her attire.
Even her red hair flowed like fire.
Easily, she could make her skirt twirl,
While giggling like a little girl.

Always displaying a big smile,
That was infectious the whole while.
Prancing and dancing, she was elated.
She only flirted, never dated.

She enjoyed the company of men,
But wanted no trouble to begin.
She flirted and some men felt ill at ease.
Others were comfortable "batting the breeze."
Never did she let men "do as they please."

Occasionally a little "peck on the cheek,"
Was planted on the bold and the meek.
When the weather was pleasant, not bleak,
She would stroll by the banks of the creek.

Spotting her red skirt, a few would ride,
To the creek to be by her side.
With them she would walk, chat, and then sit,
She flirted, but that's all there ever was to it.

—October 10, 2001

FLOWERS

Flowers of all kind,
Are pleasing to the mind.
The fragrance that some emit,
To young and old, they are a hit.
The beauty of a rose,
Is enjoyed by many, I suppose.
The scent of gardenia, along the walk,
Fills the air, as we talk.
The wisteria way up the tree,
Has reached the top I see.
The flowers look like grapes.
From many branches, they drape.
Lilies of many colors and hue,
Decorate the lawns and yards, they do.
Many of different heights and shape,
A nice addition to any landscape.
Flowers of some kind do appear,
Every season and throughout every year.
In some trees and on the ground,
Flowers are found the year round.
Flowers brighten up a gloomy room,
Be it just a stem with a bloom.
For many, a really nice bouquet,
Will cheer them up, the entire day.

—September 23, 1999

FOOTWEAR

Booties that are cute and neat,
The first footwear to adorn our feet.
Perhaps knitted by Mother or Grandmother,
Maybe handed down from one to the other.

As a toddler, we learn to walk,
Then get our first "hard sole."
Fast growing, some parents may balk,
To buy new shoes, before wearing out the old.

As a teenager, choices may vary,
Have to keep up with Tom and Mary.
Some fads may last but a short while,
But peer pressure determines the style.

Soccer calls for a special shoe,
Another for running track.
For mountain climbing, these won't do.
To skate, you can rent from the rack.

Dancing shoes are specially made,
A kind for ballet and another to tap-dance.
Hunting or fishing may require shoes or boots to wade,
Without proper gear, you don't have a chance.

Shiny leather shoes, the proper gear,
For formal wear any time of the year.
Some workers wear shoes with a steel toe.
'Tis for safety, to prevent any woe.

There are special shoes to hike.
There are special shoes to ride a bike.
For boxing, special shoes to prance and strike,
Special slippers to lounge when we like.

Cowboy boots to ride the range on a horse,
Or drive an 18-wheel, semi-rig.
They're not as popular East, of course,
As out West, where they are really big.

—January 30, 2000

FOOTBALL COACH

Coaching is a really great job,
No room here for any kind of slob.
With much "prestige" they get to "hobnob,"
With the very elite, Jane, Rob and Bob.

When winning for quite a while,
Players and fans, give you a big smile.
A winning coach, everyone does like.
A losing coach can take a hike.

A winning coach is everyone's hero.
A losing coach's popularity goes to zero.
A winning coach is held in high esteem.
A losing coach is criticized by all, even his team.

A winning coach, can't pay for his treats.
His coffee is paid for, so is his sweets.
Pity the coach, if he loses a few games.
The "treaters" vanish, it's really a shame.

Lose a few more and he cannot hide.
Everywhere he goes, fans are after his hide.
Snide remarks, chants and verbal abuse,
A losing coach must take "in stride."
If he thinks, "What the heck, what's the use?"
He'd better be careful, no one must he deride.
Soon he'll know who is on his side.

—October 19, 1999

215

FOR PETE'S SAKE

Many nights I lie in bed, wide awake.
Why can't I go to sleep, for Pete's sake?
I count sheep after sheep, until I tire.
It's difficult to sleep, no matter when I retire.

When I finally fall asleep and snore,
I may sleep for seven or eight hours or more.
When I awake, all my joints are achy and sore.
Two or three hours later, I'm drowsy encore.

Some of my medicine may be to blame.
So many I take, it really is a shame.
If they keep me alive, I shouldn't complain.
Quit the medicine and I may become sick or lame.

My daily routine is much the same.
To bed late, up late, eat, read, write and watch TV.
Write poetry when there's nothing on TV I care to see.
The time seems to zip by to me.

—March 5, 2017

FORTY-EIGHTH
ANNIVERSARY

'Twas seemingly so long ago,
Yet, so swiftly, did the time fly.
Love and joy did surely flow,
During the years, that went by.

How radiant you were,
Beautiful, and all aglow,
That memorable day, that year.
'Twas our wedding day, where many did show.

What anticipation, that April in 1950,
When a new course we did set.
Soon learned we'd have to be thrifty,
If our goals, were to be met.

Very early, you proved your worth,
When to our daughter, you gave birth.
Three sons followed rather quickly.
Hale and hearty they were, never sickly.

You were most times gentle, seldom rough.
The task, physically and mentally, was tough.
During our working, we moved a lot,
Took any assignment that we got.

All in all, we did well.
Everyone is happy, best I can tell.
Lots of credit that you are due,
I profess, Dear Wife, I give to you.

Happy Anniversary, I love you.
That's so true.
Even when you're angry, perhaps blue,
And I whole heartily disagree with you.
HAPPY, HAPPY ANNIVERSARY.

FRANK'S HORSE

This time your horse,
Put you under the knife.
It could have been much worse.
You could have lost your life.
With horses you should always beware,
That some are unpredictable, easily do scare.
Always be on the alert and take real care.
Horses are animals, they don't always understand,
What's expected of them unless there's a command.
Usually they react upon demand.
Perhaps this horse has an inherent streak,
Of mischief, or is just hell-bent,
To get you to ride him until he's tired or spent,
Proving that he's not meek or weak,
And is his way of staying strong and sleek.
Or maybe his mind, that day, was absent.
On the other hand, maybe it was meant,
To see just how willing and confident,
You are to ride him a lot more,
Enough so that your behind gets sore.
Once, twice or three times a week, at least.
Then he'll probably remain a friendly beast.
I truly hope that your "boo-boo,"
Heals well and very quickly.
Relax and get plenty of "do-do."
Maybe then you won't feel poorly and sickly.
Don't stir until late afternoon.
Rest and rest so that you don't swoon.

You might be well by the next full moon.
Ask your Mother if she does recall,
How horses busted up your "Uncle Coon,"
Breaking his arms, his legs, his nose and all.
With your horse, just take it easy,
Be gentle, calm, sure and not edgy or queasy.
Learn to read his signs that give a clue,
About what he's doing or is planning to do.
Love you. Uncle Ray.

—RRP, September 28, 2001

FRIDAY THE 13 TH

'Tis Friday the 13th today.
Be wary, if scary, some say.
If afraid, you don't have to go,
On a trip, even to the show.

Under a ladder, I say,
"You don't have to walk."
Go around, let people talk,
Even, if it is a longer way.

If a "black cat" does cross,
Your path this day,
Just be careful, but you're the boss,
Of what you do and say.

If by chance, for goodness sake,
One of your mirrors really did break,
Seven years bad luck, will you face?
Maybe not, if it, you soon replace.

In superstition, I believe not,
Yet, "bad luck" I need not enhance.
Better yet, you know what?
'Tis no need to take a chance.

—August 13, 1999

FRIENDLY PET

He's a cute dog, medium-sized.
By his owner, he's very prized.
He barked as I came near,
"Don't worry, there's naught to fear."

'Tis what my ole friend said,
About his dog, while he shook his head:
"It's okay, really, don't fret.
He hasn't bitten a sole, yet."

As I neared the fence on the farm,
The dog kept on barking, was it my charm?
O'er the fence, not expecting any harm,
For a handshake, I extended my arm.

In a flash, my arm, the dog bit.
He leaped again, didn't want to quit.
Four punctured wounds did bleed.
His warning, the barking, I'd failed to heed.

"He had his shots, it's okay,"
His owner said again and again.
Yet, 'twas my arm bleeding that day,
And not him, that suffered the pain.

'Twas my fault, I should have been faster.
The dog was only protecting his master.
'Twas his line that I did cross.
He just showed me who was the boss.

You never know about another man's pet,
When you're the stranger there.
They're very unpredictable, you bet,
And are apt to turn on anyone, anywhere.

—January 29, 2000

FROG

The bullfrog on the lily pad,
Was very lucky, very glad.
He took the only chance he had,
Leaped and caught the crawdad.

Had he not jumped when he did,
Before he let out a "croak,"
The gator with an easy stroke,
Would have had him, the dirty bloke.
He was not well hid.

On the bank, again he did leap.
Another crawdad he did seek.
In the grass he could easily hide,
As he ate his meal with pride.

He opted to linger near the pond,
Where many ferns displayed their frond.
Insects surely lurch therein.
Prospects of many meals now begin.

In the pond, alongside a log,
Waited a gar, for a frog.
If on the log, the frog came,
To the gar, he'd be fair game.

Just how long would this wait be?
Curiously, I waited to see.
Shortly, a small turtle did appear.
He sunned on the log without any fear.

The gar never moved for a long while.
Being still, lurking, was his style.
The turtle was lucky this day.
The gar was not hungry, he went on his way.

—June 3, 2000

FROM THE INSIDE

'Tis dreary today, more gloom than glee.
Of course, it's still winter, you see.
Days like this, we can expect to be.
I gaze out the window and here's what I see.

Not a leaf moves, on nary a tree.
A humming bird feeder, hangs alone, and empty.
The hummer that once flew like a bee,
Did he vanish, fulfill his destiny?

The feral cat that roams around free,
Hunts birds, squirrels, and rodents on my property.
Me thinks he's become very fond of me.
Homebound folks like me and perhaps, thee,

May have a tendency to delve in misery.
The news from reading and watching TV,
We digest and try hard to understand.
Weird, unusual happenings, occur in this land,
Caused by Nature or beings inhumane or insane.
Perhaps we now dwell on a different plane,
Than we did when we were a young, naive teen.

—February 14, 2013

FUN

Fun is what gives you pleasure or enjoyment,
Something that makes you glad.
What for many, may be merriment,
For others, may cause them to be sad.

For some, it's fun to shop all day.
For others, shopping may cause them dismay.
Making all the "flea markets," for some,
Is fun, for others 'tis boring and tiresome.

Out on the beach, bathing in the sun,
For "sun worshipers" is a "lot of fun."
For others, such as me,
We burn, so we tend to disagree.

For many, it's fun to "wine and dine."
If you enjoy "dressing up" that's fine.
On the go, others like to "eat and run,"
Sightseeing, to them, is much more fun.

Vacations are usually for "fun and rest."
Yet, some can really put you to the test.
Fighting traffic, long lines, and the heat,
Instead of resting, many wind up beat.

A cruise, many will say is fun,
But, even that, is not for everyone.
If you go to just "loll in a chair,"
Stay home, you're better of there.

Fun is what makes you happy.
What's fun for "Mammy" may not be for "Pappy."
For your enjoyment and "fun," do what you may,
But please let others enjoy their "fun" their way.

—August 1, 1999

GARDENER

He loved his garden best.
He loved to till the soil.
He'd take a noonday rest.
Then back to the garden he'd toil.

Tomatoes he grew every year,
And tasty, sweet, corn, each juicy ear.
Cucumbers by the buckets, he'd pick.
Often, they grew so quick.

Okra grew well, bountiful, too.
'Til the frost killed it, it grew.
Snap bean, butter bean and poled bean,
Were as delicious as any bean ever seen.

Melons grew 'til ripe, on the vine.
Cantaloupes were sweet, simply divine.
Turnips and mustard, very lush greens,
Were the normal, fall and winter scenes.

Producing more than they could eat,
He gave a lot of vegetables away.
He toiled, hoeing in the heat,
Many, many a hot summer's day.

I picture this gardener often, then get sad.
You see, he was my 97-year old dad.
In the "Garden of Eden" he now does rest,
But while among us, he did his very best.

—November 24, 1999

GAY HUSBANDS

Years they struggle with strife,
To understand the meaning of their life.
Some marry, take a wife.
The pain, ofttimes, must cut like a knife.
They raise a family.
Some have more than one child.
As husbands, they do provide.
Their demeanor is usually easy and mild.
Keeping the family together,
Many strive to do.
They go thru much "bad weather,"
Because their frustrated wife never knew.
The "blowout" comes one day,
When she finds out that he is gay.
Dumbfounded, aghast; it's hard to believe,
She's heartbroken, why her, did he deceive?
Will the marriage be dissolved?
Can this dilemma ever be resolved?
They still do love each other,
Yet, he's also in love with another.
The "other" happens to be a man.
He copes the best way that he can.
His family has been his life,
Yet, he thinks, "I am what I am, I am."
The children, how do they react,
Knowing that their Dad is gay, for a fact?
Their feelings are of love and hate.
Will it affect them, with any future mate?

—August 24, 1999

GEEK

Tall, skinny and weak,
Shy, timid and meek.
A change in lifestyle, he did seek,
Because he hated the word "Geek."

From history, he learned of the ancient Greek,
Admired his mind, his body, and his unique physique.
Into history, he did more than peek.
His future position was more than oblique.

From his cabin, near the flowing creek,
Fresh air would give him a rosy cheek.
His body he'd build, muscular and sleek,
By exercising week after week after week.

In a while, two months or perhaps three,
Changes in his body, he began to see.
His muscles were tighter and bigger.
Soon he'd be as fit as any "well digger."

He began to like his new lifestyle.
He smiled as he jogged mile after mile.
He'd continue this for a while.
At a glance, he admired his new profile.

—September 29, 1999

GENERATION GAP

When discussing the generation gap,
Oldsters find little, if any, overlap.
Many view oldsters with much disdain,
Unless they have something to gain.

For some, the elderly are in the way,
Hindering them, though they're loathe to say.
A child born out of wedlock,
In the oldster's day, came as a shock.

Today, the mother is very proud.
Her joy may be very vocal, very loud.
No longer is she considered wild.
Her child, though illegitimate, is not stigmatized,
But venerated, praised as a "love child."

This goes on and on, day after day,
While many depend on others, in some way.
Grandmothers very often carry the load.
While many fathers are no better than a toad.

Women and girls, not naive or even dumb,
Fall prey, to too many a bum.
It's hard and many oldsters can't figure why,
'Tis sad, enough to make "old ones" cry.
They soon learn to "chill out" and sigh.

—February 8, 2008

GETTING BY?

For a time he lived out West.
He was known then as a "desert rat."
Was he then doing "his best,"
Living with a donkey and a desert cat?
He ate cactus, snake and jackrabbit.
Prospecting had become a habit.
The lure of gold was always there.
With pick and pan he scrounged everywhere.
When it got that he could hardly hear,
He suddenly began to fear,
Became worried about his health.
Harsh winters were too severe,
And he still had found no wealth.
He decided to come south,
Where the weather was mild.
News by word of mouth,
Indicated things were not too wild.
He started "wheeling and dealing,"
Accepting trades and things to buy.
He never did resort to stealing.
He made enough for tobacco and rye.
He picked aluminum cans,
Along the roadside and street,
Junk, batteries and discarded fans,
He sold all to buy food to eat.
Soon he came to realize,
Doing this, he was not alone.
Waking up late he'd lose "the prize."

He found that the cans were all gone.
He began doing any small task,
Just so that he could "eke by."
Had old age caught up? he did ask.
On no one did he ever rely.
Would he be alone, left to die?
For the first time in many, many years,
He felt that he would and began to cry.
He could not stop the flow of tears.

—November 4, 2001

GIFTS

About this time each year,
People think of Christmas cheer.
They shop for an appropriate gift,
That will give someone a lift.

For the very small, shop with ease,
Almost anything is sure to please.
For the teen, avoid a contest.
Cash money now seems to work best.

Married children, can be a chore.
Do they need less or perhaps more?
Add their spouse, 'tis double now,
But we'll manage, somehow.

What about Mom and Dad?
It doesn't take much to make them glad.
To see their children happy, not sad,
Is the best gift they've ever had.

Christmas, is not without some woe,
For some, 'tis touch and go.
They remember the happy days of yore,
Knowing it will never be again, like before.

—December 13, 1999

GIRL ALONE

Sitting on the sand,
She gazed toward the sea.
She held a book in her hand.
Her thoughts, what could they be?

Her mind did seem to be far away.
'Twas not on this beach, this day.
Alone she sat, neither sad nor gay,
Near the edge of an inland bay.

Was she in deep sorrow,
Or suffering from a terrible grief?
Would she be better in the morrow,
Or would she seek some relief?

Was she thinking of a distant isle,
Or swaying in dance, wearing a sarong?
Or was she dreaming for a while,
Being on stage, singing her song?

Perhaps she only wished for peace and quiet,
Was brooding over a special diet,
Just wanted to be alone till night,
Had told someone, "Go fly a kite."

Alone, she was a mystery.
Was the book she held, about history?
Perhaps, she came here only to rest
And found this spot to be the best.

—April 8, 2000

GLASSES

Eye glasses are a visual aid.
Drinking glasses are used to serve lemonade.
Sunglasses help protect the eyes from the sun's rays.
Field glasses bring objects closer, that are far away.
Certain glasses many people use to read.
Some glasses are used to drink the water we need.
Tall glasses are used to serve iced tea.
Some glasses help those who very far can't see.
Glasses with a stem is a choice for wine.
Ordinary glasses, for sodas and water is fine.
Some people prefer "chilled glasses" for beer,
While others sip from small glasses, for cheer.
Celebs wear dark glasses because of the photo's flash.
Some wear glasses, makes them look more dashing.
Safety glasses protect a worker's eyes.
Dark glasses can hide someone's black eyes.
The meaning of words can ofttimes confuse,
Since the same word can mean a different thing.
Many of the words we do use,
To some, bewilderment, it may bring.
Sayings in other languages, too,
You should be aware,
May cause many to scratch their head.
*"Un ver vert dans un verre vert,"
May confuse some, but tickles me instead.
(*A green worm in a green glass.)

—RRP

GO OR NO

The mind says "go" but the body says "no."
Pain meanwhile, will let you know,
That you had better take it slow.
Sit back and enjoy a "cup of joe."
Take it easy and just "go with the flow."

Mother Nature may have no pity, you see,
For "oldsters, perhaps like you and me.
Things happen, "what will be, will be,"
It's up to you to do, no matter "the fee."
That's the way things are, there's no guarantee.

Health, at our age, is a big concern.
Poor diet, a fall, a cut or a burn,
May make us aware and we soon learn,
That our health, may take the wrong turn.

Soon our joints suffer with arthritis.
Our shoulders may pain from bursitis.
Diverticulosis may develop into diverticulitis
And other inflamed maladies ending in "itis."

—December 2020

GOLFER

He hits the ball, from the tee,
Straight down the fairway.
The next shot, the ball hit a tree,
Went into a nearby field of hay.

Better starts, he usually had.
Would this day be very bad?
Golf was a game he loved to win,
He'd done it often, again and again.

The foursome, they were all very good.
He knew this and understood.
He must remain calm, "keep his cool,"
Concentrate, must not be a fool.

True to form, he kept his swing.
Birdie after birdie, became his thing.
Much luck he had, much charm,
Much elation, it did bring.

He won the game this day.
Sand traps were narrowly missed.
Glad was he, he'd had his way.
The hero, he was hugged and kissed.

—August 11, 1999

GOLFER 1

The avid golfer on the golf course,
Kept playing, although he was very hoarse.
Eighteen holes he decided to play,
Regardless of what others did say.

Playing golf six days a week,
Few other pleasures did he seek.
His game, he thought, should improve.
His swing now had the right move.

Bright and early he teed off,
Even though he had this nagging cough.
He'd stay away only if very sickly.
When well, he'd return real quickly.

His personal clubs were the best.
He'd put each one to the test.
His irons were special to him, too.
With his putter, he'd try to pull through.

Golfing helped him to keep fit.
For his mind and body, this was it.
New friends he made now and then,
Who enjoyed who he was, not what he'd been.

No two courses are being the same.
Golfers enjoy the challenge of the game.
They play a different course every chance they get.
Ignored are the cold, the heat and the sweat.

Frustrated golfers, do they have fun?
Are they frustrated because they have not won?
Seems the harder they try, the higher their score.
Do their efforts become less fun, more of a chore?

—June 4, 2000

GRACE REBECCA

Grace Rebecca, you are a delight.
You caused a sensation, much elation.
You are a beautiful sight.
Were you crying out of fright?
Were you crying with all your might?

You appeared and your loved ones were there,
To greet you and meet you today.
Comments heard were, "beautiful hair,"
"Such a big, beautiful girl, I do declare."
Everyone had nice things to say.

Your Dad took pictures, he's very proud.
He stood out, in scrubs, in the crowd.
Your Grandparents were beaming, too.
Everyone was very happy to see you.

'Twas said that you were rated,
A high score of nine point nine.
Your Dad was pleased and elated,
When told that this was real fine.
After viewing you again and again,
'Tis unanimous, you're a perfect ten.

In a few days you'll get to settle down,
In your room, home, in your gown.
As your parents experience "parenthood,"

Let's hope that your cries and sighs,
Will always, by them, be understood,
'Cause I know that you'll always be good.

You were given a lovely name.
Perhaps, one day, it'll also be one of fame.
Much love was exhibited today.
We all love you in much the same way.

—RRP, August 24, 2001

GRACE THE FETUS

Tonight we saw a preview
Of the unborn baby, Grace.
'Tis a girl, they said they knew.
Was that a smile on her face?
Is she comfortable in that crowded place?

Tightly positioned inside the womb,
Is her hair long enough to comb?
Was that her tongue she moved about?
"Beautiful lips!" someone did shout.

"There's her feet," her Dad said.
I was still admiring her head.
Her heartbeat was easily seen.
'Tis amazing to see it on the screen.

How wondrous to capture this on tape,
To view over again, to admire and to gape,
To study the outline of her body, her shape.
Years from now, she too will say,
"Was that really me, moving that way?"
"Did I truly cause excitement, that day?"

In six weeks, more or less,
We'll know more that's for certain.
No more will we hear, "I guess."

It'll be clear when she is born.
When they open the curtain.
Mom and Dad will proudly toot their horn.

—June 29, 2001

GRASS

The greener the grass,
The more it seems to grow.
Hardly a week in summer pass,
Before you need to mow.

You cut the grass, as oft as needed,
Only as short as need be.
With proper care, won't need to be reseeded.
It should last and last, you see.

Trim around each and every tree,
Else brush and briar will grow there.
Edge the driveway, too, dear me,
Get the "neat look" everywhere.

A lawn freshly cut, looks neat.
A yard well trimmed, looks great.
Yard maintenance, you should complete,
Before the rains, then it's too late.

Flowers do a lot for a lawn,
When they're in bloom, full grown.
They may brighten things, in the right nook,
Give the yard, a "picture-book look."

—August 6, 1999

GRAY MOUSE

The little gray mouse,
Decided to leave the house.
Into the barn she went,
Where, the entire day she spent.

A decision she needed to make,
Concerning her future's sake.
Would she prefer to stay in the house,
Where a cat, all day, played with yarn?
Or to share with a rat and a louse,
A roomy old barn, with plenty corn?

The house had a pantry with cheese,
That she could get to with ease,
Just about as oft as she did please.
The corn in the old barn,
Was there in a huge pile.
She could eat it in the morn,
During the day, every once in a while.

She could compete with the rat,
But wasn't too bold with the cat.
If he saw the elusive mouse,
Head for the barn, from the house,
He could easily pounce on her,
Toy with her like a ball of fur,
Before the "coup de grace."
What to do, je ne sais pas!

—September 12, 2001

GREAT NEIGHBORS

Riding her "Zero Turn" mower, she mows their lawn.
It cuts so fast that she need not start at dawn.
Though covered with dust, she cuts on and on,
Until she finishes and her work is done.

A good wife to her husband, she's also his pal.
From where I sit, she sure is quite a gal.
'Tis apparent that she enjoys yard work,
As much as did my late wife.
Yard work and gardening may enrich one's life.
When enjoyable, it may relieve stress and strife.

Just to be outdoors and out of the house,
Can be good, especially when it's helping a spouse.
To maintain and care for a well-manicured yard,
One has to be dedicated and work very hard.

The end results usually does say a lot.
It shows pride and defines the ethos one's got.
Her husband tends his garden with love and care.
It produces vegetables as good as you'll find anywhere.

He, too, does not mind doing hard work.
Neither one is lazy nor do they shirk.
It's a pleasure having neighbors like these two.
If you see them as I do, you would agree, too.

—May 16, 2015

GREETINGS

"How do you do?" people may ask.
An answer today, is somewhat of a task.
Nothing seemingly is going my way.
It's very difficult to appear "happy and gay."

"Have a nice day," other people may chime.
They'll do it, time after time.
Not knowing your "tale of woe,"
Merrily, they just come and go.

Do many people truly care,
When they casually inquire "how you fare"?
Are they saying what they mean,
Or is it a habit, so oft seen?

Now if someone asks, "How is your back?"
You think, "He's right on track."
He remembers that you had much pain,
Which may reoccur, again and again.

People frequently inquire about one's health.
Many may even wonder about one's wealth,
But one is truly a dear friend,
Who's concerned about you to the very end.

GUMBO KREWE

The Gumbo Krewe from Norco,
Is headed for "ground zero,"
To feed the workers and they know,
Exactly what is needed when they go.
They'll work with little rest or "deau deau."

They've become famous for their gumbo,
Will serve seventy thousand bowls or so.
Their Jambalaya, red beans, and rice,
New Yorkers also think is very nice.
"King cakes" they also did take.
Workers munch on them on their break.
Free meals uplifts the morale of the crew.
'Tis a great job these men do.
Louisiana is proud of the "Gumbo Krewe."

New Yorkers welcome this bunch,
Gladly greet them and enjoy their lunch.
Meals are cooked there on the spot.
They're served to workers piping hot.
All work hard and seem to have fun.
'Tis a remarkable job that's well done.

A third trip is already being planned.
Their Cajun cooking is really in demand.
The "Gumbo Krewe" is received with glee.
When they arrive 'tis happy workers they see.
Knowing that so many people do care,

Makes the job a little easier to prepare.
Allowing many others to give and share,
Also makes the load much easier to bear.

—October 31, 2001

GUNSLINGER?

Circumstances placed him in a spot,
Where events turned chaotic, real hot.
Two gunmen were mysteriously shot.
How he got a gun, he remembers not.
To others, he too, was a gunslinger,
Resembling the man on the "wanted poster."
He actually was a "dead ringer,"
But, woefully, inept with a gun in holster.
Of him, people became scary and wary.
Upon seeing him, few men did tarry.
None would look him straight in the eye.
Women and children hid, some did cry.
Perhaps they feared they would soon die.
'Twas the same in every cow town.
People looked, ran or gave him a frown.
Some had their horse prance on the ground.
A few drunks and clowns hung around.

One day in a smoke filled saloon,
He'd expected it would happen soon,
He came face-to-face with a goon,
Who loved to shoot off his mouth and gun.
Shooting someone, to the goon, was much fun.
Pity the mother who bore such a son.
But alas, before they could exchange a shot,
From nowhere came a bullet the goon got.

Now his "exploits" seemed to grow and grow,
Preceding him everywhere he did go.
He began to enjoy the attention and fame.
'Twas to him, just a big OLE game.
But then, the ill-fated day finally came.
An unknown shot that came from behind,
Caused him to become permanently blind.
He's alone without pain, fame nor shame,
But maneuvers around with the help of a cane.

—September 29, 2001

HAIRDRESSER

She is a "hairdresser,"
One of notable fame.
"Stylist," appears next to her name.
Don't rush or press her.
She'll tell you it's work, not a game.

Many years she's done people's hair,
Has always treated them fair and square.
Sure, at times, she's put to the test,
Yet, she treats them too, like the rest,
Takes care of their hair does her best.

She and the ladies gossip a bit, at times,
Sometimes catty, always chatty,
Discussing celebrities, events, or crimes.
'Tis hard work on your feet, but enjoyable, too,
Creating new styles with a new hairdo.

Doing this for over forty years,
Physically, she's about worn down.
Backache and other aches cause her many tears.
It's now difficult for her to get around.

Her customers are now but a few.
Her chores are getting harder to do.
She must ease up, her body is crying.
She still wants to do, keeps on trying.
(Dedicated to Rosemary)

—September 14, 2000

HAS HIS WAY?

The Chap who wears a "bolo,"
When all others sport a tie,
Is not unlike he who goes "solo,"
When in the sky he wants to fly.
He's the guy, who won't conform,
To what others deem to be the norm.
He lives his life, day by day,
Perhaps differently, but his own way.
Some say he's a real sport,
But he seldom attends games of any sort.
He won't start or run from a fight.
When pressed, he'll use all his might.
He doesn't seek or give advice,
If not left alone, is not very nice.
He doesn't drink, play cards or shoot dice.
No one says if he has any vice.
Like in days gone by, he's a certain breed,
That follow a certain code and creed.
He's like the old-time mountaineer,
Who lived among wolves, bears, and deer.
Living off the land, far and wide,
Wearing clothes fashioned from hide.
Single, he won't even discuss marriage.
Would a wife only be excess baggage?
To some he is considered a hero,
A few girl friends see him as a "zero."
'Tis his life, tho, need others care,
If his clothes is untidy and shaggy his hair.

He's an adult, man with a brain,
Who can be mighty mean and gruff.
When intruders invade his domain,
Things can get pretty rough,
If they indicate they plan to remain.
People say he doesn't have sense enough,
To just come out of the rain.
I think that remains to be seen.

—October 3, 2001

HAT OR CAP

Hats or Caps, I very seldom wear,
Although thin now, is my hair.
Also, my skin is thin and very fair.
No need to cover my head whilst in my chair.

If I venture out in the sun,
To avoid a heatstroke, which is no fun,
Then it's wise to cover my head.
I'll wear a cap or hat instead.

In summer, a straw hat may keep my head cool,
Wintertime, for warmth, a hat made of wool.
Years I spent in the Oil Field Pool.
Wearing a "hard hat" was strictly the rule.
Not wearing one, one would be a fool.
Long retired, I'm as hardheaded as a mule.

I wear what I feel like, if I'm hot or cold.
Because at 90, I'm now considered to be old.
Years ago, in the olden days of yore,
Men's hats were part of the dress code.

Today, that's passe, seems to be no more.
Bare heads with suits is now the mode.
Stetson hats, many westerners wear still,
Cowboy hats and cowboy boots, they always will.

"To each his own" are words often said,
It's true, when it's about covering one's head.
Do people still cover their head, at night in bed?

—July 25, 2019, 1:00 a.m.

HATS

Hats are not commonly worn these days,
A big change, from the many yesterdays.
Hats, the "dressy chapeau,"
What happened, where did it go?

Today, when donning "formal wear,"
Hats are seldom seen anywhere.
Men usually wore a hat,
With a suit, coat or vest.
Now you rarely see anything like that.
Formal hats have been put to rest.

A few women wear hats today,
But very few, it seems, down our way.
In church, a hat once covered most every head,
Tho at times, a shawl, was used instead.

"Cowboy" hats are worn a lot out west.
With "cowboy boots" they go best.
"Cowgirls" wear western hats, quite a bit.
"Country singers" may sport a similar "outfit."

On the job, "hard hats" are the hat most worn.
They protect the heads, of the working men.
"Caps" may cover the "tetes" of so many they adorn,
Retirees, sportsmen, servicemen, teens and yes, women.

—December 2, 1999

HAVE-NOT

The less than average "have-not,"
What has he really got?
He's got too many of "not and un,"
Which creates problems in the long run.
That's why he has so little fun.

To his wife he is very untrue,
Which makes her unhappy and blue.
He tells many lies, untruths.
He's also crude, lewd and uncouth.

He's perceived as being unreliable.
His actions confirm it, it's undeniable.
He is, 'tis a fact, not dependable.
To many, this is not acceptable.

A good job he simply does not seek,
Tho he's apparently not sick, not weak.
He's not meek and is not a geek,
Does not earn much money each week.
His future is unclear, dim, and bleak.

The "have-not" usually has not,
A strong desire, a drive, and is unwise,
May be educated but does not capitalize,
Take advantage of opportunities he's got.
He may see himself "as gifted, a prize."

Too many a "<u>have-not</u>,"
Envies anything that others have got.
He blames others for his "sad lot,"
For his being in such a tight spot,
For his failures, for being such a flop.

Tho he dearly loves to shop,
He's <u>un</u>willing or cares <u>not</u>,
To change, he's such a sot.

—August 30, 2001

HE DID BRAG

Spotted by two dogs,
Near some old pine logs,
Their tails did wig and wag,
While they seemed to zigzag.
Were they playing a game of tag?

Down the craggy hilltop,
Came the beautiful stag.
He often came to a stop,
Behind the herd he did lag.

Upon the shaggy ole nag,
Rode the lad who does brag.
Once, such a stag, he did bag.
For which he was presented a red flag.
Was it a joke or just a gag?
Inhaling on his cigarette,
He took a very long drag,
Claimed he had no regret.

Later he spied an old hag,
Who covered her head with a rag.
Then he got on this jag,
Gossiping 'til his jaws did sag.

—October 13, 2001

HEALTH CARE

Just once, I'd like to be awake,
And not have some kind of ache.
At times, aches are one, two, or more.
Why, why, am I so sore?

My pain is generally just an ache,
A result of arthritis, I'm sure.
Few activities, I'm able to participate,
And for arthritis, there is no cure.

In my arteries, six stents are now in place.
Another, in my aorta, I still must face.
Each, were an option, I had the choice.
As I was spared the knife, I do rejoice.

Medical teams do wonders, today.
They're always, constantly, striving,
Seeking, to find an easier, better way.
Consequently, more of us are surviving.

Some people, I find, choose to criticize,
Health Organizations known as a HMO.
Very early, I came to realize,
For me, that was the way to go.

I do praise my HMO,
For giving me good health care.
Treating my health needs, I know.
They've been effective and fair,
Are as competent as you'll find anywhere.

—September 29, 2000

HEART AFFAIR

"He's got such a big heart," some say,
A comment that's often heard.
Taken literally, word for word,
It would mean, his health is in a bad way.
"Have a heart," means to "be kind."
Yet, even an ogre, we find,
Has a heart, has this eluded the mind?
"From the bottom of my heart," does imply,
A gesture, that is very deep and sincere.
But, we all know, and on this you can rely,
Only blood flows from the heart, my dear.
To have "your heart in your mouth,"
Indicates nervous anticipation or even fear.
Don't we know, without a doubt,
You'd be dead, unless hooked up to other gear?
"Set one's heart at rest,"
Is to set aside, one's fears, worries or doubts.
That would be quite a test,
Since you'd be unable, to sing or shout.
"Eat one's heart out,"
Means to be keenly unhappy over some regret.
If that happened, you'd be wiped out,
No heart, no life, want to bet?
"Knowing something by heart,"
Memorized, it's what it means.
How does the heart become a part,
Of such wordings, or schemes?
"Heartache," is that really sorrow or grief?

If a heart does ache, that's physical pains,
That requires immediate attention and relief,
Utilizing all available means.
A vital organ, is this heart of mine,
Without "any hint," of a mind.
A hollow muscle, albeit, one of a kind,
That pumps my blood, I find,
Continuously, time after time after time.

—February 12, 1999

HELPLESS?

Retired, old, helpless and alone,
All the "helpers" that were known,
Have been, for some time, gone.
Do the "new helpers" have hearts of stone?
When the A/C runs low on gas, Freon,
A new "technician" must be called "today."
The senior hopes "it won't take an eon,"
Won't cost more than she can afford to pay.
A "dispatcher fee," forty-three dollars, plus four,
Agree or don't agree, sign must she,
If any work needed to be done by he,
Which will additionally, cost considerably more.
Her unit required three pounds of gas.
The small "roof vent" motor was out too, alas.
The total was three hundred and seventy-five,
She wondered, "How will I stay alive?"
Her senior friend had problems, too.
Knew not whom she could turn to.
Her sink was clogged, what could she do?
Her options, she knew, were few.
A plumber, in the morning, around eight,
Had promised to be there by one.
He'd try his best not to be late.
Unable to leave his early job undone,
Much delayed, 'twas nearly four,
Before he came knocking at her door.
She'd waited, 'twas not any fun.
His delay would cost her much more.

After four-thirty, he went on "over time."
The senior must pay, 'tis not a crime.
Had he mentioned this beforehand,
"Go home, return tomorrow,"
Would have been her demand.
She would've paid less, had less sorrow.
Seniors with only a "social security pension,"
Find it impossible, their house to maintain.
Plumbers, electricians, A/C technicians, I must mention,
Charge as much as some doctors, 'tis a shame.
When they hear they need a mechanic,
Their heart races, they become frantic.
"Overhead costs" today are higher than yesteryear,
But greed, more so than need, is there, too, I fear.

—August 15, 2001

HE'S JUST OLD

His hair is very thin and white.
His eyes are blue, but not as bright.
Most of his teeth are now gone.
The enamel on ones left is very worn.

An upper plate helps him to chew.
Lower partials are very new.
Sounds, his ears fail to receive.
Hearing aids don't help, would you believe?

A pacemaker keeps his heart beating.
Pill after pill keeps his blood flowing.
"Depends" keeps dry his bottom, his seating.
Now he needs a miracle to keep his skin glowing.

With a "walker" he's less likely to fall,
If only he remembers to use it at all.
Toenails grow fast and often need a trim.
A diabetic, he can't chance it, not him.

He depends on others for some of his needs,
Especially with a cut, when he bleeds and bleeds.
His mind still functions, but he's forgetful, too.
An octogenarian, he's like many, perhaps me and you.

Once he was strong, hardy, brave and bold.
Now he's frail, weak and always, always cold.
The problem is that he's alone and he's old.
His family is gone and so is most of his gold.
May God have mercy on his poor ole soul.

—July 20, 2016

HOMEBODY

Within the confines of his home,
Was as far as he dared to roam.
Very reluctant to take a trip,
He feared he'd leak more than a drip.

Wherever he planned to go,
Foremost, he needed to know,
If a bathroom was available, or no.
He wondered why Mother Nature treated him so.

Many oldsters envision a scene,
Where they're tethered to a machine.
What's in store may be rough and tough.
Then some say, "No more, enough is enough."

Some of their biggest concerns,
Are to exist gracefully on their own terms.
A decision difficult for some to accept,
Even if an "oldster" with the Internet is adept.

Is to give up their home and go away,
To a "Nursing Home" to stay until their dying day.

—January 26, 2007

HOMEGROWN

Many vegetables my Dad grew.
That's what he liked to do.
Mom planted a yard full of flowers.
She too, toiled in the soil, many long hours.

Vegetables were Dad's pride and joy.
All sorts of flowers Mom did enjoy.
Nothing but her "green thumb" did she employ.

Homegrown produce, we ate a lot.
With fresh meat, all went into the pot.
The beef we ate was "grain fed."
Never were we hungry before going to bed.

Milk, eggs, butter, and pork, we had aplenty.
By "home canning" we stocked our pantry.
Fresh baked bread was an after-school delight.
Homemade ice cream, we enjoyed day or night.

We ate well, without any complaining.
Our plates we did empty, nothing was remaining.
Mom and Dad did well, 12 children they did raise,
For their loving care and efforts, they deserved the praise.

Despite much hard work, the struggle and strife,
Mom and Dad did have a very long life.

—third child, October 17, 2019

IT COULD HAPPEN

I have diabetes, so I pamper my feet.
Careful am I, doing so, very discreet.
After a bath, I massage and massage each foot.
Is this good or bad? The question is moot.

If you have a small callous on a big toe,
Take care of it soon, don't allow it to grow.
Otherwise, you may lose it, don't you know?
For some reason, the soles of my feet get rough.
To smooth this out can be difficult, very tough.

Next, on a foot you may develop a sore,
An ulcer on the heel that just won't heal.
Perhaps, very soon, you have one or two more.
This is very bad and 'tis terrible you feel.

First the toe, now the foot, gone by amputation.
If you're unlucky, the next sign is mortification.
Gangrene, now your leg may have to come off.
This is mortifying, with chagrin, you may scoff.
Like some say, "The truth hurts," but it's true.
Be aware, take good care, don't let it happen to you!

—Wednesday, November 7, 2019, 9:20 p.m.

IRMA AND NORRIS

Irma and Norris, the only two,
Remaining children of Adeline and Menville Malbrough.
Both widow and widower live in Bayou Blue.
To adulthood, twelve siblings grew,
Married, raised children and grandchildren they knew.
Their mother, "Tante Deline," and her siblings numbered eleven.
She was the first of them to go to heaven.
She died at age 56 in the year 1952.
Filled with wanderlust, was "Uncle Menville," their Dad,
E'en tho twelve children he and "Tante Deline" had.
Was he, perhaps, more Nomad than Galahad?
Irma, was the third daughter born, Norris, the third son,
Six more siblings came, born one by one.
Having lived four scores and much more,
They're lucky to have children they adore,
Who are able to keep the wolf away from the door.
They'll not know hunger nor be poor.
Each live alone, in their own home.
Nowadays, not very far do they roam.
They see each other once a week or so.
Not too many places do they go.
Few, if any, luxuries must they forego.
They live their lives the best way they know.

—May 2011

KISS

The Kiss is an act, a treat,
E'en with one, when first you meet.
Perhaps it's only a peck on the cheek,
But it's great, for the bold and the meek.

'Tis an informal way to greet,
Family and friends we admire.
Even babies, they're so sweet,
Reach out for that kiss they desire.

The Kiss, a sign of affection,
Puts one's mood in the right direction.
It can say "hello," "thank you,"
"I'm sorry" or perhaps "I'm blue."

It may say, "You, I forgive"
Or "With you, I'm glad I live."
But one thing it will surely do,
Is surely say, "I love you."

So don't be afraid, don't be,
To give and receive a kiss.
'Cause if you do, you'll see,
There's a lot you'll surely miss.

Kissing, as ofttimes seen on TV,
Can be gross, and I think unwise.
The "sucking of lips," take it from me,
Is uptown shopping for downtown merchandise.

—June 28, 1999

KITTEN

The "two-year old" was smitten,
By the cute "six-week-old" kitten.
Unaware that she might be bitten,
She tried to pet her without her mitten.

Chased the kitten, she did,
Just like a much bigger kid.
Too slow, she was, natch,
The kitten she could not catch.

Yet, give up, she would not,
As she chased the kitten around the lot.
It's amazing, the stamina they've got,
Even though it was fairly hot.

Never close was the race.
It was more of a playful game.
Both moved at an easy pace.
The distance between them stayed the same.

When the chase finally did end,
Into the house, the tot came in.
Back to the games of "pretend,"
She was ready to play in the den.

—Rudolph Ray Porche, September 28, 1999

KITTY IN THE BOX

In the large box, the poor kitty cat,
Looks pitiful, hopeless and forlorn.
Her mother vanished, weeks after she was born.
She stands on her hind leg,
Trying to figure where she's at.

Saved from coons, she's in a box, in the house.
Outside, her life is no safer than a mouse.
Her tiny claws are sharp as a razor,
Cuts on her skin could be from a laser.

Vienna sausages, pasta with sauce, she devours.
She's ready to eat every few hours.
On the walls of the box, she tosses a ball.
A plastic alligator she plays with, too.
She's named "Miracle," Seth made the call.

Anxious to play, she welcomes me and you.
What do you think we should do?
A woman adopted it, she loved it, too.

—June 16, 2016

KNIT OR CROCHET

Some women love to crochet.
They stitch, stitch, all the day.
Afghans small, baby size,
Or large, they all make a great prize.

Some require many ounces of yarn,
Many, many hours, of work, gosh darn.
For the women, it's relaxing,
Especially when daily chores are taxing.

At the polls, like today, it's a good way,
To break the monotony, pass the time of day.
Very few voters are coming today,
So "knit away and crochet," I say.

Is it a strain on their eyes?
Their fingers, how many, tires?
To them, it seems to be automatic.
They love it, but are not fanatic.

'Tis a labor of love,
And not at all a chore.
It's something others will adore,
Later, perhaps, as part of a treasure trove.

—October 7, 2000

LABORER

Coffee, an egg and toast,
Two slices at the most.
Not unlike an Army Post.
Awakened by an early alarm,
They rushed to eat it while warm.

Then it was early to the field,
To harvest its early yield.
Lunchtime came mighty quick.
Two sandwiches did the trick.
Time allowed to eat and rest,
One hour, no more, no less.
Then 'twas back to work again,
Unless it happened to rain.

They usually worked until dark.
Six days a week, it was no lark.
So it was late before they had supper,
Though it was generally a "pick me upper."
Two vegetables, a roll and some meat.
Dessert was included as a special treat.

Food and lodging usually did suffice.
Lodging was adequate, not that nice.
The work was hard and lasted long.
The pay was minimal, very low.
Though they did as told, did no wrong,
What was right, where could they go?

—September 8, 2001

LADY OF THE HOUSE

The Lady of this house,
Had been timid, quiet as a mouse.
Occasionally she'd gotten her way,
But never without her hubby's okay.

A mundane life she'd lead,
From the time she awoke,
Until she went to bed.
Seldom a word she spoke,
While making sure he was fed.
Silently, she'd done every chore,
Even when he piled on more.
Never, even when she'd felt,
She'd been wronged did she complain.
Always on her knees she'd knelt,
Praying for guidance, again and again.

Married a bit over a score,
She'd decided she'd have no more.
No more abuse would she ever take,
Listen to no excuse, true or fake.

She would now go after her dream,
Regain her composure and self-esteem.
With her husband or without,
That's what life is, she realized, all about.

She could and would get by alone,
If or when her husband was gone.
Her ability to cope, she had confidence.
She was ready and willing to take a chance,
No longer would she do anything in silence.
Her Lord spoke, she had her guidance.

—September 7, 2001

LAKE CABIN

The cabin by the lake,
Was a refuge they did take.
It was rustic, comfortable and secluded.
When she was baking a cake,
An aroma was also included.

The sweet-smelling fresh air,
Smelled of jasmine everywhere.
They were overjoyed to be there,
But feared an occasional bear.

They come to the cabin to find,
Solitude, quietness and to rest.
It offers them peace of mind,
And good fishing they love best.

The husband loves to fish.
To fish was always his wish.
She loves to whip up a dish.
When she "stuffs a trout,"
He has much to "talk about."

Springtime they "set out a trout line,"
Because catfishing then is fine.
The weather then is not severe,
Usually fair, calm and clear.

In the winter they opt to hunt,
Geese, duck, squirrel and rabbit.
With strangers they're sharp and blunt.
Too many "friends" can become a habit.

—September 4, 2001

LARK IN THE PARK

His moped died, no spark.
How would he get to the park?
To the park, just for a lark,
She raced to be there before dark.
Spotting the moped, that was just ahead,
She slowed down to render aid.

With pride, he accepted the ride.
To the park they rode side by side.
Under the trees in the breeze,
On a bench, next to a wench,
They sat, it was a tight squeeze.
Abruptly, both did sneeze.

Oh, they thought, this is not fair.
Pollen was everywhere in the air.
Dampness messed up their hair,
But neither seemed to care.

Was it fate, had each found their mate?
By chance, it was not even a date?
Hand in hand, they did walk,
Lots of smiling, very little talk.

As if on cue, they both knew,
The next thing they would do.
They'd go park in the dark,
Where it was quiet, no sound, no bark.

—September 10, 1999

LATE IN LIFE

My time on earth is drawing nigh,
Faster and faster, time seems to fly.
I sigh and cry and know not why.
What will transpire before I die?
My, my, oh my, of little use, am I.
Many a chore, I can do no more.
To some, I'm probably just a bore.
I suppose my life is nearly o'er.

Most things are no longer fun.
It's difficult for me to walk, I can't run.
I cannot be exposed to too much sun.
At night I ponder and wonder on things to do.
Day comes and I cannot follow through.

Aches and pains occur again and again.
Much of my muscle loss I'll never regain.
As my memory seems to fade and wane,
I wonder, how much will I retain?
It's enough to rattle my weakening brain.

In the future, not knowing what's in store,
Chills my bones, to the very core.
Will help always come knocking at my door,
Especially when I'm much more than just sore?
Nevertheless, I cannot hide so I must abide.
The fact is that I'll live until I die.

—November 5, 2008

288

LE CHAPERON

Very easily our heart he won.
He's not unlike our very own son.
'Tis a pleasure to just sit and chat
With him, talk about this and that.
As a World Traveler, he does well.
He's outgoing and loves people, I can tell.
An "Ambassador of Goodwill" is he.
He's a pleasant guest, of my wife and me.
Our wish is that he enjoys his stay,
That he does exciting things, day after day.
Enjoy the people he does meet,
Visit many places, with little exposure to heat.
Taste the many foods that we're famous for,
Learn our many customs and see sights galore,
Including our marshes, swamps, and seashore.
See all of them and many more.
"Host Families" deserve a "big hand."
What they do is no less than grand.
Their time, energy, shelter and food,
They gladly give to put their guests in a good mood.
Some go much out of their way,
So, that the kids may have a pleasant stay.
They give parties such as a "barbeque,"
To meet kids, like you, you and you.
The kids he chaperons, all from France,
Will do great, let's give them a chance.
Some may appear quiet or even shy.
Others may be very energetic, very spry.

I hope all the kids enjoy their stay,
Exchange ideas and not be sorry in any way.
Leave with memories that will last and last
So that in years to come they may say,
"I had a really big blast."

—August 15, 1998

LEGACY

In our footsteps, who will follow?
Will our imprints just remain hollow?
What inspirations will they need,
For our works in life to proceed?

Will anyone attempt to fill our shoes?
Who will care after we've paid our dues?
In less than a century, will we be forgotten?
Will signs remain of all we've begotten?

All our forefathers, will our progeny know?
Who they were and where they did go?
Whence they came and if they traveled far,
By ship, by barge, by wagon or cattle car?
How strong was their religious belief?
Did they go thru life suffering much grief?

Will our descendants remember our life?
Will they know our struggles and our strife?
Will the values instilled in us,
Remain the same to descendants we know,
Or will they ignore all and act as though,
They just got off the bus?

—March 7, 2003

LETTING GO

Parents reflect on events past,
Wondering, if truly, they did their best.
Their baby, their child, their last,
"Flew the coop" like the rest.

A Mother remembers the void, the ache,
When the first child left, a choice he did make.
Tho instinct told her, "Let him go,"
She suffered greatly, this we all know.

"Letting Go" is not taught in schools,
But, are there, any set of rules,
That guides a parent toward their goal,
To rear and prepare a child to leave the "fold"?

A parent may find solace and relief,
That may ease and alleviate their grief,
When they see and are proud of the result
That transformed their child into an adult.

Be proud you taught them to be fair and just.
Now let them simply do what they must.
Go out into the world, start a new life.
It may be tough, they must deal with strife.

When the last child goes out "on his own,"
There is that feeling of "being alone."
This emotion is called "empty-nest syndrome."
It is very real to parents at home.

Stay busy, don't allow yourself to brood.
Many things can put you in a "blue mood."
"Keep in touch" with children, show you care,
As new "family units" begin here and there.

LIGHT DISPLAY

"Celebration under the Oaks,"
Is more than fine food and cokes.
The artistic displays of light,
To all that visit is a delight.

Adults and children gaze and stare,
Bewildered by what they see there.
Big swans, sea serpents like "Nessie,"
A pirate ship lit up, neat, not messy.
Two rocking horses rocking away,
'Twas drizzling but they rocked anyway.

Santa, his reindeer and his sled,
Suddenly loomed just ahead.
Santa's workshop was operating "full swing,"
Making toys and scores of other things.

Squirrels and acorns were lit in a tree,
A large American Flag displayed for all to see.
Hot air balloons were suspended in air.
Stars and tree decorations were lit here and there.

A giant angel shaped by beautiful lights,
Created a view enhancing other great sights.
Symbolic of peace was the dove.
Beautiful, was all the above,
Shaped by lights, a labor of love.
Colorful displays shining these Yule nights.

—December 22, 2001

LIGHT

Morning sun, "daylight," is a welcome sight.
People "rise and shine" with energy and delight.
The sun emits lots and lots of light,
Enabling living things to grow and reach their height.

Sometimes the sun is much too bright.
People may get "sunburned" and it's a painful sight.
Without "sunlight," we'd surely have more blight.
The dying of plants would be more than slight.

Darkness, for some, can be a time of fright.
They may feel uneasy during the "dark of night,"
And don't change unless they "see the light."
At night, a handy tool is a "flashlight."

Old-time lamps using coal oil or kerosene,
Are hard to find and are very seldom seen.
Lamps with "led bulbs" are much better.
Using "long-lasting batteries" they're a "trendsetter."

They're easy to use and are much safer, you see.
A child can use them as well as you or me.
"Solar Power" from "sunlight" to many people's delight,
Provides cleaner electricity and seems to be all right.

With the high cost of living and money so tight,
Solar, wind, and water power, may save you money, right.

—February 23, 2020, 1:00 p.m.

LITTLE GIRL

I got the news, just heard,
In fact, tonight I got the word.
A little girl entered the fold,
Arriving at the Robichaux household.
Healthy, beautiful, too, I'm told.

Everyone is happy, all are thrilled,
For the grandparents, a wish is fulfilled.
Grandchildren are great, a real joy,
Whether they are a girl or a boy.

How quickly we realize,
They're the most beautiful, deserve the prize.
They become the brightest, the smartest we know,
As we watch them develop and grow.

They have a way of touching our heart,
As we get the first glimpse, from the start.
Soon, in a very short while,
They recognize us, and smile.

We know then that they did bond,
So ofttimes, we want to be around,
To hold them, hug them, steal a kiss.
You'll really enjoy all this,
With your dear, sweet "Little Miss."

—RRP, December 5, 1999

LIVE AND LET LIVE

It's 2:30 a.m., very peaceful and very quiet.
That's the best time for me to read and write.
The phone doesn't ring and ring,
Not even for a lousy "scam call."
After my bath, I wasn't sleepy at all.
Earlier today, Glenn, my son, did say,
Reggie, my daughter, would cook today,
Chicken with dumpling and something good,
Things that she usually fixes for her brood.
At her house we're invited to go.
That's a good way to spend a Sunday, don't you know?
Hopefully, grandchildren I'll get to see.
Lately, seldom do they come to see me.
Busy as a bee, everyone always seem to be.
I understand, but that means less joy and glee.
Today, everyone has their own life to lead and live.
I see no need for me to intercede or advice to give.
"Live and let live" is a good motto.
As long as everyone is happy, I'm good to go!

—Sunday, October 20, 2019, 2:30 a.m.

LOG HOUSE

The log house at the lake,
Had hand hewn logs, none were fake.
Badly needed was a rake.
Leaves were high, kindling they'd make.
It was a fire hazard, for Pete's sake.
In the hot sun leaves did bake.
It could cause a sudden fire to break.
It's a chance some people take,
A foolish chance, a big mistake.

Life is not always "a piece of cake,"
But it can be enjoyable at the lake.
When fishing, one is not annoyed.
Boating and skiing is also enjoyed.
A pair of ducks, a hen and a drake,
Faced a fast boat making a huge wake.
A fast break, the hen and drake did make.

At the sign of the first snowflake,
More ducks may flock to the lake.
Hunting blinds hunters will make,
When good locations they stake.

On the lake, their finger they shake,
At any boat who makes a big wake.
Furious, they may quiver and quake,
Shout and obscene gestures make.

—October 17, 2001

LOOTERS

Ye that plunder, burn and loot,
Ye we're justified to shoot.
More miscreant than galoot,
Just a cruel, stupid brute.

Treating authorities with much disdain,
They rob and steal for personal gain.
When innocents get in the way,
Their pleading holds no sway.

With savagery, they will hold them at bay.
They may continue this day after day.
With orders to "shoot on sight,"
What is required is "military might."

Civilians, too, assume the right,
To shoot looters during their plight.
Looters are a low form of life,
Roaming during disasters, amid the strife.

They loot and loot, then shoot at anyone,
Offering succor, aid and relief.
To many during their time of loss and grief.
Getting rid of looters needs to be done.

—September 14, 2005

LOST TRAIL

Along the running brook,
A path, the youngsters took.
Soon they left the obvious trail,
Got lost and began to wail.

Deeper into the woods they went,
'Til they were tired, nearly spent.
They decided it was time to eat,
So they set up their tent.
Into the supply of dried meat,
They quickly made a big dent.

Into the woods, not knowing how deep,
Scared and exhausted, they fell asleep.
At the break of dawn,
Refreshed, they stretched, with a yawn.
Again, they were ready to eat.
Breakfast was eggs on whole wheat.

They ate then quickly broke camp,
Packing their gear while still damp.
They headed in the direction of the sun,
Hoping into a highway they'd run.
With no compass, no map, they had no clue,
As to their whereabouts, what should they do?

After walking mile after mile,
They stumbled on a logger's road.
They followed it for quite a while,
Then met a truck hauling its load.
They hugged, they cried, they each
Gave the driver a great big smile.
Happy that safety, they finally did reach.

—September 14, 2001

LOUISIANA

Louisiana, my beautiful, scenic state,
Its greatness, let me try to relate.
Moss covered oaks along southern bayous,
Cypress, maples, ash, pine, and tupelo trees too.
Flora and fauna are abundant, that's true.

Hunting and fishing is enjoyed by more than a few.
Weekly festivals are nothing new.
Somewhere, there is always something to do.
Mardi Gras, known worldwide by all,
Parade floats after floats, then have a great ball.

Sport teams are generally much admired,
Even when, too often, they are apt to lose.
Education, some think, is less than desired,
But celebrations and fetes, where food and booze,
Is never denied, perhaps are more than required.

Nearly every weekend, there is some type of Fest.
Yearly, "Fest goers" return and claim their Fest is best.
Our crawfish, in the USA, is well-known.
Crawfish boils are great, with wild crawfish or pound grown.
Today, at the good ole age of seventy-seven,
I see Louisiana as truly my part of Heaven.

—July 5, 2006

LOVE

What is the boundary of love?
Is it beyond the sky up above?
Love has no boundary, many agree.
What is it about love, many don't see?

Mutual love means "each give and take."
It's sharing everything that you make.
It's bending so that you don't break,
Admitting fault after any mistake.

Love is a feeling that's hard to describe,
Feels better than medicine, anyone can prescribe.
Many deeds are done, in the name of love,
Some good, some not so good, my little dove.

Love can break a strong man's heart.
Love has caused many to really fall apart.
Love given, but not received can be rough.
It can destroy the toughest of the tough.

For love, many will do anything,
Do their best, give their all, everything.
Love makes them happy, makes them sing,
Yet, rejected love, that awful sharp sting,
Too often, much unhappiness it does bring.

Love is something we all need.
In the name of love we sow our seed.
The more we love, the better we are.
Love is the greatest of emotions, by far.

—January 20, 2000

LOVED ONES GONE

Some days I wake up feeling tired and spent,
My "get up and go" done "got up and went."
Seldom do I attend any event.
On many days that I spend alone,
I think of all the loved ones now gone.
More seem to die, year after year,
Parents, siblings, relatives, and friends, all dear.
Neighbors too, their voices I no longer hear.
Sometimes I wonder, why am I still here?
White hair and tired, worn-out aching bones,
Reality kicks in, then I surmise,
There must be a reason, though I'm no prize.
I go to bed late, sleep long past the sunrise.
Then I play it by ear, when from bed I arise.
Seldom am I awakened by any surprise.
Out of town, I no longer drive.
Medications help keeping me alive.
Many doctors I see, perhaps is why I survive.
My routine is much the same, day after day.
I generally do things as much as I can, my way.
At 86, my limitations are more than a few.
Many things, too many, I can no longer do.
My children, grandchildren, and neighbor, help a lot.
Many thanks for all the relatives and friends, I've got.
Now a widower, life is not the same.
Widowhood is a whole new ball game.

—December 7, 2015

LULLABY

Hush my angel and please don't cry.
Paw-Paw will sing to you a lullaby.
When you cry your eyes get red,
That you may ache we fear and dread.

Now, now, please don't cry.
Give your eyes a chance to dry.
You're not dirty or wet, I see.
Why you're crying is beyond me.
What, oh, what, can it be?

Hush, sweet baby, why do you wail?
Is stomach gas causing you to ail?
Are you cutting teeth, my sweet,
Or do you want a special treat?

Hush, hush, please don't cry anymore.
Stop before your throat gets sore.
You're not hungry, you've just been fed.
Hush, hush now, it's time for bed.

Close your eyes and go to sleep.
Don't you cry, don't you weep.
Go to sleep, a sleep that's deep.
Then Daddy will ride you in his Jeep.

—December 18, 2001

MALADIES THAT I'VE GOT

Arthritis, believe it or not,
Causes many of the ails that I've got.
My joints, at times, all feel shot.
Creams and steam don't seem to help a lot.

At times when I'm happy and rejoice,
For some reason I suddenly lose my voice.
I'll begin to stutter and stammer.
No longer can I hold a hammer.

Too often I feel weak and frail.
To drive a nail I now fail.
Slow as molasses, I move like a snail.
My breathing is impaired because of COPD.
Too many years I smoked, yes siree.

Although I quit smoking 35 long years ago,
Much damage was done, now I know.
Now that my internal organs are in decline,
Many changes occur and that is fine.

I realize that bad choices made were mine.
Being choosy, is necessary now when I dine.
That my "taste buds" changed, I have no doubt.
Seldom am I hungry, so I don't eat a lot.

Now I won't eat anything that's too hot.
I must watch my diet, 'cause I've got the gout.
So many maladies I've got, that I could yell and shout,
But then people would say, "What's that all about?"

—April 9, 2020, 2:30 p.m.

MARRIAGE

Marriage is a contract, sealed with a verbal vow.
It's a simple fact, a union the law does allow.
Many marriages remain intact,
Especially if they give each other some slack,
Respect and scratch each other's back.

Depending on how the parties act,
Determines if they will stay on track.
Too often marriage vows are broken.
Too often angry words are spoken.

Where once they were often "cheek to cheek,"
Weak arguments occur every day of the week.
Many profess that they live in harmony,
Without constraints nor "bonds of matrimony."

Perhaps it's commitments they dislike,
Want to be free to "anytime" take a hike.
Should marriage be redefined or refined?

A Church Wedding Ceremony is the right sight,
For this type of "Rite Site."
There is a saying, "With a happy wife,
You're bound to lead a happy life."

MARY, THE MAIL LADY

Mary delivers my daily mail,
When on duty, without fail.
A large package, she'll bring to my door.
She goes "out of her way" to do more.

She's very energetic and does her job well.
Her attitude and aptitude with gratitude,
Convinces me that she loves her job,
At least as best as I can tell.

Always smiling, I've never seen her pout.
Cool, calm, and collected, she doesn't shout.
She's a great lady, with much charm and grace.
I always enjoy seeing her smiling face.

If more people were like her,
The world would be a better place.
Thank you, Mary, you're a credit to the Human Race.
Your friend and admirer.

MEMORY 2001

Memory is a strange thing.
Joy or sadness, it may bring.
Events that happened years past,
In my memory they returned to last.

Some night, out of the blue,
I dream about someone I knew.
Why that person, why now?
He was a memory, is he back somehow?

Do we always separate,
Actual events from the dream?
So vividly we may relate,
To the dream, or so it does seem.

Things we did as a child,
Was long ago forgotten, I must say.
Now it sort of feels a bit wild.
Has the memory returned to stay?

Are we just actors on "life's stage,"
Where roles change as we age?
Memorizing only the "lines we need,"
Deleting others not needed to succeed?
Occasionally we get a "flashback."
Maybe 'twas something we did lack?
Perhaps our "role then" we didn't play well?
Perhaps we just tried too hard to excel?

Did our "director" reprogram our memory chip?
Was it the wrong switch he did flip?
Memory flashbacks after so much time,
Is the meaning perhaps sublime?

When our memory fails us much more,
More surprises may be in store.
If we suffer a "total memory loss,"
Who, then, will become our "boss"?

—October 27, 2001

MEMORY

I must admit, 'tis true,
And at times, it makes me blue.
That my memory is getting bad.
It happens and 'tis very sad.

I may see a familiar face,
Approaching, it's an old friend.
Just then, the name, I cannot place.
I'm embarrassed, to no end.

Other times I do feel shame,
When I try to introduce,
A lifelong pal, named Bruce,
But lo, I can't think of his name.

Some days, while using a tool,
I suddenly feel like a fool.
The tool, I can't seem to find.
This simply, "blows my mind."

I cannot put the blame on "so and so,"
'Cause, I was using it a moment ago.
No one else is there but me.
I've been working alone, you see.

On days when my hands begin to shake,
I think, "My medicine, I must take."
Then suddenly, I realize, I don't know.
Didn't I take it an hour ago?

My wife has this problem, too.
I think, what are we going to do?
We must now, check on each other.
Even if she makes the comment,
"You're not my mother."
I may respond, "Oh, brother."
Is this a howl of dire portent?

Cooking with electricity or gas,
A dire situation can easily arise.
Fire can erupt and spread really fast,
So, alone in the kitchen, is unwise.

—February 12, 1999

MINNIE THE MORKIE AND ME

Minnie loves to sit by me,
With her head resting just above my knee.
When she feels the urge to pee,
She dashes outside and goes under the oak tree.

Looking at me, she does not beg,
But looks mournful, alongside my leg.
All day she never drank nor ate,
Not until tonight, late at eight.

Quiet she has been and very still,
Following me everywhere at will.
Strangely, I've yet to hear her bark,
Not even when outside, in the dark.

I wish I knew what she thinks all day.
She must really miss her "Mimi" that's away.
Like a child who is away from home,
She sits by me, or near me, does not roam.

I am her "pal" and she knows very well,
That she is safe and secure where I dwell.
She seems very happy, as best as I can tell.

MIRROR

Mirror, mirror on the door,
Everything I do is a chore.
Help me again, once more,
As oft I've looked before.
Show me the spot that is sore.
Is it a carbuncle with a core?

Mirror, mirror, is it me,
That you really do see?
I see and am without glee.
Why do I feel like,
That can't be me, yipe?
But I can't really gripe.
I don't think, don't believe,
That me, you would deceive.

Surely, I'm not that fat.
I feel skinnier than that.
Yet, mirror, I alone am facing you,
So it must be me, that's true.

Mirror, mirror, do you share,
The burdens that many do bear?
What people say when they stare,
At you, divulge their misery, do you care?

Mirror, mirror, here's my plea,
I must lose much fat to be free.
Join forces with the scale and me.
Help me, help me overcome obesity,
In a way that we three can agree,
Painlessly and easy as can be.

—July 11, 2001

MIRRORED LOOKS

I gaze into the mirror and decide,
I must do better, I have too much pride.
My beard surely must go,
No matter how fast it really does grow.

I need to cut my hair,
Just as short as I dare.
'Tis easier to groom it that way,
Feels better to me, too, I must say.

My pants, I'll buy the "wrinkle free."
The crease remains forever on them, you see.
My shirt will be neatly pressed.
This will help to be neatly dressed.

My everyday shoes, don't really shine,
But, they're "loafers" and that's fine.
A belt, I don't always wear.
"Suspenders" I wear occasionally, here and there.

Whatever I wear, comfort is a must.
Sizes, when buying, I cannot trust.
Try everything on, I must do,
Lest I be sorry, how about you?

—December 1, 1999

MODERN STORES

Modern stores are very different today,
Than the earlier ones of yesteryear.
They differ in many, many ways, I must say.
Bigger and much bigger they get, oh dear.
Many of our needs are still on a shelf,
But nowadays, we must help our self.
The modern "self-serve" stores of today,
Drove most of the small stores away.
"Put it on my bill" is now rejected.
Cash, check, credit or debit card only, is accepted.
Few, if any, "ole corner grocery or general store,"
When "charging until payday" are no more.
Then, total faith and complete trust,
In the grocer or storekeeper, was a must.
Big, big stores of today, are too much for me.
I search and search, but items can't be found.
Where are the "help"? No one is around.
Frustrated, I'm ready to leave, you see,
But, my need compels me to shop more, I must eat.
Though fast my heart does beat,
Whilst I'm, by now, dead on my feet.
Far is the car, parked near the street.
Therefore, much distance I must walk in the heat!
I survive somehow, it's too late to retreat.

—August 1, 2013

MOM '99

You've made it, Mommie Dear,
Today you became ninety-two.
Sadly, 'tis the first year,
That Daddy is not spending with you.

'Tis very hard to adjust,
To living your life all alone.
But once a lifetime mate is gone,
In God, you must trust.

Your situation, not bleak nor gloom.
Thankful, that your daughter has room.
She accommodates you very well,
In everything, best I can tell.

Other children, too,
Are ready to help, no doubt.
All you ever need to do,
Is tell 'em, just sing out.

Your sons-in-law, too,
Deserve a real "big hand."
What they "put up with" is not new.
'Tis more than some husbands could stand.

It's your birthday.
I hope you can enjoy it a lot,
With friends and family, today,
And anyone who "comes about."

Happy, Happy Birthday,
We love you.
Phyllis and Ray.

MON PERE

Je pensee a toi bien souvent,
Tous les semaine.
Je pensee, comment etre ta sante,
Toutes les temps.

Le pretemps et proche ici,
Il fait pas trop froid aujourd'hui.
Votre bras et votre jambe et pied,
Pas faire mal, j'espoir, pas des malade.

Que tu peu pas aller dans la court,
Quel dommage.
Dans la maison, toue les jourd,
C'est difficile, cela ne faire rien,
Quel-que age.

Un autre annee, un autre fete,
Avec gratitude, c'est quatre-vingt-dix-sept.
Votre sante, pourquoi pas mieux?
Dependre sur toi, le docteur et le Bon Dieu.

That's all my French for today.
Hope all is well, down your way.
Have a Happy, Happy Birthday.
We love you. Phyllis and Ray.

—March 21, 1998

MONEY, MONEY

Newlyweds, on their way to a famous fete.
When the husband decided to have a "tête-à-tête,"
Said he, "Money, money, will we ever have enough?
Honey, honey, times ahead may get tough.

"Before my monthly salary is all spent,
We need to save enough money for rent.
Utilities, too, we'll have to pay,
Else they may take the electricity away.

Water is something we can't do without.
If we don't pay the bill, they'll shut it out.
Bills, bills, every month they're due.
How we spent our money, is up to me and you.

We can plan a budget and follow it through,
Or amass debts like many people seem to do.
We can live well with my monthly pay,
If within our budget, we do stay.
I don't think there is no other way.
Do you agree, what do you say, yea or nay?"

—February 5, 2020, 1:00 p.m.

MORE NONSENSE

Poor Horace was dating Doris,
Knowing that she had a "thing" for Morris.
Gene, planning to date Irene,
Called, hoping they would "make the scene."

Jake planned to go out to the lake.
Who, just who, would he decide to take?
Marie, with Henri, baked her cake.
Warily, she eyed Henri, giving Jake a handshake.

Gloria, claimed she'd been to the "Astoria."
Gale was a regular at "Bloomingdale."
Tonight, they said, "'Twill not be right,
To go out with just any ole male."

Florence gets along fair with Lawrence.
They know 'tis best to "go slow."
Usually not venturing beyond their fence,
Tonight they will go out for a bowl of gumbo.

Tomorrow, Marci and Darsy Munro,
Along with Dorcus and Lewellyn Marcus,
Will choose and rent a video.
Staying home, they'll watch a movie by Lucas.

Casey, Lacy, Frances and Gracie,
Are considered to be very energetic, racy.
Planning a shopping trip at Macy,
They contacted their dear pal, Tracy.

Adolph, Rudolf and Dolph Roth,
Impeccably dressed in the finest of cloth,
Went looking for Randolph, with his betroth,
Completing a foursome, for a round of golf.

Everyone apparently has something to do.
Planned or not, it seems to be true.
Most are happy, get along well.
The others, well, they simply won't tell.

—January 29, 1999

MOTHER NATURE

Awaken this morn, by a loud clap and rumble,
I thought, something cause Mother Nature to grumble.
A disturbing event may have aroused Her ire.
Things may be far worse than She does desire.
Is She about to set the world on fire?
Is there any place where I may inquire?
No more being gentle, nice, and humble,
Forget all the hogwash, the mumble jumble.
Prepare for the fall, the tumble and the crumble.
Hereafter, it'll be rough, tough, and no mumble.
Crime is rampant in many a city street.
Criminals are brazen, no longer being discreet.
Be careful about new people you meet and greet.
Even if they appear to be congenial and sweet.
Politicos fight each other, 'tis a "free for all."
Instead of working together for the "good of all."
Some seem to enjoy this, they're having a ball.
It's appalling that some have that much gall.
Let's face facts, they were elected.
By many people, they were selected.
So it appears that the people they represent,
Like them and their style, so they laugh and smile.
No matter who they may hurt, meanwhile,
If you don't agree and them you resent,
Try to change their view and your opinion present.
Debate, don't argue, they have rights just like me and you.
Perhaps Mother Nature is sad and that's too bad.
Will the world ever change to make Her glad?

—July 22, 2019

MOWING THE FIELD

Mowing grass on a summer day,
I noticed some activity that came my way.
Very soon, an egret did appear.
It came close, very near.
Is it the same one that came last year?

Suddenly, a redheaded woodpecker swooped,
Caught a cricket in midair.
English bluebirds, too, flew and looped,
Joining other birds, who gathered there.

Soon a field mouse scampered full speed,
Missing the lethal blades of the mower.
In a flash, it was in taller weeds,
Hiding from reaper and sower.

Riding the mower, that very day,
A tree branch, even with my arm, did sway.
On it a long black snake was stretched.
It rubbed my arm, that memory, in my mind, etched.

Startled I was, my heart skipped a beat,
As it slithered away, a simple feat.
Soon it disappeared out of my sight,
Oblivious that it had caused me fright.

Occasionally a wild rabbit is seen,
Nibbling on new grass that's green.
Usually 'tis before dusk when they show.
Leisurely they hop, like they have no place to go.

—November 5, 1999

MUST I GRIN AND BEAR?

Today my age is eighty-eight.
I admit that I have a slow gait.
I don't walk but waddle like a duck.
That is because my left leg isn't straight.
Cautious I must be, to fall would be my bad luck.

What caused my weak bones to bend?
I see others like me, is it a trend?
Perhaps it's all about my genes,
Or have radical cells made the scene?

I get out of breath so, so fast,
When I walk, my stamina just doesn't last.
Sit I must, or I may black out.
It's difficult to breathe and I cannot shout.

After a spell, all may seem well.
Indeed, I can proceed if there is a need.
I do declare, it doesn't seem fair,
But it is a burden that I must bear.

—April 24, 2017

MY BODY

My body has doubled in size.
What happened, did I do something unwise?
If my diet changed, I didn't realize.
My physical activity, I do surmise.

Did decrease after a series of event after event.
Most procedures for this or that, was to prevent,
A stroke, a heart attack or even death.
I had quit smoking to maintain good health.

My medication increased at an alarming rate.
Gradually it began, an increase in weight.
Nothing I did helped, was this my fate?
How this all happened is a matter of much debate.

I am not qualified to speculate or elaborate.
So I just go on living from day to day,
Doing things I'm able to do in my own way.
I heed my doctor's advice, what more can I say?

—June 14, 2017

MY CARDIOLOGIST

My Cardiologist and his office personnel,
Are very professional and do their job well.
He installed a "Pace Maker" when he saw a need.
I trust them, their advice I always did heed.

During this COVID-19 pandemic,
They saw me in the office, without panic.
I wore a mask and gloves, that did suffice.
He and the NP seeing me there, I thought was nice.

Cooperating with my other Doctors, I also like.
He does this, to me this means a lot.
Since I no longer exercise or ride a bike,
I depend on the many medications I've got.

My heart and my kidneys, get a lot of attention,
Especially when it comes to "fluid retention."
The "cancer cells" are supposedly "all dead,"
According to the "Pet Scan" that was read.

"Virtual Doctor Visit" may work for thee,
But "Face-to-Face" seems much better for me.
Whatever the Doctor wants, I won't disagree.
I place my life in his hands, you see.

—May 3, 2020

MY CLOTHES

Do you really suppose,
That it happens only to my clothes?
A loose thread, a rip or a tear,
Spotty stains here and there?

Certain knits, again and again,
Get small holes in the cloth.
That's not made by a moth,
And apparently not by acid rain.
Is the culprit the washing machine?

Stains on my trousers mystify.
'Tis as if 'twas spilled some dye.
No other clothes in the same wash,
Seems to be affected, by gosh.
'Tis a mystery that's difficult to track.
Only stained are the legs and the back.

Washing was done in water cold,
As suggested and often told.
No logical explanation or reason,
Is there for such a blue stain.
Nowhere are berries now in season.
What's to blame, the mystery does remain?

When I eat, juices somehow do squirt,
For no reason, land on my shirt.
The front of my shirt is a "catchall."
I need a bib like the good ole "overall."

—November 1, 2001

MY DAYS ARE NUMBERED

My days are numbered, I know 'tis so.
When it's time, I must let go.
Time goes by fast, but I go slow.
My mind wanders, I forget things I used to know.

During my last doctor visit, I got a low blow.
It's my kidneys, something about "the flow."
At 22% they're working, that is bad.
No advice to remedy the situation, that's sad.

What can I do? What should I do?
My mind goes into a fog, then it's blank.
I'm like a "bump on a log,"
Or a car with any empty tank.

I read and read, my doctor's advice I heed.
I tend to my needs, the best way that I can.
In a careful way, I'm no longer an agile man.
Instead of walking, I waddle like a duck,
But with a "walker" I get around, I'm in luck.

At home I'm at ease and at peace.
So far, so good, but someday all will cease.
I do hope that it's a painless release.

—June 9, 2016

MY FIRST LOVE

I was just 18 and 5 feet seven, the year 1947.
She was 19 and stood 5 feet eleven.
I was a paratrooper and our uniform was neat.
People noticed us as we strolled down the street.

The uniform must have attracted the girls.
We were very happy to give them a whirl.
I met "Elizabeth" on a "blind date."
It must have been a real case of fate.
A "knock 'em dead," redhead, she was 1st rate.

For eight months we went steady.
She called me "Porche" and I called her "Betty."
As a pal, she was my only gal.
We never "crossed the line" and that was fine.

Her parents were gone, she and a brother were alone.
A Telephone Operator, she lived in mansion,
With 60 women and an elderly "House Mother."
Disobey and you suffered according to the sanction.
Well supervised, rules were very strict, oh brother.

During the 8 months, we got along very well.
Prior to my discharge, the decision was where to dwell.
She had "lined up" a job for me, thru a friend,
At J.C. Penney, in Fayetteville, North Carolina.
The disagreement was the beginning of the end.

I was adamant about returning to Louisiana, you see,
To resume my studies toward a college degree.
With a very sad heart, I did finally depart.
Never did we ever meet again.

—February 22, 2020, 2:00 a.m.

MY IMMUNE SYSTEM

My Immune System must be confused,
By the amount and types of medicine I've used.
I'm certainly not the least bit amused,
But have not yet dared quit or refused,
The meds, tho my Immune System may feel abused.

Of drug abuse, I've never been accused,
Nor have I ever knowingly, any drug misused.
A pill or a capsule for this or that,
A cream for pain, while in my chair I sat,
I rubbed my knees, where the pain was at.

I think and feel sorry for the poor "lab rat,"
Who is injected or tested while kept safe from a cat.
Today on the "Smart Phone" there's an APP,
That may help you wherever you're at.
All this is available while I'm trying to lose fat.
I lose a little, gain a lot, just like that.

—April 10, 2020, 11:00 a.m.

MY OAK TREES

Oak trees in a yard are beautiful and nice.
In a small yard, one or two will suffice.
Many oak trees I planted years ago,
Amaze me how fast and big they did grow.

In the winter, their leaves may cover the ground.
Squirrels love them, acorns abound all around.
In summer, lots of shade the oaks provide.
Birds like them too, there their nests they hide.

Oaks are a buffer, when strong winds blow,
Preventing damage, at least we suppose 'tis so.
Perhaps there are more beneficial than we know.
They remove carbon dioxide from the air,
Then emit lots of oxygen that we breathe there.

Oak is a hard wood, good for a floor.
Is it as much in demand now as 'twas in days of yore?
For "firewood" oak is still in much demand,
It's wise to have a cord or two in winter on hand.

Every oak I see is a great wonderful tree,
And yes, each one I have is dear to me.

—September 21, 2019

MY, OH MY

My, my, my, how clumsy am I?
Why, why, why, no matter how I try,
Something always seem to go awry?
It's awful, yet I just wonder and sigh.

Things, at times, are hard to understand.
When so easily, items slip out of my hand.
My mind seems to function well,
But why physical mishaps occur, I can't tell.

Once my spelling was great, now words I oft misspell.
I suppose my brain is slowly failing, cell after cell.
I do my best and on somethings I opt not to dwell.

Some days I dawdle, more and more.
Things seem unreal, blindly I grope and grope.
That things will improve, I hope and hope.
Money is not the problem, I'm not broke.

I miss my late wife, hearing words she often spoke,
Or relating an e-mail, a real funny joke.
Memories are treasures, that's really true.
Dreams I welcome, when I feel blue.

There's so many things I need to do,
Yet, time goes by so fast,
I'm unable to follow through.
Is any of this happening to you?

—October 17, 2015

NAIVETÉ

Naiveté may be our downfall.
We condone many things we should appall.
We hear foul language and turn a deaf ear,
So gutter talk gets worse each year.
Movie Stars are role models to so many,
Yet, they spout, too often, the f-word.
Other professionals, too, 'tis uncanny,
Use words that would be best left unheard.
Mentors, you'd think they would know better.
Many use words with the infamous "four-letter."
Tiny tots, as young as the age of three,
"Pick up" on the many things they hear and see.
What's happening, whom do we blame?
No one seems to care or have any shame.
Some parents allow their children, alone,
To go to movies, perhaps the worst kind.
They drop them off and they're gone.
Who watches the movie?
Those kids, with their young vulnerable mind.
To them it probably seems "groovy."
Do parents care, or do they just don't know,
That many movies, for their children are unfit,
Especially an "R-rated" show,
Regardless if it is an acclaimed "hit."
Watching a movie with someone they adore,

Perhaps shocks a "senior citizen" more,
Because some movies contain "filth" that they abhor.
Some movies may not even have a plot,
But you can bet, many f-words it's got.

—December 27, 2000

NAKED AND ALONE

A woman, to win a prize, was naked and alone,
In the Amazon Jungle where she had gone.
She weaved a mat with leaves to sleep on.
A machete, fire starter and a big pot,
Were the only tools that she'd got.

To ward off predators, she built a fire.
A lighted torch was handy, when the situation was dire.
Now she could boil water to cook and drink.
It's amazing how well she did work and think.
A shelter of some sort, she did desire.

With branches and leaves, one she did erect.
She seemed very adept, before she slept, by heck.
Eating reptiles, insects and grubs to stay alive,
Was part of her diet to try and survive.

With her fish trap, she snared some fish.
Now she ate more proteins and a tasty dish.
It was an answer to her daily wish.
The challenge was to survive for 21 days.
It must have been a large prize, that really pays.

A raft built with logs, she made to cross a lagoon.
Infested with alligators, she was picked up, very soon.
She had survived 21 days as was required,
But lost 20 pounds. Was that desired?

—February 23, 2020, 9:00 p.m.

NEEDS

Some people have not a lot,
Yet seem happy with what they've got.
There's a lesson we can all learn,
Money is not made, "to burn."
Wanting more than you need,
Is that not a sign of greed?
Many of us could do with less.
"Wanting more" is natural, I guess.
More one has, more one does desire.
The struggle can be a strain.
Some seem to set "the world on fire."
Money and power they hope to gain.
Husbands permit their wives to work,
To achieve a better "lifestyle."
Is the load heavy, or does he shirk?
Do the children suffer, in the meanwhile?
To be fair, many wives enjoy their job.
Some must work to "make ends meet."
Many husbands are no "slob."
They do housework, are very sweet.
Happiness, many do seem to lack.
They just can't "get right on track."
Their "need" is misguided, you see.
There's this constant, too much, "me, me, me."

—September 6, 1999

343

NEW YEAR

Another year has swiftly gone by,
My, oh my, I don't know why,
I have much mixed feelings, somehow.
Should I jump with joy or maybe cry?

Forget the things that were bad in the past,
Or just think of the good and hope that it'll last.
Look to the future in a positive way with hope,
Face my problems, deal with them and learn to cope.

Try my best to never be a pest, a boor or a dope.
Keep busy, not just sit around, moan, and mope.
Property taxes are still on the rise.
Will insurance companies give us another surprise?

Cost of essentials may continue to increase.
I see no signs that this trend will soon cease.
Gasoline prices change and change and change.
This seems to me to be rather strange.
Who decides, who should we really blame?

Speculators, regulators, oil companies or OPEC,
Stock market, crude oil market, or the government, by heck?
No one cares to truthfully tell the public and explain.
It seems of little use for anyone to complain.
Just try to figure who has the most to gain!

—January 2, 2011

NEWS 2001

In the morning when I arise,
Before I even wash my eyes,
I stretch each leg and arm,
To ease pain and prevent any harm.

At the start of each day,
I ask myself, "Self, I say,
What events will occur today?
Will there be surprises along the way?"

Daily news can be very depressing,
Fires, natural disasters, as before.
Accidents and murders happen by the score.
Mystery of missing people keep many guessing.

People suffering seems to be worldwide.
Many have no place to go, run or hide.
Despots who care not at all,
Kill and harm many before they fall.

Prisons everywhere are overflowing.
Crime and mayhem meanwhile keep growing.
Why do so many, to crime turn?
Will criminals really, ever learn?

Bad news and sports dominate the air.
Commercials use the rest of the time there.
"Good News" seems to share very little time.

Is it because it's hardly worth a dime?
I'm beginning to prefer my news in "print,"
"Good news" front page, hint, hint.

—November 26, 2001

NIGHT CREATURES

Creatures of the night,
May or may not be a fearsome sight.
Yet, they give some people a scare,
Just by knowing that they are there.
Try, try as they might,
Because 'tis night, and of their fright,
They're too fearful to go out anywhere.

Without warning, some creatures may strike,
During the night, at whatever they like.
Some people are fearful of man, beast and fowl.
They jump after an earful from the screech of an owl.
They freeze at the sound of a dog's growl,
Or when they hear, near and clear, a wildcat's howl.

Some creatures, like the rattlesnake,
Give fair warning that one needs to heed.
In the wrong direction, 'tis a mistake,
If too many steps towards it you make.
Then move fast to "make a break."
He'll rattle, then give you a battle, yes, indeed.
'Tis best to stop when you first hear its rattle.
Not such are they ways of cattle.
Startle a cow in the dark,
She is likely to just say "moo."
But a bull, loose in the park,
Like a flash, may dash, straight for you.
Cattle are easily spooked at night.

Many things may cause their fright.
On cattle drives, you always read,
At night after they were herded together,
Many things caused cattle to stampede,
Lightning and thunder during stormy weather,
A bear out of his lair, when the weather was fair,
The snap of a twig, from a foot or a rig,
When an eerie feeling was in the air.

Many creatures that hunt at night,
Are equipped with very good eyesight.
Some have a hearing that is very keen,
They detect their prey before it's seen.
Sometimes the hunter becomes the prey.
The bigger and the faster get to live.
The survivor may get to see the break of day.
The next night, his life he may give.

A fearful creature is the humankind,
Especially one with a wicked, evil mind,
Who thinks he was seen committing a crime.
Anyone at the wrong place, at the wrong time,
He will seek out and probably find,
Any victim, because he enjoys crime and slime.

—August 14, 2001

NIGHT OWLS

They always work at night
And sleep during the day.
Try, try as they might,
'Tis difficult to adjust, some say.

During the day it's difficult
To sleep without, ever being disturbed.
Their deep sleep, someone may interrupt,
Causing them to become a bit perturbed.

The telephone, they may take off the hook.
Earplugs, they may also wear.
But somehow, by hook or crook,
Someone will disturb them without care.

Early in the morn
When many people arise out of bed,
Night owls arrive, tired and worn,
Ready to rest their weary head.

If they dillydally much too long,
Stay up a big part of the day,
Enough sleep won't ever come their way.
The lost sleep will forever be gone.

When they get a few days of rest,
Night owls try their very best,
To sleep at night, but 'tis not so easy.
Their disturbed pattern, makes them queasy.

—April 1, 1999

NIGHTFALL

The sun, slowly it does fall,
Out in the distant, western sky.
Like a giant orange ball,
'Tis a beauty, that meets the eye.

It has such an ethereal glow,
That is quite a heavenly show.
Slowly it sinks, ever so slow,
Is it telling me, "Watch, don't go"?

I watch as night shadows fall,
Till it's gone, the golden ball.
The beauty of such a serene expanse,
I watched, while I had the chance.

Now 'tis totally, completely dark.
I can't see a star or the moon.
In the distance, I hear a dog bark,
But not at the moon, it's too soon.

Darkness brings an eerie hush,
Throughout the meadow that is so lush.
Wildlife seek their den, roost and nest.
Mother Nature designed this time for rest.

Nightfall, nighttime, for most a need,
Time for peace, rest and sleep.
But for some, it's time to feed.
No rest for the weary, for them we weep.

—August 10, 1999

NIGHT BEAT

Drums, the natives furiously beat,
Then dance wildly in the night heat.
The tempo quickens, what a feat.
With rhythm, they move their feet.

They continue, all night long,
Dancing, while singing a song.
Into a frenzy, they do seem to get.
Sweltering heat makes them wet.

Special meaning, this has for them,
Much like one feels singing a hymn.
They move with passion, or is it a trance,
They get into, while dancing the dance?

Young and old, they dance about.
While the drums beat, they sing and shout.
Happy they seem, glad as can be,
Enjoying the night, so gleefully.

But, is this a ritual, a special rite,
That they perform on a given night?
Perhaps it's to put everyone in a good mood,
Or simply for enjoyment, by everyone, understood.

—October 15, 1999

NIGHT NURSE

"Grab some shut-eye,"
Her husband did cry out.
"You need the rest, so don't pout."
She was so tired, she could cry.
Would she nap or at least, try?
Would she allow the time to slip by?
More often, she needs a break.
Too many chores she does undertake.
She's under a lot of stress.
Really, she should be doing much less.
She works at the hospital all night,
Twelve long hours at a stretch,
Then she babysits during the daylight,
While this and that she will fetch.
She loves her job and won't quit.
Her grandchildren she loves to "babysit."
A homemaker, she does most every bit,
More than she does care to admit.
Sadly, I notice that she's not alone.
I say "sadly" because that's how I feel.
"Husband's pride," where has it gone?
Is it the "extra things" they're able to own,
That gives "this deal" so much appeal?
Do they demand the added income,
Their wives contribute, by gum?
The husband generally earns enough,
For them to live a comfortable life.
Spending, like they do, may be rough,

But the wife would have much less strife.
Her life, she may easily extend.
Feeling better, she would not pretend,
Everything may be better in the end.
More family activities she could attend.
She could do her chores at a slower pace,
No longer would she be in the "rat race."
That "tired look" would leave her face.
She'd be resting home, her favorite place.
Eager to welcome a good embrace.

—November 7, 2001

NO CLUE 2001

She felt that he acted rather odd.
When asked a question, he gave a nod.
Did he not want to discuss,
His problems, to avoid a fuss?

The hurt seemed deep inside.
Was it physical or just his pride?
Like a mute, he acted dumb.
Was there really pain or was he numb?

Had something at work gone wrong?
Was something not where it did belong?
He seemed sad, listening to her song,
E'en tho she wore little more than a thong.

She thought, "Of me he did tire,
No longer do I light his fire.
Gone must be the love and desire.
He's so miserable he could cry.

Had she not even one clue,
As to why he was so sad and blue?
Was his anger bottled up?
Were his emotions about to erupt?
He felt that he was in a stew.
What to do? He wished that he knew.

He really didn't want to hurt her feelings,
Yet, things needed changes in their dealings.
He felt as one caught in net.
His "freedom" he wouldn't lose just yet.
Their "romance" he'd cool or simply forget.

—December 8, 2001

NO EXCUSE FOR
HOUSING ABUSE

He was tall and muscular at six foot seven,
Living alone at the age of forty-seven.
His dad he never, never knew.
His mom died at the age of seventy-two.

Living in Public Housing all his life,
He and his Mom struggled with strife.
School he did abhor, so he quit in grade four.
Never did he learn to read nor write,
So, though big, he was never considered bright.

Odd jobs he did now and then, when in dire need.
Driving was limited, 'cause signs he couldn't read.
"Katrina" came and all he owned was gone.
After his Mother died, he remained alone.

Evacuated to a great Northern State,
FEMA funded his housing and what he ate.
His clothing, donors gladly did provide,
But friends he lacked, now on the outside.
Yet drugs he bought, his habit he did hide.

Church doors opened, he was beckoned inside.
His great voice, he then used with much pride.
In the choir he began to sing and sing.
Good fortune, his way did swing.

A private tutor, with no strings,
Began teaching him many, many things.
Lady Luck, every day now brings,
Hope for a future, he professes to yearn.
But to New Orleans, he will not return.
Now that he's made a complete turn,
He is content to live in obscurity,
Until he's old enough to draw Social Security.

—October 16, 2007

NO REMEDY OR CURE

We wake up and face each day,
Wondering if things will go our way.
If no, what do we do or say?
'Tis a fact, very true and very sure,
What we cannot remedy or cure,
We must simply do our best and endure.
It doesn't help to moan or cry,
E'en if we feel we're about to die.
Will we violate Mother Nature today,
Or are we just old and are fading away?
Will Mother Nature demand that we pay?
Has our time on earth finally come?
Did we dare defy Mother Nature and overstay?
Are we worse off or better off than some?
Is there a quota that must be filled?
If not enough die, must blood be spilled?
Perhaps Mother Nature is not always nice,
Some time She may demand a price.
In the past, in days of yore,
Some people offered their Gods a sacrifice.
Does Mother Nature now demand more,
Or much less than She did before?
Some may wonder, what's the score?

—October 2010

NONSENSE TWO

Sam was seen moping at the dam.
A scam had put him in a jam.
During the bedlam, he heard "scram."
The guns went off, "bam, bam, bam."
He mumbled, "Damn," froze like a clam,
Was caught with more than a gram.
"It's a sham, must call Pam,"
He thought, as he heard the jail door slam.
To get out of jail,
Someone had to post bail.
Who could he depend on, without fail?
Perhaps, his ole buddy, Dale?
Dale came by, he really did try,
It was no lie, Sam did cry.
The bail was set way too high.
Now on whom could he rely?
Dale called Lew and between the two,
They'd come up with a compromise.
They called a judge they both knew.
A decision, that proved very wise.
The bail was reduced,
Because the judge had deduced,
There was the possibility of a "plant."
Bail was paid, Sam was elated with the "grant."
Now Sam was facing a trial.
Would it be soon or after a long while?
For now, he's deep in thought,
About evidence brought, denials sought.

Tho it was "planted," he well understood,
His chances were not all that good.
He'd always thought everyone was "fair."
Lesson learned, be alert, always, beware!
What if he lost the case?
How could he ever save face?
Being "not guilty," was not enough.
He must be strong, really tough.
The "key," he was told,
"Get a lawyer who is aggressive and bold."
One who knows "his way in court,
Works hard, not just at being a sport."
The lawyer was a true gem.
He threw everything he could at them.
Sam was acquitted and set free,
But the stain on his name remains, you see.
Where would or could he go?

NORTH SHORE

What can it be, about the North Shore?
Is it what I noticed, twelve years ago,
That attracts people by the score?
How pleasant people were everywhere I did go.
Is it because the people, are more laid back?
Or is the woods, the ozone, that other places lack?
The traffic is less hectic in our town, it's true,
Probably not for long, if the migrations pick up anew.
The schools are now bursting at their seam.
Such a rapid development was more than they did dream.
The building industry flourished last year.
Everyone was working, everything was in gear.
If you need work done, be prepared for a stall.
Some may just come late, some don't show up at all.
The majority are dependable and good,
Will do a good job, fairness to them is understood.
Shopping is great, everything is close at hand.
Eating places are bountiful, varieties abound,
In one town alone, six of one famous eatery, is found.
Many places are available to hunt or fish.
Boat lunches are nearby, go to any place you wish.
Wildlife refuges, some are very close, nearby.
Swamp tours are available if you so desire.
An eagle's nest is available for many to see,
Over seventy years, I'm told, in the very same tree.
The atmosphere, to me and many, is great.
The politics no different though, sorry to relate.
Churches are many, different religions worship here.

Schools are rated high, have been every year.
A good place to raise a family, more peace and harmony.
Much to offer the elderly and the retirees,
A large Senior Center, nursing homes and other facilities.
Yes, to the North they're flocking, not the West.
Must be something here, that many like best!

—February 28, 1997

NOUVEAU RICHE

Proud he was, with his business and his work,
Just as he'd been his entire adult life.
Never did he ever shirk.
It had been a struggle, a strife.

The past few years,
He'd really fared out well.
Millions he made, after shedding many tears.
Now he was prosperous, you could tell.

The "high society," the elite,
Snubbed him, because he was "Nouveau Riche."
Not accepting him, they were very discreet,
Denying him, his most ardent wish.

Now that he had enormous wealth,
Many friends he did acquire.
Along with his very "good health,"
He enjoyed fulfilling other peoples' desire.

Eventually, the "elite" did recant,
Accepting him within "their fold."
After all, 'tis not for the "Nouveau" they chant,
But for the "Riche," which counts, I'm told.

—September 13, 1999

NURSE ANNETTE

You made it.
You earned it.
We're all so very proud.

Now you're a hit,
And along with your wit,
You stand above the crowd.

You achieved a lot
With the good attitude you've got.
Keep up the good work,
Don't tarry, nor shirk.

Honor your profession,
Vow, no transgression.
When faced with any concession,
Let ethics be your obsession.

We praise you.
We know you'll do good.
We love you,
That's Understood.

—RRP, April 20, 2000

NURSING HOME

Today she resides in a Nursing Home.
She decided 'twas best, 'twas her choice.
'Tis limited, the space to roam,
Limited activity, few reason to rejoice.
Privacy, not much to be had, as expected.
Gifts of any kind to her, by her, are rejected.
Personal items, she says, seem to disappear.
Do wandering residents come too near?
The food is good, but she may hesitate to eat,
Not because it's too bland nor too sweet.
Digestive problems she may try to defeat.
She loves the wheelchair, is comfortable in that seat.
She's well cared for, they tend to her every need,
But 'tis still very different, very different indeed.
People get lonely, even when in a crowd,
Even when all are singing and the music's loud.
Visitors come many days of the week,
Yet, her daughter's daily visit, she awaits, does seek.
What are her thoughts, is it about the infirmity, the meek?
What will become of me at that age, when I'm weak?
What are the choices when you require 24-hour care?
You just simply cannot go just anywhere?
You rely on caregivers, hope they do their best.
With senility, daily, they are put to some test.
Their mind may wander, be in a far distant place,
Back in time, when they were happy, full of grace.
It can be difficult for everyone, in any case.
That's the penalty for growing old, in the Human Race.

—January 27, 2000

OAITW

As we approach our "end of days,"
Expect changes in many, many ways.
You may no longer "have your say."
Many wish, hope, deny and pray,
Yet, they become "Old And In The Way."

Your memory fails, things you forget.
'Tis embarrassing at times, you bet.
You want to cry as you wonder, why?
At times, you may wish you could die.

Dear ones that you love and trust,
May have to take over your life and your home.
They do what they think they must.
Your activities are restricted, you must not roam.

Cooking things you wish or desire,
Is a "no-no," you may set the house on fire.
"Menial tasks" you're told not to perform.
They wish to keep you from harm.

They prefer if you "stay out of their hair."
Don't despair, even if you don't think it's fair.
Be calm, no need for anger or alarm.
'Tis "their way" or a nursing home.

No longer welcomed is your advice,
You're expected to just "sit and be nice."
Perhaps, you are OAITW, are you?

—May 26, 2015

OCEANS

The ocean is a vast open saltwater sea.
When calm, on it, it is a pleasure to be.
But if there's a raging storm, believe me,
It's not a safe place for me or thee.

Rogue waves in oceans have claimed many ships.
Suddenly they appear, ending many trips.
Five oceans cover about 71 percent of the Earth.
Teeming with life, very much is their worth.

The Pacific Ocean, largest of the five,
Between America, Asia, and Australia,
On islands many people live and thrive.

The Atlantic Ocean, between Europe, Africa, and America,
Many ships, boats, planes and lives were lost, too.
In the Bermuda Triangle alone, more than a few.

The Indian Ocean, south of Asia, between Africa and Australia,
Tsunamis, huge waves caused by earthquakes
and volcanic eruptions,
Have caused much damage around that area.
They have killed many and caused very much destruction.

The Arctic Ocean surrounds the North Pole,
North of the Arctic Circle, harsh weather, not nice.
Antarctic Ocean, parts of the Atlantic, Pacific and
Indian Ocean surrounding Antarctica.
Land area about the South Pole, completely covered by ice.

It's hard to believe, with weather so severe,
That living creatures do exist, yet they do, here.

—January 23, 2020, 10:00 p.m.

ODETTE

Lying down on her back,
Inside her room and atop her bed,
Comforts, she does not seem to lack,
Yet, at the moment, I was taken aback,
Wondering what was going through her head.
'Twas early afternoon, we found her thus,
Gazing upwards, quietly, without a fuss.
Then she seemed in awe, surprised to see us.
Every day, everything, 'tis a daily routine,
That begins in early morn, 'till bedtime.
For her, will it change, this scene,
Or will loneliness become her "pastime"?
Never, never to be all alone,
Does she ever want to be.
Afraid of falling down, breaking a bone,
Is her big fear, 'tis plain to see.
Visitors, she gets quite a lot.
'Tis a large family that she's got.
A daughter, living nearby, visits every day.
Other children, for daily visits, are too far away.
Her children visit as oft as they can.
They discuss and listen to any plan.
If better, her life can possibly be,
They will come together and try to agree.
She says she's well-fed,
That she's treated very nice.
Yet, what is really the price,
To be paid, as to where she will rest her head?

—August 23, 1999

OH, WELL

Bad back, bad knees, loss of hair,
Am I slowly falling apart?
What will fail next, my heart?
Things I can't mend or repair,
Puts me in a state of grief and despair.

What once I was eager to do,
I'm now unable to follow through.
Mentally, what seems a simple task,
Physically, I can't perform or endure.
In the sun, I can no longer bask. Why you ask?
Because I'll burn or ail, for sure.
For this, is there really cure?

Paper-thin, is my skin, as thin as onion skin.
Thick hair is only on my face and chin.
No hair left on my legs, not even my shin.
When did all this begin?
Shucks, it seems I just cannot win.
Pain persists externally and within.
The same thing happens to some kith and kin.
Are we being punished for a particular sin?

—April 13, 2009

OLD BONES

My old bones are tired and weary,
At times so painful, my eyes get teary.
From my hips to my ankles the pains radiate.
I take "nerve capsules" to ease the pain,
But they seem to aggravate rather than eliminate.
A situation such as this rattles my brain.

Should I continue, as the doctor did advise,
Taking the capsule or as I feel and surmise,
Reduce or eliminate the medication?
Either way, I perceive it as a great risk,
But is this not so of such a situation?

I should weigh the pros and con,
Perhaps, use a "gut instinct" to rely on.
I may follow the doctor's advice a bit longer.
Take Tylenol until I get a little stronger.

Right now, I'm weak in the knees, but just a little.
Hopefully, tomorrow I'll feel "fit as a fiddle."
The weather may be partially to blame.
Many feel the same, so I feel no shame.
With a pocket knife and a piece of wood, I can whittle.

—June 20, 2016

OLD COOT

They came, the usual, same old bunch,
Every day, at the Senior Center, for lunch,
A hearty meal with milk or tea, no punch.

One was considered, "just an old coot,"
That few cared for, or gave a hoot.
Was it because, his horn he did toot,
Or his shabby suit and unpolished boots?

At four scores and eight, alone he usually ate,
Yet spry, he was always ready to debate.
His oafish criticisms, another aspect,
Why he commanded little or no respect.

Living a life of simplicity and neglect,
Was his feeling, "What the heck"?
Some days, he just wished to die.
Other days, afraid to die, he'd cry and cry.

His moods changed and he knew not why.
Sad days he spent and as time went by,
Shopping nearly ceased, fewer things he did buy,
Even though his "well had not run dry."

Lately, when quizzed, he would just sigh.
Are his days on Earth drawing nigh?
What's ahead for this poor old codger,
A nursing home, where he'll be a permanent lodger?

—January 23, 2008

OPOSSUM AND RACCOON

Cat food left on the patio, in a pan, for a feral cat,
Must have been smelled by a big old raccoon.
Especially on nights with a full moon.
It's like the raccoon knew exactly where it was at.

First one raccoon, then a handsome pair, pretty soon,
Would appear, eat and disappear, just like that.
Another shabby raccoon would soon come seeking his share.
He'd nibble a bit, then quickly scoot out of there.

A young opossum, unaware of a cat, would soon scan the pan.
Seeing that it was empty, it spoiled his plan.
He'd meander about, sniffing with his snout.
Then, it too, disappeared into the night.

Meanwhile, the cat had stayed out of sight.
Had she eaten earlier, was she bright or was it fright?
Perhaps, she just wanted to avoid a fight.
This went on night after night after night.

Until, one day, the feral cat disappeared for good.
The raccoon and opossum no longer came seeking food.
Why or what happened to the cat, we never understood.
Was she captured and adopted, or by a coyote, slain?
So far, the mystery does remain,
Will we ever see her again?

—July 26, 2019

OUR FIRST DATE

At work with Schlumberger, was this young, lovely girl.
To date her, I decided to give it a whirl.
Though she was "engaged," she finally did relent.
Perhaps because of a strange event, was it "godsent"?
An engineer friend bought a new Packard, a luxury car.
Then on a 4-day job he had to go.
He said I could use the car, if I didn't drive very far.
It needed to be serviced and I was happy to do so.
The next morning, going to work as usual, Phyllis walked.
I offered her a ride, she didn't balk, we talked and talked.
"How do you like my new car?" said I.
She looked at me "eye to eye" then shook her head.
Laughing and laughing, she then looked ahead.
"If you don't believe me," I said,
"How about a date tonight?"
"Okay," she said, "if what you say is true, then alright."
The date was great and we did kiss.
It was a chance I didn't want to miss.
She laughed and said, "You may be sorry."
I said to her, "Don't you worry."
For two years hence, she was the only girl I did date.
Was I just lucky, or was it really fate?
Born 2 days apart, was she predestined to be my "soul mate"?
After we both became 21, we did finally wed.
For nearly 63 years, a good life we led.
Children and grandchildren, because of her, were well-bred.
Because of 3 massive strokes, it came to an end.
Nine months in "hospice," then she was dead.

It was 63 years, 8 months, and 11 days since we were wed.
I'm alone now that she is gone.
Many friends that I have are gracious and kind.
They do their best to give me "peace of mind."
If some day, a compatible comrade came to stay,
What would I do and what would I possibly say?
Who knows, it may "make my day."

—October 26, 2019

OUR SKIN

What's happened to my skin?
Changes, changes, where do I begin?
Acne plagued me, as a teen,
As unsightly a skin, as I'd ever seen.

For many years, my skin looked nice,
After a shave and a little "old spice."
My arms and legs had nary a bruise,
I'd have looked good, on the beach or a cruise.

Eventually, wrinkles began to appear.
They seemed to increase, year after year.
Blotches, too, were noticed, here and there.
Before long, they seemed to be everywhere.

Looking in the mirror, I now dread,
Parts of my skin are blotchy, red, or dead.
Purple bruises I see, when first out of bed.
Did I bump myself? I just shake my head.

Our largest organ, is our skin.
Some parts are thick while some parts are thin.
Through our skin, the sense of touch, we feel.
Though bruised, burned, or cut, it normally will heal.

Why can't we be like some reptile,
Shed our skin, every once in a while?
Renewed, it would be blemish free.
Scars would disappear, too, you'd see.

—August 22, 2000

OUR TEETH

Our teeth, we do brush,
Until it becomes routine.
Daily, even when we're in a rush,
To keep our mouth and teeth clean.

Early in the morn,
After we first arise.
To brush our teeth, is the norm,
To not do so, is very unwise.

We often choose toothpaste,
According to how it does taste.
Leaving the mouth fresh, is a plus,
But cleaning power, is a must.

Toothbrushes do wear down,
But may be bought everywhere.
Every Grocery and Drugstore in town,
Plus General Stores, here and there.

Toothbrushes come, very oft,
In as many colors as the rainbow.
This, too, you ought to know,
Bristles are hard, medium or soft.

To brush your teeth is not a must.
This you can believe, can trust.
Don't you worry or lose any sleep,
Brush only the teeth you want to keep.

—February 18, 1999

OUR WEDDING PICTURE

On the wall, near the foot of my bed,
Hangs the picture taken when Phyllis and I were wed.
Every night before I rest my weary head,
I look at the picture and I think of the past,
Thankful how long our marriage did last.

A wonderful wife and great mother of four,
Each grandchild and great-grandchild Phyllis did adore.
Two more great-grandchildren were born since she did die,
Lovable and feisty, Phyllis would "eat 'em up and cry."

I think of the vacations we enjoyed year after year.
When our children were home and had nothing to fear.
Together we watched our children and their children grow.
Most are wed and their children we got to know.

It's 2:30 a.m. and looking at our picture now,
I see us smiling, shortly after we'd taken our vows.
Lovely she looked in her beautiful wedding dress.
I think she really did dress to and she did impress.
If so, she was a real big success.

The picture was taken April 30, 1950.
We headed for Chicago, Illinois after we changed clothes.
Our wedding guest celebrated, I suppose.
Glad I was that Phyllis said "yes" when I did propose.

—September 21, 2016

PAIN AGAIN

So sad and sorry am I,
Hearing you experienced such pain, such woe.
So hurt that you could cry,
But your "gallbladder" had to go.

Why must it always be,
In the middle of the night,
To get such a scare as Ye,
Giving you such a fright?

Were you surprised, taken aback?
Were the symptoms like a heart attack?
Was your suffering very long?
How long to discover what was wrong?

Did you get, at the hospital, immediate care?
Was you doctor made aware,
Of your anguish and despair,
Just as soon as you got there?

How long were you kept,
Waiting, before they operated?
Surely, they were not inept.
Meanwhile, were you sedated?

I hear that the operation went well.
That alone is a relief, Belle.
Hopefully, you'll recover very quickly.
Only medical personnel gain when you are sickly.
Heal very soon and begin a new day.
Once all your pain goes away,
You'll feel better, happier and gay.

Now, on a positive note,
Is the ole saying and I quote,
"She's got a lot of gall."
Now this can never apply to you,
Since now, you have no gall at all.
'Tis plain, no one can misconstrue.

Get well, Belle.
We love you.

—Phyllis and Ray, October 3, 2000

PAIN, PAIN

What is there to gain,
By enduring constant pain?
Do I misunderstand my brain,
Telling me not to overdo, not to strain?
Should I welcome pity, to get a hug,
Or chance relief, by taking a drug?
Perhaps 'tis only a bug,
That threatens me worse than a thug.
Relief may come after a simple shot,
Or taking pills (capsules or tablets), there's a lot.
However, to ease the pain I've got,
May require rest, in a bed or cot.
The brain must know whether or not,
To apply something cold or something hot,
Unless all it receives is a blot or dot after dot.
The answer may be chicken soup in the pot.
Too much pain, at times, we endure,
'Cause we don't know or won't try a cure,
Simply because we can't be sure,
If it's safe or if ingredients are pure.

—April 2010

PARATROOPER 2001

The paratrooper is a soldier elite,
Who never thinks in terms of defeat.
Thoroughly trained he'll jump into hell.
If he must die, he'll die well.

He keeps himself trim and fit.
He's combat ready and won't quit.
A certain job he's trained to do.
He'll follow orders and see it through.

Trained to strike and strike fast,
The first to go, not the last.
Swiftly and decisively his unit will strike,
Intelligently and fearlessly with all its might.

He's patriotic and very proud.
Easily he stands out in a crowd.
"La crème de la crème," is he not?
Lots of confidence he's got.

He's been excited, really pumped,
Since the first time he jumped.
He felt then that he was over the hump.
Ever since, each jump is a thrill.
He loves action, can hardly keep still.

—September 14, 2001

PATIENT, PATIENT

In a doctor's office, I did wait and wait.
I arrived early, as asked, but he was late.
Fifteen minutes early, they requested that I come.
I complied, but as I did wait, I wondered, "How come?"
Now I did sit, twiddling my thumb.

An hour later, they called my name,
Led me to one of four rooms that looked the same.
Another half hour and I was ready to scream,
"What on earth is this game?"

My dear wife goes to the desk.
They seem to think, "Who is this pest?"
"What is going on?" the wife inquires.
"Unexpected emergencies" are the replies.

Are they truths or are they lies?
Emergencies do arise, I know and realize,
But every time? No way, I am wise.
One doctor, four rooms gives him away.
That's four appointments, same time, day after day.

He's more "businessman" than healer, I say.
The "scar on my nose" is still there today.
He offered to reoperate, but I said "nay, nay."
Highly recommended and high was his fee,
I feel to this day that it was a bum deal for me.

The operation was not successful and he offered to redo,
For a mere $100, did he fear that I would sue?
I wouldn't, but with him I was through.

—2010

PEDICURE

My toenails are too long, I'm sure.
What I really need is a pedicure.
A pedicure I'm always happy to endure.

Things they do is real neat.
In warm water, they first soak your feet.
Then your toenails, very gently, they clip.
One by one, 'tis snip, snip, snip.

Massaging your feet, every toe,
Feels divine, that's the way to go.
Vick's Salve they rub, on and on,
And scrub the bottom of your feet,
Until all the roughness is gone, gone.

Next, as a very, very, special treat,
They massage your lower leg,
All this without you having to beg.
All the work they do is quite a feat,
Which, in my book, is hard to beat.

A manicure, I'm still able to do,
But, not a pedicure, how about you?
A necessary luxury, simple and pure,
Is a "feel good" pedicure.

—October 20, 2019

PERSIMMON TREE

The wild persimmon tree in my field,
Every year, lots of fruit it does yield.
When ripe, the yellow fruit hits the ground.
They're very tasty, but are seldom found.

Squirrels love them too, you see,
And they are more agile and hungry than me.
The tree is now very, very tall.
It bears fruit a bit smaller than a Ping-Pong ball.

The fruit may ripen in September, in the fall.
It's usually enjoyed by one and all,
With a few exceptions, as I recall.

It's the only persimmon tree that I've found,
Although I've covered every foot of ground.
The tree is over 35 years old and is very sound.

Beside squirrels, birds may like the fruit, too.
That means that less remains for me and you.
I'm lucky if I get one to chew or even taste,
Although when ripe, I search for them in haste.
But I'm happy that no fruit will go to waste.

—February 25, 2020, 2:30 p.m.

PILLOW WITH
A PICTURE

A pillow with a picture of Phyllis and me,
Is on the side of the bed where she used to be.
She slept on the left and I slept on the right.
Many years, that's how it was when I was home at night.

In bed, I don't remember ever having a fight,
Or Phyllis experiencing any kind of fright.
We did have very many nights of pure delight.

Some of the happy memories that I do recall,
Is when all four of our children were very small.
On Sunday mornings, I'd read the comics to them,
While we were all in our "king-size bed."
I can still hear them laughing, as I read.

When small, grandchildren enjoyed our bed, too.
Even our great-granddaughter, who is now 22.
After Phyllis died, I gave the "king-size bed" away.
Now I'm alone in my bed every night and day.

Every night I look at the picture on the pillow,
A gift from my oldest grandson.
Who, as a baby, like the others, our hearts he won.

He was such a dear, lovable little fellow.
Today, he is also a grandfather, too.
It's hard to believe, but it really is true.

—Friday, November 15, 2019, 1:00 a.m.

PINE TREE

Pine trees are many where I reside.
They abound in the forest and the wayside.
Tall tops with few branches is one kind.
Shorter ones, with many branches, I also find.

Its shape and beauty I do admire.
Some are taller than a steeple's spire.
Pine cones large and small are found.
Many, many, oft fall to the ground.

Squirrels gnaw them when they're green.
Certain times, around the tree, they're seen.
Lightning seems to favor a tall, tall pine.
It's killed several pines of mine.

When it strikes it peels a strip of bark,
From the treetop, down to the ground.
Whether 'tis daylight or dark,
'Tis not a place to be anywhere around.

These are trees with few disease,
But strong winds they cannot take.
Little more than a slight breeze,
Pine branches may snap and break.

During a gust of strong wind,
Tall pines may bend and bend,
Then break midway with ease.

Yes, a common tree is the pine,
But frankly, 'tis not a favorite of mine.

—July 13, 2001

PLASTIC CONTAINERS

Plastic bottles people take,
Poolside, out on picnics and to the lake.
Like the glass bottles some make,
They contain the same and don't break.
Plastic jugs are also used a lot,
For nearly all the liquids we've got.
Cooking oils, fruit juices, vinegar and bleach,
There's a plastic jug that's used for each.

Sodas, colas, teas and drinks of every kind,
Many, many more that may come to mind,
On shelves in every store you'll find,
Most, if not all, in bottles made of plastic.
The popularity of plastic is utterly fantastic.
On a picnic or patio barbeque,
It's paper plates and plastic forks for you.
When finished, into the trash they go.
Clean up is easier, less messy and not as slow.
For landfills, though, it's a no-no.

Plastic buckets contain things such,
As detergent, soap powder, bird seed,
Dried pet food, the list has so much.
They fill such a great, great need.
Reusable, they're likely not to fail,
When replacing a rusty ole metal pail.
In many sizes, they're handy for use.
They can also take a lot of abuse.

Plastic containers are made to store or freeze,
Varieties of foods efficiently and with ease.
Shapes and sizes vary quite a bit.
With homemakers, they're a big hit.
Plastic containers, everywhere are seen.
They're also a big reason highways are not clean.

—September 30, 2001

POISON IVY

Poison ivy doesn't care which,
People tall, short, black, white, poor or rich,
It affects them all and really does itch.
The more people itch, the more they scratch,
Then the more sores they get, natch.
Sores may spread over their body and face,
Everywhere they touch, every place.

Remember when you roam in the woods,
It may be nice but not necessarily divine.
It would help if everybody understood,
Much more about each plant and each vine.

Poison ivy, poison sumac and poison oak,
Can cause much misery and that's no joke.
Pity the laggard, the poor slowpoke,
Who may lean on tree after tree,
Perhaps on one a poison vine will be.

Care must be taken when cutting the vine,
Then placing them in a big pile.
You may suppose that all will be fine,
After waiting quite a while,
But for now, just wipe off that smile.
Setting the pile afire to burn,
A lesson you may soon learn.
The smoke can also irritate you too,
Cause more misery before you're through.

—September 29, 2001

POTATOES

Potatoes, potatoes, we eat a lot.
Nearly each meal, potatoes we've got.
Breakfast, 'tis potatoes hash brown,
Fried as a patty, perhaps made round.

For lunch, many choices, many tries,
One that is popular, is "french fries."
Boiled potatoes is a choice of many.
Scalloped potatoes are enjoyed aplenty.

Meat and mashed potatoes, what a combo,
Eaten a lot, by every Jane and Joe.
Lots of potatoes, in a hearty stew,
Is a wholesome meal, for me and for you.

When boiling crawfish, boil potatoes, too.
They pick up the flavor, they surely do.
New, small red potatoes, is the choice of most,
A "hit" with your guests, makes you a good host.

Steak and potatoes, a diner's choice everywhere,
The baked potato is loaded with "stuff."
This is a very popular dinner fare,
Usually with a salad, it's quite enough.

Sweet potatoes and candied yams,
Are popular holiday treats.
They satisfy a "sweet tooth" as do jams,
And compliment a variety of meats.

—November 15, 1999

PRECIOUS MEMORIES

Her eyes in the picture on the shelf,
Seem to gaze at me wherever I go.
When I'm in the room alone, all by myself,
I sense that the picture has a certain glow.

There she is smiling at me,
Making me remember how it used to be.
In our bedroom, so many memories I recall,
Especially when our children were very small.

In our king-size bed, all four would meet.
On Sunday Mornings, reading comics were a treat.
Now grandparents, all four have children of their own.
I hope they treasure the memories they have known.

As babies, at times our grandchildren slept with us.
Never do I recall, any creating a big fuss.
Phyllis loved them all with a passion supreme.
Now she is gone, I only see her in my dream.

The picture on the shelf seems to say,
"I loved you, so I wish I had not gone away."
But, as a preacher once said, "We're all born to die."
Precious memories help, even when I'm about to cry.

—June 15, 2016, 3:00 a.m.

PRETENDING

In the "Movie Business" pretending is considered an art.
Great actors are very adept at playing their part.
They "make believe" from the bottom of their heart.
That's why Hollywood and some Politicos aren't far apart.

Do some people who act at "making believe,"
Learn and practice to lie, cheat, steal and deceive?
"Big stars" who play their roles very well,
Earn big money and their endorsements really do sell.

Many fans, to be politically correct, perceive,
That what some "Notables" spout they did conceive.
Is what these people do and what they say,
In agreement with most and does it really hold sway?

'Tis hard to decide, yea or nay,
Since their tales may change from day to day.
Many may wonder what games they do play.
Fans, friends and many listeners they easily sway.

What is real and what is totally untrue?
Uneasy, many may feel, don't know what to do.
I feel befuddled at times myself, don't you?
Some of them are probably confused, too.

—February 23, 2013

PROBLEMS

Problems, problems, we all get.
Some get more than others, I bet.
Solutions, solutions, where are they?
In the imagination, some will say.
A faucet suddenly springs a leak.
Is it not a plumber that you seek?
Perhaps a "self-help" book will do.
Simple advice may be enough for you.
The lawn mower just won't start.
You've changed the plug, done your part.
Perhaps you can remove, clean the head,
Or take it to a repair shop, instead.
The A/C won't put out cold air.
You're so hot, you could even swear.
This is not a "do it yourself" repair.
"Certified help" is needed here, mon cher.
Outside the city, out goes your water well pump.
'Tis a long weekend, no one answers you call.
Before long, you're "way down in the dump."
It is evident, you can get no help at all.
After a week, help is finally on the way.
What he thought would take an hour,
Now takes him the entire half day.
He's dismayed, his mood turns sour,
Says he will try to return the next week.
You agree, 'tis that or someone else you must seek.

Problems come, yet solutions are generally there.
You look around, find out it's the same everywhere.
When you have a problem, try to keep your "wit."
Usually you can find a solution that will fit.

—August 5, 1999

PROJECTS

Projects, projects, they never cease.
They don't decrease but constantly increase.
Just when you finish a very long one,
Seems that two or more have already begun.

Some projects you simply hate to start,
Knowing that it will take a long while.
Yet, you know, deep in your heart,
You'll do it, you have it on file.
You'll do it, before things fall apart.

Delayed projects just don't go away.
You know you must do them some day.
Some of us really do procrastinate,
Put things off, 'till a much later date.

Projects pile up, they accumulate,
So you consider hiring help, a pro.
You ask for quotes, the going rate,
Then tell yourself, "Whoa, whoa, whoa."

Some charge by the job.
Others charge by the hour or the day.
Some appear neat, a few look like a slob.
They seem anxious to help in any way.

Retired, many of us still have lots to do.
Project after project comes our way.
Some think we're idle the entire day.
'Tis not so here, how about you?

—October 29, 1999

PUPPY LOVE

Is it infatuation, "puppy love,"
The two are together quite a lot?
Like some lonely, "cooing dove,"
Heartaches, they claim they've got.

Youngsters, they're both fifteen,
Think that their parents are being mean.
During the week, they can't go,
Anywhere out past ten, including the show.

After all, they're still in school,
Must obey each and every rule.
Weekends, more freedom they get,
May stay out a bit later, not too late, just yet.

At school, they hold hands in the hall,
Sneak an occasional kiss, 'tis all.
Weekends they date, hug a bit more.
Romancing begins, as they exit her door.

They're both smart, have a lot of respect,
For each other, and for their parents, by heck.
Their hormones rage, yet, they don't exceed,
Certain limits, they have their creed.

Perhaps their love is real and true.
They appear to know what they want to do.
For their age, they seem very mature.
Their goals are set, they feel very secure.
In their hearts, they are sure and feel pure.

—November 8, 1999

PURITY

She is all of thirteen,
Naive, but sweet, innocent and pure.
Pure evil she had never seen,
Except what she saw on the TV screen.
Of nothing, can she be sure.

Much violence she sees on TV.
Movies, she knows are unreal.
How bad can the real world be?
Could she believe all she did see?
Then came Tuesday, September eleven,
Did all that died end up in heaven?
The evil ones, where did they go?
How long before we ever know?

She shows an interest in boys.
They are now more fun than toys.
Some boys are too interested in her.
Which ones do her parents prefer?
Several years she has to decide,
Before she'd consider being a bride.
She is still too young to date.
"Not until sixteen," her Dad did state.
"That is three long years away,"
She thought, but did not say.
Three years she has to sway,
Her parents to see things her way.

Pure and chaste she would remain,
Until her beautiful, wedding day.
From using liquor, tobacco and dope,
She would honestly, truly, abstain.
Her future is bright, she has high hope.
She knows that this is the best way,
Especially, in a world that's in such disarray.

—September 13, 2001

QUITE A LADY

She's three scores plus eleven,
But looks much younger than that.
She's like an angel from heaven,
Brightens things up, wherever she's at.

A very good and desirable friend,
She'll stand by you, to the very end.
Simply a joy to be around,
Rarely, is a dearer person found.

She loves to shop very much,
Visits her favorite shops and such.
Bargains, she seldom will resist.
Shops during vacation, she may insist.

Very talented, she loves to sew,
Works wonders, with material, I know.
She can alter, mend and create,
Be it a dress, a gown, pants, or things to decorate.

She stays on the move, loves to travel,
Takes several trips a year.
Rests at her Lake House, before things unravel,
Quietly, with her husband, the dear.

She and my wife get along great,
Enjoy each other's company a lot.
They travel together, without their mate,
Meet with other friends they've got.

—September 18, 1999

RABBIT 2001

Did the dogs just happen by?
Could he outrun them? He must try.
He had a slight head start,
If immediately, quickly he did depart.

The rabbit ran very fast,
Knowing this run could be his last.
He zigzagged and zigzagged, turned and turned,
So much that his paws burned.
Two dogs were enjoying the chase,
Going about it with gusto and haste.
Barking and barking as they ran and ran,
They started to bark when the chase began.

The rabbit thought that as long as he leads,
He'd try to run into some thicket.
Perhaps briars, bushes or very thick weeds,
Might help him, those dogs looked wicked.
He came upon a log nearly hidden,
That he knew had a long hollow spot.
The dogs sniffed but were they forbidden?
Clawing and crawling inside they could not.

Safely and patiently waiting, the rabbit did nap.
Until he no longer heard the dogs yap.
Finally giving up, the dogs went about their way.
The rabbit lived to enjoy another exciting day.

—September 28, 2001

RAIN

Today we had lots and lots of rain,
Most of the day, enough to rattle the brain.
Hour after hour, it was shower after shower.
Luckily, between downpours, the water did drain.
At 9:30 a.m., there wasn't much daylight.
It may have rained since late last night.
They predict this weather will last 'till noon tomorrow.
If it rains relentlessly, we may feel much sorrow.
I do hope it's nice tomorrow in the afternoon,
And that the sun does appear real soon.
Then grocery shopping, I may decide to go,
To take advantage of the bargains they show.
I may go with my sons, Brian and Glenn.
It's good to shop with them, now and then.
Reggie, my daughter, shops with us at times, too.
But she's going to the game tomorrow at LSU.
That's where she and husband, Eric and friends love to go.
It's good to stay in touch with the old friends they know.
At least I happen to think so.

—Friday, October 25, 2019, 10:00 p.m.

RAINBOW

In the sky, a Rainbow did appear.
My, my, is it a sign of good cheer?
In the fields, wildflower far and near,
Beautiful they are in full bloom.
Today is not a day of gloom and doom.

Maybe the coronavirus will be over soon,
And people may again "spoon by the light of the moon."
A lot of sunshine in the weather,
Will surely make people feel much better.

After being "cooped up" for a spell,
A bit of sunshine may do very well.
A sky with a beautiful Rainbow,
Like a lovely face with a big smile,
Both may "cheer you up" for a while.

So, life can be beautiful, don't you know?
Therefore, enjoy yourself today.
As you self-quarantine, in due time,
Your woes may go away.
You obeyed the law and committed no crime.

—March 27, 2020, 10:30 a.m.

RAMBO

He looked pitiful and poor,
A miserable, forlorn pup,
Sorrowful, at my back door,
Not knowing which end was up.
Out of the blue, from nowhere,
He suddenly did appear.
His seedy, patchy hair,
Was nearly gone, I did fear.
He was evidently very, very young,
Four to six weeks, perhaps more.
By hard luck, he'd been stung,
Covered by more than one sore.
'Twas more than a rash.
Perhaps, it was the mange.
I didn't see any cuts or any gash,
Yet, it all seemed very strange.
Surely, he was brave and bold,
Had a stout, strong heart of gold.
No telling, how far he did travel,
Before everything began to unravel.
I decided I'd treat him myself,
Using salves from my shelf.
Carbolated Vaseline, I did find.
It did work, gave me peace of mind.
My grandson, named him "Rambo."
Good healthy signs began to show.
Would we keep him, let his stay?
Discussed the pros and cons all day.

Yes, me, my grandson did sway.
For him, I said he could stay.
My wife chimed in that day,
"I knew he'd get his way."
Eventually, my grandson did depart.
With a sad heart, he left Rambo behind.
I guess, I knew from the very start,
That Rambo would really become mine.
He was a Pit Bull, but he did "mind,"
Much like a very small child.
He loved to roam, run and unwind,
Yet, he did not really act wild.
For nine years, he greeted me every day,
Jumping up and down, ready to play.
Then early one cold, dreary morn,
I found him by my tractor, where he lay.

RATE YOUR MATE

It shows, he's definitely hurt.
She has demeaned his self-worth.
'Twas like a dart to his heart,
When she told him to please leave.
She needed space, they should part.
Silently, now he does grieve.
Married to her for several years,
Her children he did help her rear.
He has naught to show for it now,
But heavy debts, a heavy heart and tears,
And much confusion somehow.
He loves her, he does confess,
But he can't take the stress.
It' is all a big mess,
The tremendous pressure and strain,
Every time she "yanks his chain."
One day it's "honey this and honey that."
Next day 'tis "leave and take your hat."
She uses him to satisfy her need.
Where money is involved, is it greed?
Manipulative, she wraps him around her finger.
She pleads, "Come," he goes and does linger.
Mismanaging their money, they're deep in debt.
It's happened to her before, she's inept.
Too many debts have piled up, by heck.
They're way overboard, over their necks.
He's unwilling to face the fact,
That what she does, is no way to act.

Married to her, he must realize a thing or two,
Her debts are his debts, too.
His options now, are but a few.
Divorce is a very serious action,
I usually recommend couples not do.
For him, I have a different reaction,
In order to start anew, a new life,
And to rid himself of such strife,
He should sever ties, divorce his wife.
The reason for this suggestion,
Is to keep him from more depression.
She faced this situation once before.
With bankruptcy, her debts were no more.
She was married to another, then.
Her allegiance now, as it has been,
Is only to her cat and her (not his) children.
                              —September 17, 2000

RATTLESNAKE

A venomous American snake with a tail that rattles,
Fighting in the wild, it may win many battles.
When walking in the woods or field, almost anywhere,
Be wary, watch your step, a Rattler may be there.

Cautious though you may be, if you hear a rattle, beware.
It's a snake, ready to strike. What do you do?
Try to avoid it if you can and if you dare.
It may try to avoid you, too.

The rattle is a warning, that's their way.
If you're not aggressive, it may just slither away.
An untreated Rattlesnake bite, can cause pain or death,
So wear boots when hiking, it's good for your health.

When you see a Rattlesnake, your instinct may be to kill.
For once, forgo the kill, just go against your will.
Is the Rattlesnake a friend or is it a foe?
I'm really no judge, so I actually do not know.
They eat rodents and small varmints, but perhaps birds also.

Its venom may have good medicinal use,
So there's no reason, this snake to abuse.
I seem to recall that in parts of the South and West,
Some days, Rattlesnake hunting becomes a sort of contest.
People will capture, dress, cook, and eat Rattlesnake meat.
To them, it may be a very special treat.

—Thursday, November 7, 2019, midnight

REFRIGERATOR

Refrigerator, an appliance that cools and makes ice.
Having one in the house is useful and very nice.
The ones with a small freezer may suffice.
Half and half models may come with a higher price.

After 12 years, many models may need replacing.
Now, how big a bill will you be facing?
A few hundred or a few thousand dollars it seems,
Depending on your choice and your means.

You ask yourself, "Why only 12 years, do they last,
When they worked 40 plus years, or so, in the past?"
Then they were made in the "good old USA,"
While many may come from Asia today.
When and why the change? I cannot say.

Now they cost more and don't last as long.
What can be done to right this wrong?
Surely, they could make them to last longer.
The sooner they're replaced, many more are sold.
Then the price goes up, they're very bold.

Only a fixed budget, many people have to live.
With surprises like this, somethings have to give.
On credit, a new one they must buy.
With another bill to pay, it's harder to get by.

—October 25, 2019, 1:00 a.m.

RELAX AND LEARN

Not having to work, he's happily retired.
He may stay up late, even if tired.
In his "easy chair" he's the master.
There he controls the "remote."
Whether he "clicks" slower or faster,
Some time, to TV, he does devote.

With "nature programs" he's fascinated.
"History" may show where things originated.
"Travel channel" highlights unusual places.
"Biography" depicts people with their true faces.
"Animal Planet" show how animals survive,
How they eat and hunt to stay alive.

His "lounge chair" faces the TV.
What better place could it be?
Watching a game, can he relax?
If it gets too exciting, will he in fact,
Be subject to having a heart attack?

So comfy is his "lounge chair,"
That every spare moment, he's there.
Snacking on chips and dips,
Will his tummy get bigger than his hips?
This "comfy feeling" is so good,
That "by others" it's oft misunderstood.
He feels lazy, but don't much care,
Life's a bit hazy, here and everywhere.

So, you can be comfortable while learning,
Depending on what it is you are yearning.
"Sci-Fi" pleases the young and the old.
"Sitcoms" have become very bold.
Yet, they are watched by many, I'm told.

—October 26, 2001

RESIDENTS

They are in nursing homes everywhere,
Fading away in their wheelchair.
All some display, is a blank stare,
Oblivious, of the fact, that they're there.
Too early in the morn,
They're shaken to awaken.
Tho perhaps, some pain they've born,
To the showers they are taken.
In their wheelchair then they sit,
Longer than common sense should permit.
Many fall fast asleep in their chair.
Others gaze about; their mind is elsewhere.
For some, 'tis not all dismay and gloom,
For they can visit, from room to room.
Some attend festivities, even play bingo.
Some are confined to bed nowhere can they go.
Visitors, most residents really do enjoy,
No matter if it's a man, woman, girl or boy.
Relatives and friends they're glad to see,
As often, as can possibly be.
Many visitors do get depressed,
Upon seeing how loved ones look.
The state they're in, how they're dressed,
They're physically and mentally stressed.
Degeneration, such a heavy toll it took.
"The golden years" are they really fair,

For many who are residents there?
Once wonderful, fulfilling, active, lives they led,
Now debilitated, they're waiting to die in bed.

—August 15, 2000

REST AND EAT

Early in the morning, the sunrise they greet.
Other "walkers" on the trail they meet.
They chat and chat then decide to go eat,
At a Café that's just down the street.

Cold and frosty, it's about to sleet.
A cozy spot with a temperate heat,
Will warm the body with each heartbeat.
No need to worry about being discreet.

They're only too glad to rest their feet.
After walking three miles, 15, 840 feet.
For some old people, this is quite a feat.
Yet, no one wants to admit defeat.

All are ready to occupy a seat,
Before they are really, really beat.
Coffee or tea, with something sweet,
For some will be lite and neat.

For others, sliced meat on whole wheat,
A salad or spinach, cheese, tomato and a beet.
Whichever, it will be a special treat.
They'll enjoy as soon as they find a seat.

—January 21, 2008

REST, REST

That I'm often forced to rest,
Is as much a cure as being blest.
Am I being put to a test?
Or to prevent me from going on a quest?
Who knows, but me, what is best?

Exhausted, some days, I easily get,
This, with very little exertion, yet.
Things my brain suggests I do,
My body simply cannot follow through.
Am I frustrated, yes indeed, you bet.

Life is much simpler, in a sort of way,
Since I have much less to do each day.
Although 'tis not by choice, I must say.

Perhaps its "past dues" that I need to pay,
To keep the "angel of death" away,
Else I'm destined to go astray.
Therefore, I take it easy, day by day.
Oh well, what more can I say?

—September 26, 2010

RESTLESS

Awake, 'tis late at night,
I'm restless in the bed.
Tossing about, left to right,
I'm unable to rest my head.
Is it the pain in my knee,
That's causing me such misery?
Or is it my aching back,
That won't cut me any slack?
This business of getting old,
Just as I've been told and told,
Can be frustrating, leave you cold,
Even for the hearty, the bold.
I read, trying to ignore the pain,
Yet, somehow, it does remain.
Watching TV, I try to forget,
My worry, that cause me to fret.
Few months go by without some woe.
We're a big family, as families go.
I try not to worry, yet I do know,
We all worry and it does show.
Does the Lord give us,
Only as much as we can bear?
Or do we just seem to fuss and fuss,
Thinking that we get more than our share?
We must accept life, day by day,

Handling whatever comes our way.
The good, the bad, what can we say,
Life goes on, we're not made of clay.

—July 31, 1999

RETIREE

How happy is the retiree?
Did he retire willingly,
Or was it a bit forcibly?
It makes a difference, you see.

Retiring young, 'twas my choice.
Changes were coming, I'd heard the voice.
I was lucky, got a good deal,
Embraced the change with zeal.

Retirees are now seen everywhere,
Here, yonder, and over there.
In the casino, en masse,
They are the supporting class.

To the store, on discount day,
Retirees slowly make their way.
Dollars saved now really count,
However small, the amount.

Retirees frequently "babysit."
To their Grandkids, they're a hit.
Some take care of their Mom or Dad.
For some it's rewarding, for others sad.

Some Retirees get another job,
Just to mingle with others, hobnob.
The extra pay, some may need.
Seldom is it ever, just greed.

Retirees may do volunteer work.
Where needed, they don't shirk.
Their time and valuable expertise,
They give willingly, with ease.

The loneliness, it is very hard to take.
For some retirees, 'tis a heartache.
Forced to retire, they feel 'twas a mistake.
They're mad, they quake and shake.

Many retirees are unable to "get around."
They or their spouse, are down.
It's sad, when both are "down and out."
Depressed, they want to scream and shout.

RISE AND SHINE

Seldom do I rise before nine,
Yet, it may be later, that I shine.
My decisions, of late, are all mine.
Although I'm awake at an earlier hour,
I may stay in bed and skip my morning shower.

Sometimes breakfast becomes brunch,
If I get up when it's time for lunch.
This is not a problem either way,
Since I have no special time to begin my day.

A light breakfast is usually my first meal.
But even that depends on how I feel.
No meal, for me today, is no big deal.
In fact, much today, does not seem real.

Beans, a stew, or perhaps a gumbo,
I may decide to cook, nice and slow.
Breads, potatoes, pizzas and brown rice,
I eat sparingly, I watch my glucose.
Since the death of my wife, nothing is as nice.
Compared to her cooking, my meals are not close.
But, so far, my cooking seems to suffice.
Sometimes I may eat out and pay the price.

—March 2014

ROBOT

'Twas a real fancy robot,
That the lad had made,
From the many parts he'd got,
For the money, that he'd paid.

The robot obeyed his every command,
Did what the lad would demand.
He would protect the lad every day,
Prevent harm from coming his way.

The town bully and his pals,
Harassed most of the boys and gals.
Then one fateful afternoon,
The lad encountered the bully and his goon.

Held by the goon and the bully,
The lad asked the robot to react.
The robot understood fully,
Opted to set them on the "right track."

Grabbing both firmly by the neck,
He picked them up abruptly, by heck.
Startled, they knew not what to do,
But kick up their heels, bang their shoe.

Hearing the lad command to "let go,"
The robot obeyed and did so.
The bully and his pal, the goon,
Sped away, they wouldn't be back soon.

—September 5, 1999

ROCKING CHAIRS

Rocking chairs were everywhere,
As long as they both lived there.
The front porch had three or four,
One was wide, could hold two or more.

In the living room,
I picture in my mind,
Two platform types loom,
And two of the regular kind,
Used by relatives or a guest,
In a rocking chair they rested best.
A rocker was the first seat,
Offered to people they did greet.

In the kitchen was a rocker, too,
Used every day by one or two.
All family members loved to rock.
They could rock, rock, around the clock,
In a rocking chair, brother or sis,
Talking and rocking was bliss.

But lo, the rockers are there no more.
The old ones are gone, too.
Only memories remain in store.
Fond memories of those two are not few.
'Tis three years ago today,

That Daddy passed away.
Mom's been gone a little over a year.
We miss both very much, the dears.

Their old neighbors have also died.
Changes affect us all in some way.
This or that, we should have tried,
Things we didn't do or say,
Questions not asked, pertinent today?
Life must go on, it does go on.
For the "old ones" we still mourn.

—October 11, 2001

ROMANCE?

Poteet loved his honey, his sweet.
She was neat, petite and discreet.
"Bonnie is my honey," claimed Johnny.
But was Johnny too bony for Bonnie?
Sandy thought Andy was her "Dandy,"
But Andy was seldom handy for Sandy.

Desiree assumed that Rene was her finance,
But he said his love for Desiree was passe.
A bore that Lenore did adore,
Having dated him for nearly a score,
Was now looking elsewhere for more.

Elaine said her "swain" was now a pain,
After she heard he'd been dating Lorraine.
To hear about this "Prince Charming,"
Was all too unforgiving and very alarming.

Joe courted Flo after taking her to a show.
He realized that her "no" meant that she'd go.
Roe had a row with her new beau,
Her "no" was the reason that he didn't show.

Did Mary Jo and Flo really not know,
That they each had a beau named Joe?
Sal admitted that his gal was more than a pal.
Ella found her fella in the cellar with his cello.
Every note he played was soothing, very mellow.

—October 9, 2010

ROOSTER

The rooster with his cock-a-doodle-do,
Annoyed the late sleepers, the entire crew.
Night workers, one thing they knew,
He could be silenced, perhaps cooked in a stew.
The meal enjoyed, even if by only a few.
Any chicken who flew the coop,
Became a target for chicken soup.
Even if he's the "cock of the walk,"
He'll taste good with a celery stalk.
To some, a rooster is a pet.
To others, he is just a foul fowl.
He's no different to a late sleeper,
Than a pesky dog's, annoying howl.
Roosters who live on the farm,
Are less likely to suffer harm,
And they may replace a clock alarm.
They are admired as they crow and crow.
Farmers will tell you, they all know.
At daybreak, a rooster may start crowing.
He wakes the farmer who wants to start hoeing.
But in the "hustle and bustle" of the city,
Things may be more "rough and tough,"
For the poor rooster, and that's a pity.
Close neighbors say, "Enough is enough."
They may wish to sleep very late.
Anything that wakes them early, they hate.

Many are awakened, using their personal clock.
They don't "give a hoot,"
May even be tempted to shoot,
A crowing, "fancy feathered cock."

—February 7, 2001

ROSES

A very beautiful flower,
Is the lovely Rose.
A climber, it may cover a tower,
And admired by many, I suppose.

Roses grow on bushes or on a vine.
Today, many varieties you can find.
Fascinating, pretty and sweet smelling,
They're grown on estates and small dwellings.

Some roses have big, luscious blooms,
That may bring life into many rooms.
Some are planted outside a window,
Where they may be admired,
Or for scenery and greenery, in a furrow,
To enjoy beauty and fragrance, as desired.
Some miniatures do well in pots,
While Climbers decorate arbors a lot.

Old Garden Roses, some like to grow,
They're appealing, planted alone or in a row.
Different kinds, people seek to plant in their bed,
Like Cornelia, Safrano and Annie's Red.
Some Rose Growers are like in a cult,
To gather and meet, from afar they roam.
Exchanging ideas, they expect some result.
From cuttings, they swap and take home.

Long Stemmed Roses, by the dozen are sold,
Admired nationally, by the young and the old.
They send a message of high esteem,
From some, reflecting a hope and a dream.

Sometimes a simple Rosebud,
Says it all from the start.
The sender hopes it's not a "dud,"
That the recipient acknowledges his part,
About sending a "gift from the heart."

—October 6, 2000

SAD HEARTS

Departing without a fuss,
She left on the Greyhound Bus.
She did what she felt she must.
'Twas no one left that she could trust.

Her mother's heart, she did break,
Tho she'd left town for her sake.
Misunderstandings always took place.
One was forever "having to save face."

The truth, her mother had withheld,
Born was she, tho her mother had never wed.
She was really all her mother had,
But lo, the relationship had turned bad.

She decided to leave town for good,
E'en tho 'twas much that she misunderstood.
Her mind was unclear, she was in a bad mood.
She left hurriedly, without money, without food.

How she'd get by, she gave no thought.
In the past, when necessary, she'd fought and fought.
It would be tough, this future she sought,
But her body and soul could not be bought.

Independence, at long last,
No more drudgery, as in the past.
Freedom, freedom, the die was cast.
The sky was the limit, the territory vast.

—April 7, 2000

SAD LAD

The sad lad, the poor dear,
Had a tired, weary look on his face.
Just like some of his peers,
His wish is to venture into space.

With Sci-Fi, he's fascinated,
He reads all the available books on the subject.
Movies about space, to him, are never outdated,
To discuss these topics, they never do object.

Computers are neat, really okay,
Especially the games he can play all day.
Comic books, too, have great appeal,
Superheroes deal harshly, with killers who steal.

Now, on the matter concerning school,
Some subjects, he finds not too cool.
Math is difficult, he feels like a fool,
Perhaps, he doesn't use the proper tool.

History, is it necessary to know,
About events, that occurred eons ago?
English, he can understand the need,
For communication, to travel, and to read.

An education, he knows he needs to get,
If he plans to amount to anything.
The discipline needed, he's not acquired yet.
As he matures, what will the future bring?

—January 30, 2000

SAILING

He sails and sails for pleasure,
At his own convenience and leisure,
On his twenty-one-footer, his treasure.
He gets excited, grins with joy.
He's like a lad with his favorite toy.

He enjoys sailing the nearby lake.
Few risks he at times does take.
His skills he tries to hone.
He works his hands to the bone.
'Tis less fun to sail alone,
So he invites others, one by one.

Does he dream of faraway places?
Of sailing, in daring "ocean races"?
Many who now live on their boat,
Speak of adventure, of days afloat.
Uninhabited islands that some went to,
After sailing for days on the ocean blue.
Other islands with natives galore,
Some said that they loved to explore.

Prevailing winds can take you very far.
'Tis cheaper sailing than gas for a car.
Sailing demands that you be adept, awake, and alert.
One mistake and you may easily get hurt.

—November 30, 2001

SAILING AGAIN

He launched his sailboat,
For an outing, on the lake.
Just repaired, would it float?
You bet, make no mistake.

His brother, he took along.
He'd be his "first mate."
They'd sail a while, not too long,
Return soon, not too late.

But lo, a sudden squall,
Swiftly upon them came.
Hopes of "having a ball"
Were gone, but no one's to blame.

'Tis just some things you must face,
Whenever you sail the lake.
It can happen suddenly, any place.
'Tis just a chance you always take.

Always be aware and be prepared,
So sailing can be safe and fun.
In an emergency, you may be spared
From disaster, when right things are done.

—November 21, 1999

SANTA

He's the Jolly Ole Man who comes every year,
In a sleigh, boat or van, to spread lots of good cheer.
I know that this is true, once in my house I knew,
That he was close, very, very near.
The night was still, the sky was unusually clear.

The stars were bright, there he was, oh! What a sight!
A big fat belly, that shook like jelly,
A suit bright red, hair and beard of white,
Flowed from his face to his head.

He opened his sack, as I peeked thru the crack.
Lo and behold, toys, presents and candy like gold,
He began to unload and unpack.
Large eyes twinkled, they seemed to say,
"You were good, I'll reward you today."

My eyes popped wide open, my hands began to shake.
I was stunned with joy, not a sound could I make.
In a daze, I ambled to the Christmas Tree.
I gazed as he placed presents for Mom, Dad, Brother, and Me.

In a flash he was gone, this Jolly Ole Man in red.
He had spread his tidings and whisked back to his sled.
Away they went, quick to disappear,
The sleigh, Santa and all the Reindeer.
I'm glad I'm good, 'cause I'll see him again next year.

—Rudolph Ray Porche and Kayla, December 7, 1996

SARGE

Not so very long ago,
He was just a playful pup.
But you should now know,
Sarge has really grown up.

He did attend "obedience school,"
Learned very well, I'm told.
His master says, he's real cool.
He's now very strong and bold.

Being part of a "search and rescue team,"
Is his master's aim, his hope, his dream.
Locating someone, he does very well,
His master says, and everyone he does tell.

A new truck, his master just bought.
"Need it for Sarge," he thought.
A special carrier he places inside the truck bed,
So that Sarge can ride without cracking his head.

Now Sarge also has a new "yard mate."
She's a much smaller but older female.
Smart too, she's also great,
Does not bark, whine or wail.

—October 6, 1999

SCARED 2001

Many people live in fear,
The world over, overseas and over here.
They sense that "doom" is near.
Today, 'tis the fear of getting anthrax.
They fear it even with all the facts.
It's true, you may contact a spore.
It's easier today than ever before.
Be aware and be ever on the alert.
When necessary, take the pill, it doesn't hurt.

For this terrible disease,
There is also a vaccine.
Inoculation may put many at ease,
If the disease makes the scene.
The probability of getting it is low,
So go about your activities, just go.

Being scared occupies the mind,
Clutters it with a foreboding scene.
Fear after fear, the everlasting kind,
May even drive some people insane.
Danger seems to lurk everywhere,
Over land, at sea and in the air.
Taking safety precautions help us survive.
We need to "be aware" to stay alive.

When up the proverbial creek,
Without the proverbial paddle,
Many will panic and yell for help.
Their brains they allow to rattle.
'Tis when you're "down the creek,"
Without the needed paddle,
Returning home may look bleak.
You're facing an "uphill battle."

—October 16, 2001

SCHOOL IS OUT

School is finally out
And everywhere I see,
Children who yell and shout
With joy, with glee.

Three months out of school,
What will they do?
Some will swim in a community pool,
But "loners" will be more than a few.

Many will go to camp and be,
With children about their own age.
Some will be home alone, you see,
With their computer games, it's the rage.

How many will have to go,
With their families, on a vacation,
Visiting many sites, some they may know,
Or perhaps touring a foreign nation.

Teachers, too, are very glad,
For the time, that they may rest.
So much stress, it's very sad.
What they endure, 'tis quite a test!

—June 4, 1999

SCHOOL

When I was a lad in school,
Which now seems so many years ago,
My Dad didn't want to raise a fool,
So to school, we definitely had to go.

Tho his schooling had been cut short,
My dad had been put to work while young.
He made sure that he'd do his part,
About our schooling, we'd not be stung.

Twelve children, he put through high school.
Some also attended college, while on their own.
To him, quitting school would have been cruel,
For an education was needed when one was grown.

School tuition was free, even back then.
Later, transportation was provided by bus.
Books, too, were free, yet excuses were given when,
So much was done to educate all of us.

Too many people are illiterate today.
'Tis sad and inexcusable in a way.
Too many dislike school, now as then.
Many succeed, but too early, some are a "has-been."

—November 17, 1999

SCUM

He was evil, wicked and cruel,
Who didn't obey any rule.
A barbarian, he was impudent, very rude.
He was unkempt, boisterous and crude.
Tho he led a life of crime,
Somehow, he did very little time.

He quit school while still a teen.
Now with hoods he was oft seen.
A petty thief he quickly became.
Stealing was not unlike a game.
The longer he stole, the better he got.
Scruples, by now, he had not.
For compassion he had little use.
He was very familiar with abuse.

Run-ins with the law,
Occurred nearly every week.
He once got a broken jaw,
Then realized a certain flaw,
In his defense, made him weak.

As expected, soon came a time,
When he graduated to a bigger crime.
One day he killed for a purse.
Then things got really bad, much worse.
A true devil he had become.
In the eyes of everyone, he was scum.

He reached the end of his rope,
That he would live was little hope.
His life so far had been one of rejection.
Would it end with a simple injection?

—September 13, 2001

SEAFOOD FEST

"A party with a purpose" was the theme.
Many charities would benefit, was the claim.
It would help many fulfill a dream.
It would be a big success, it did so seem.
This great Seafood Fest, may be the best.

After many miles he'd ridden,
Could he go unannounced, unbidden?
He would succeed someway, somehow,
Fulfill a promise, he did avow.

To simply beat the heat,
Whilst lounging in a comfortable seat.
It would be neat, no great feat,
Yet surely, more than a treat.
But how long could he stay on his feet?

He'd grab a crab or a dish of fish,
At the festival, whatever he'd wish.
Three days of food, music and fun,
He'd get in the mood and run, run, run.
Surely there would be something for everyone.

—2008

SEAFOOD

Some of my favorite seafood is fish and shrimp.
When I dine with them, I don't skimp.
Crawfish, in place of shrimp, if you wish,
Can also be an excellent dish.
Boiled crabs, no longer do I eat in their shell.
Because of diabetes, I may not feel too well.
'Tis a bad situation, I hear tell,
So I'll give them up for a spell.
Lobsters, to me, are not worth the price.
They're bland and too much butter is not nice.
Scallops I like, but they're hard to find,
Wild caught or fake, whichever kind.
Clams, I can usually eat a few.
At Asian restaurants, I generally do.
Raw oysters, I no longer eat.
Cooked in a gumbo, they're hard to beat.
Oysters "en brochette" is a special treat.
In a bread dressing they're divine.
For thanksgiving this works out fine.
When it comes to escargot, the snail,
My in-laws brought them home by the pail.
Squids, two or three times eating them, I dared.
We caught them trawling, they were well prepared.
Everyone enjoyed them when we shared.
In a seafood soup, I ate octopus, one day.

'Twas in Mexico City during a one week stay.
The food was delicious and the octopus was okay.
Conch, a large mussel, I like in a salad best.
After eating a seafood platter, I like to take a rest.

—Monday, October 21, 2019

SEAGULL

The seagulls o'er the lake,
Were all very real, nary a fake.
They would feed then take a break.
Watch for the next net to shake.
When a shrimper pulled up his trawl,
The gulls too, made a haul.

The shrimp boats trawled fairly slow.
The gulls followed everywhere they'd go.
"Trash fish" caught in their net,
Was "manna" for the seagulls, you bet.

Some trawlers are out in the early morn.
Some drag their nets all night.
Seagulls also are flying at dawn,
But they roost and rest all night.

Seagulls are seen close to shore.
Food is plentiful and so are places to nest.
Boats stir up seafood galore.
There are many places to roost and rest.

Predators catching seagulls are few.
They are fairly safe most any day.
But coons and other varmints can do,
Much damage to the eggs seagulls lay.

Seagulls have gray or white feathers.
Their skin may be tough as leather.
They may be seen in some foul weather,
Usually perched or flying together.

—August 9, 2001

SECLUDED ISLAND

Mulling inside his head,
Was always this constant notion,
To sail away, without any dread,
Across the vast and mighty ocean,
To some secluded islands,
And watch natives make leis and garlands.

'Twas always his dream, I guess,
To sail away, seeking lots of fun.
He thought, "Fun begins with an s,"
As in sea, sand, surf and sun.

With apparently little sense,
And very little money,
But with guts and no pretense,
He did sail away with his Honey.

Tho small, his dreamy sailboat,
Was sleek, sturdy and well-built.
It sported a glossy painted coat,
And was stocked well, to the hilt.
He said he could easily keep it afloat.

The motion of the ocean,
Was something his Honey did not foresee.
For him, great was her devotion,
But seasick she got, tho not he,
On their first day sailing out to sea.

Eventually, within their sight,
Was a tropical island paradise.
There, they knew, day and night,
Their dream they would realize.

Loll on the beach.
Soak up the sun.
Hear the seabirds screech.
Sail, but not far out of reach.
Fish, swim, surf and just have fun.
Occasionally, on the beach run.

—July 31, 2001

SECURITY

How secure can we feel today,
Just living in an ordinary way?
Seems that in every burg or town,
People are harassed, mugged, or brought down.

Peacefully walking with his "honey,"
A couple are "held up" for their money.
Stopping at a traffic light,
May get you "carjacked," what a fright.

A cashier, in a drugstore,
Killed, by a robber, as she raced for the door.
In a restaurant, most of the workers slain,
Their pleas for life heard, but were in vain.

Students were slaughtered at their High School,
By their classmates, no less.
Had the killers been teased, called a fool?
Something triggered their hatred, I guess.

Some parents slay their offspring.
Some children murder their Mom and Dad.
Murder-suicide, is another thing.
These events happen, It's very sad.

Until all people learn to "value life,"
The fears will continue and be justified.
Awareness, is a must, during this strife.
A change of lifestyle may be tried.

—August 26, 1999

SEEKING RELIEF

When your back feels like it will break,
With every step you carefully take,
Causing your hips and knees to ache,
Then even your whole body begins to shake.
You may be willing to try every pill they make.
Gullible, you may try many pills, real or fake.

Seeking relief from much pain and grief,
Certain foods that you cook or bake,
Foods that you eat, may be a grave mistake.
Happiness, true happiness, is hard to fake,
Especially when, your well-being is at stake.
Living with pain, from the time that you awake,
Then all day and until you go to bed at night,
See no hope of relief in sight, try as they might.

Perhaps to manage pain, again, again and again,
It may become necessary to retrain your brain.
Close your eyes, imagine being on a plane,
In the rain, flying over a vast terrain, a plain.
Enjoying the scenery and fields lush with grain,
From lamenting, you may suddenly refrain,
When you have much, so much, to gain.

—June 22, 2006

SENIOR YEARS

He spends his days being sedentary,
Taking only an occasional stroll.
His condition makes him wary.
Inactivity is taking its toll.
No longer does he cavort,
With family or friends, any sort.
Quiet days at home is now his style.
How we change in so short a while.
Watching babies doing a fast crawl,
Is enough to make him bawl.
So soon, they'll walk and run,
Play games, have so much fun.
Teenagers, they'll suddenly be,
No longer playing, climbing a tree,
But eyeing the opposite sex with curiosity.
A movie, a trip to the mall,
Becomes and adventure and that's not all.
Oh, how quickly they seem to mature,
Yet, about so much, they're unsure.
They struggle, lead with a certain thrust,
Do what is necessary, what they must.
He knows how very fast,
Time flies, 'twill soon be past.
They too, will become like him,
Old and spent, perhaps a future less grim.

—February 17, 2000

SENIOR'S DAY

Aisles are crowded in the salvage stores.
Seniors are shopping by the scores.
It's discount day, says signs on the doors.
Besides discounted prices, seniors get 10% more,
So they flock and shop for bargains galore.

Seniors are a definite majority,
On these special discount days.
Like women in a sorority,
A kind of "bonding," exists in some ways,
Among senior shoppers, you might say.

They discuss, compare, bargains they make.
After all, a bargain, is a bargain, is a bargain.
The clothes are name brands; nothing is a fake.
Who knows, you may never see such low prices again.

'Tis not always a question of need,
Nor does it have anything to do with greed.
A bargain, most of us cannot pass up,
Be it clothes, canned goods, a pretty cup,
Or tools, supplies for school, or a dish for the pup.

It's a "treasure hunt" as they advertise.
'Tis a salvage store full of merchandise,
And foreign measurements may denote size.
Unusual items may come as a surprise.
Buying them is like claiming a prize.

Items must be examined very carefully.
Time is required to choose selectively.
Goods are salvaged from fires, floods, etc.,
Then sold for much less than they're worth.

Goods may sell as low as 80% to 90% off.
Enjoying the savings, seniors care not who does scoff.
'Tis also a way for retirees to spend the day,
Looking, comparing prices, passing the time away.
For some, savings may keep "the wolf at the door" at bay.

—September 5, 2000

SERVICE

Service, how good is it, today?
"Poor, poor," I oft hear people say.
On many service people, you can't rely.
Too many, too often, tend to lie.

In the shop, for some repair,
Over three weeks, my van was there.
Some major items they did work on.
All had to be reworked or redone.

Two more weeks it took.
More money too, I was on the hook.
Told that it was ready once more,
It wouldn't go into gear, as before.

Three more days it stayed in the shop.
Again they said, "It's ready to go."
Later that day, a window glass went "plop."
Would it come up, no, no, no.

Now all this was not their fault.
The van is old and many parts are worn.
Some things you're told, take with a grain of salt.
Other places are no better, just a different yarn.

Business, for some, may be "too good,"
Or, too many things are not understood.
On others, can we really depend,
Even if we think, he's really your friend?

Why do I continue to go, still do so?
A right and just question, to ask.
Because, the owner, I trust and know,
That he will be true and complete the task.

—November 1, 1999

SEVERE DOWNPOUR

Suddenly, around 2:00 p.m. came a severe downpour.
Moving fast, it rained harder than it had before.
Rain was welcomed after a dry spell.
Everything everywhere is cleaner, you can tell.

Overnight, the weather may change rather quickly.
People with arthritis, their joints may feel more sickly.
With sunshine and rain, happy everyone will remain.
Stormy weather, we hope to never see again.

Tornadoes cause much destruction in their path.
Is it a terrible expression of Mother Nature's wrath?
Oak trees I planted, years ago, in my yard,
Become a buffer, when the winds blow very hard.

Floods are occurring in more places these days,
Too much concrete blocking the soil's soaking ways.
New construction in nearly every town and city,
Affect the drainage in some way and that's a pity.
Few people are concerned about the "nitty-gritty."

Now that the thunderstorms have gone away,
Weather people predict that tomorrow will be a gorgeous day.
I hope 'tis true what these forecasters say.

—Monday, October 21, 2019

SHABBY HAG

At first glance, she appeared to be a Wag,
This shabbily clad, shaggy, unkempt, Hag.
"Thumbing" by the roadside, in tattered rags,
She seemed to prize her moth-eaten bag,
Like a cowboy might cherish his Nags.

She was trying to catch a ride.
But would a Trucker permit her by his side?
Was she headed very far?
Would she be allowed inside someone's car?

Passersby must wonder if they should,
Do what a "Good Samaritan" would.
Pick her up, let it be understood,
They would take her as far as they could.

Then, with her permission, I suppose,
But certainly not against her will.
Tell her they'd buy her an attire, clothes,
At a "thrift store" or the local "Goodwill."

And lo, feeling sorry, about her plight,
Having much sympathy during "her ordeal,"
With zeal and great delight,
Treat her to a very sumptuous, delicious, meal.

She may readily accept,
Just like she may easily decline.
For is she adept or inept,
'Tis hard, at this point, to read her mind.

A book, you might judge by its cover,
A Hag, no telling what you might uncover.
If, by the wayside, they sit and wait,
No telling what's to be their fate.

—September 8, 2000

SHADES

The window has a beautiful "shade."
It's one of the best ever made.
When it is lowered just right,
It keeps out unwanted sunlight.

When sunlight is wanted inside,
The shade is rolled up high.
As the sun rises from where it did hide,
The shade is lowered a bit, with a sigh.

At noon, during the "heat of the day,"
Again, the shade is lowered all the way.
Then later, as light begins to fade,
Higher and higher, goes the shade.

When darkness comes, 'tis nighttime.
There's use for a shade, and then some.
Perhaps 'tis an aid to deter crime,
By blocking the view of a "peeping tom."

By preventing a thief from seeing inside,
What to steal becomes hard for him to decide.
If the need arises, where should he hide?
So display your shades with pride.
They look good from either side.

—August 18, 2001

SHOOTINGS

Every day, it seems, we hear,
That someone has been shot.
Occurring everywhere, far and near,
Be it an adult, a teen or a tot.
Children fear to attend school,
During their normal, regular season.
Who knows when some crazy fool,
Will open fire, for no reason.
The awful threat of violence,
Is now felt throughout this nation.
Classrooms, no longer a place of innocence,
Everyone should prepare for this situation.
Day care centers have been hit,
Wounding children in their care.
Does it matter, where you go or sit?
Will you really be safe, anywhere?
Public buildings, are they secure,
From any lunatics, I'm not too sure?
Disgruntled employees, have shot their boss,
Their fellow workers, needlessly, what a loss.
Parents, too, have shot their offspring.
Some have killed themselves, after.
What causes them to do such a thing,
Home life that lacks much fun and laughter?
Shootings occur, they make no sense.
The shooters, how are they motivated?
Is it racial, hatred, or just a pretense,
Of being different, which need to be investigated?

—August 10, 1999

SHRIMP

Invited to go catch shrimp,
With a pal, in his "flatboat."
We brought essentials, he doesn't skimp,
Including rain gear, with a good raincoat.

The first "pass" with the trawl,
We made a very good haul.
We struggled to get the trawl on the boat.
In fact, 'twas difficult to stay afloat.

Picking shrimp, out the catch, from the rest,
Catching crabs as they scoot about,
Can be exciting enough to shout,
Depending on the catch, after the test.

Peeling shrimp can be a chore,
Especially, one hundred pounds or more.
Your fingers stay wet and they get sore.
They get slimy, down to the core.

After being pricked a few times,
Your hands hurt, you begin to wonder if,
The felons, who have committed crimes,
Suffer as much, your hands are stiff.

You try "alum" so the shrimp won't slip.
You desperately try to get a better grip.
Gloves don't work, least won't for me.
They're too cumbersome, you see.

But, when you later relax and dine,
Enjoying shrimp dishes that are so divine,
Even if you have tea instead of wine,
You think, "It was all worth it," and I'm fine.

—October 27, 1999

SIMPLE LIFE

The young teen watched a "screen scene,"
Featuring a lovely "movie siren,"
Who appeared very calm and serene,
As a happy and revered "island queen."

Living on a pacific island paradise,
Where the local bounty seemed to suffice.
Bananas, coconut, taro, lobsters, oysters and fish,
Provide sun tanned natives with food, a daily dish.
They frolic and play or loaf, anytime they wish.

Very happy and crime free, they all seem to be,
As they live joyously, openly with glee.
A very simple lifestyle they do enjoy.
Simple tools and means they employ.

Waterfalls by a pristine crystal lake,
Provide fresh water, all they can take.
"What a life, what a scene," thought the teen,
To live on such an island with a lovely queen!

Perhaps, someday his wish may come true.
He will seriously consider what he needs to do.
To live such a life could be great.
Just how long of a simple life could he take?

—April 2011

SLEEP TIME

Sleepyhead, 'tis time for bed.
'Tis late, yet I hate, even dread,
To go to bed early, and instead,
Find a need to read, relax my head.

There's nothing great on TV.
"Paid programs" fill the screen.
Some late shows are unfit to be seen.
Who wants to see a Nurse giving an IV?

There I go again, a great big yawn.
I must go to bed before dawn.
Surely, I will sleep very late.
Tomorrow, this is my fate.

Now I'm really getting sleepy.
'Tis very hard to stay awake.
'Tis nothing eerie or creepy.
'Tis 3 a.m. for goodness sake.

I'm getting sleepier, reading this book.
I really should go to bed.
My wife is giving me another "dirty look."
"Time for bed," she says, nodding her head.

On the sofa, she too does nap,
While she "does an afghan," crochet.
A "catnap" feels good, old chap.
Did I dream, or this hear her say?

—September 8, 1999

SLEEPING LATE

In his comfortable bed he lay.
'Twas long past, the break of day.
All night long he'd tossed and turned,
His back and leg ached, his eyes burned.

Now at ease in his bed,
Getting up and about, he did dread.
Perhaps he'd remain in bed instead,
Even go back to sleep, rest his head.

"Why get up?" he thought and thought.
A way to ease his ache and pain, he'd sought.
Now he felt good, but it was late morn.
A nap was justified, for the pain he'd born.

He didn't care how it did look.
Retired, he no longer "went by the book."
No chore was too important to delay.
He could do them some other day.

Sleep he did, two hours more,
Though he surely did snore and snore.
He dreamed about making a job offshore,
Like he'd done, many, many, times before.

—November 4, 1999

SLEEPLESS NIGHTS

When some night,
People can't go to sleep,
After trying, with all their might,
Counting sheep after sheep,
They shut their eyes very tight,
Then sigh, or cry and weep.

Insomnia, to many, is like a curse.
They get fidgety, nervous or worse.
Many seek help from a doctor or nurse.
Affected by the tensions of the day,
They're just unable to sleep, many say.

Resorting to a "sleeping pill,"
They can't go to sleep at will.
Many are relaxed, it soothes their ills.
They sleep while their "sheep" run over the hills.

When lucky, their slumber is deep.
All night, they enjoy a restful sleep.
They wake up with a good attitude.
Peaceful sleep has improved their mood.
Then they feel too good, to be rude.

—August 28, 2000

SLIPPERS

Nice slippers made from good leather,
Are comfortable and light as a feather.
I don't wear them outside in bad weather.

Slippers with a good lining of fur,
In cold weather are the ones I prefer.
The outside is suede and they are handmade.
Some slippers are old made of a fancy cloth.
They may have been eaten a bit by a moth.

Slippers made with an "open back,"
Won't stay on my feet, stability they lack.
Socks, I don't usually wear with slippers,
But I like soles on slippers with grippers.

Some slippers with "shoelaces" become untied.
If I'm not careful, I'll trip and fall.
That slippers are comfortable is not denied,
But they're not proper attire at a "ball."

In the house, I may wear them all day.
Seldom do I go anywhere, so it's okay.
Yes, when it comes to slippers,
I keep more than one kind.
That's so that I'm not caught in a bind.

—May 28, 2020

SLOTS

It's a thrill to hit,
On slot machines, a few jackpots.
And from where I sit,
Some do, playing the slots.

Some people play, play and play,
Seemingly, throwing their money away.
"I've been playing here all day,"
Is what I hear some people say.

Occasionally, you hear a yell,
Followed by the ringing of a bell.
Thinking that luck, they do not lack,
Some say, "Now I've gotten my money back."

Many players, in casinos, seem luckier than others.
No skill is required, you know.
They flock in, Fathers, Mothers, Sisters, Brothers,
To play, to eat or perhaps, to watch a show.

Winning makes most anybody very elated.
Losing, on the other hand, makes some feel degraded.
Win or lose, to quite a few, is fun.
For those addicted, great harm is done.

The slots, is it just pure luck,
When you hit, for more than a buck?
But lo, hear what I say,
You may lose it all, if you continue to play.

—August 10, 1999

SMILE

Smile and your eyes may twinkle.
Frown and you may create a wrinkle.
Laugh just a few times a week.
'Tis good exercise for your cheek.

Life, with its ups and downs,
Is reasoning enough for many frowns.
But frowns don't help a bit,
Better to endure woes with humor or wit.

Perhaps a great and wonderful way,
Is to begin, with optimism, each and every day.
Without worry, but with concern,
When facing obstacles at each turn.

In life, we may have many woes.
"That's how the ball bounces," some say.
On and on, it goes and goes.
We must constantly seek a better way.

Going thru life with a smile,
May ease some strife once in a while.
But if we always wear a frown,
Self-pity, grief and pain will wear us down.

Attitudes, many need to change their ways.
They should do so with few delays.
Grief and sorrow, we may get more than our share,
But smiles and humor make them easier to bear.

—May 6, 2000

SNIFFLES

Everyone, I'm sure knows,
The aggravations caused by a leaky nose.
Drip, drip, drip, continuously it goes,
Until its bound to get raw, I suppose.

Is it an allergy or is it a cold?
"It's hard to say," I'm told.
"It's my penalty for living here,
But it'll go away, so have no fear."

Now I'm like the rest of them,
Coughing, having a lot of phlegm.
So much, I just don't understand.
Is it all getting out of hand?

Earlier I had Flu shot,
So the Flu is not what I've got.
The nasal drip gets much worse at night.
Soon as I hit the bed, 'tis a fight.

It tears me up to see my darling tot,
Constantly blowing her nose full of snot.
When 'tis an awful runny nose she's got,
Her misery just breaks my heart.
'Tis on and off, stop and start.

—December 17, 2000

SNOOZE

My, oh my, it's afternoon, already three.
The time, how it does flee?
It does go too fast for me,
But lo, little can I do, you see.

For just a little bit, I'll rest my eyes,
Maybe even snooze, a while.
What the heck, 'tis no surprise,
I can dose off, with a smile.

Gee, I must have fallen asleep.
My slumber must have been deep,
But, it's no cause to weep.
I have lots of time today,
To nap, or simply idle away.

Oh, Oh, I was suddenly awakened,
By my loud, resounding snore,
As I've done many times before.
Was the room really shaken?
Did the noise carry, outside the door?

Some people take a snooze every day,
On a regular basis, they say.
'Tis a habit that they enjoy a lot,
So why not, lots of time, they've got.

—September 23, 1999

SNORER

How high a number, counting sheep,
Must we go to, when trying to sleep?
Is it ten or more, even a score,
Before our slumber is finally deep?

Very loud we're apt to snore,
Disturbing our mates that we adore.
Some names called snorers, we bleep.
Ofttimes they're worse than "creep."
Few may whistle while asleep,
Causing troubles to pile up "like a heap."

"Sleep Apnea" comes to mind.
'Tis the "life-threatening kind."
A special "air pump" we find,
May help getting you out of this bind.
It's cumbersome, unpleasant to wear,
But aids by pumping much needed air.

Snoring, when we consider the source,
Can it really be a cause for a divorce?
To the snorer, 'tis an uncontrollable force,
That may also leave him or her a bit hoarse.

Separate beds, is one solution.
For some, 'tis the wrong conclusion.
Tension may remain with much confusion,
But should not be enough for a dissolution.

—August 6, 2007

SNOWMAN

Snowmen, we seldom do see,
In the southern part of the country.
Because snow seldom does fall,
The weather is not right, not right at all.

It does get cold enough to freeze,
Often, cold and chilly, especially with a breeze.
With the humidity high and a damp cold,
We chill to the bone, both young and old.

If snow does fall, it's exciting for all.
Schools may be closed all day.
At home, children will play and play.
In the snow, it's an event,
That so seldom comes our way.

Roads may close, we're not prepared for snow.
No salt is available and no snow plows to go.
Most people stay off the street.
Hazards, they are not anxious to meet.

A snowman is seen here and there.
They don't last very long anywhere.
Seldom does snow last a full day.
We're too far south, is about all I can say.

—November 9, 1999

SO IT GOES

Living in freedom, with much latitude,
Our wants, needs and desires, we do include.
Our dislikes, when possible, we exclude.
Never do we go naked, completely nude,
Even though no one is considered a prude.
Thankfully, we express our gratitude.

A life once full of grit and fortitude,
Now is lacking in fitness and aptitude.
Some days, our feelings and general attitude,
Is approached in a state of ineptitude,
Caused by a worn-out state of decrepitude.
Sweat, these days, we very seldom exude,
Spending most of our time in solitude.

We dread what we see that is crude and rude,
Tho some sights we can't seem to evade or elude.
Serene scenes, less oft seen, except at high altitude.
Brutality and killings seem condoned by a multitude.
If these things we could foresee and preclude,
Without violating laws or in any way intrude,
The Golden Years, we would be ready to conclude.
Don't you agree, Dude?

—April 30, 2008

SOFA

The sofa near the door in the den,
Was well used, well used.
So many slept on it, again and again,
That the material was worn thin.
Some might think it was abused.

It was comfortable and very long,
Could easily accommodate four,
Or in a pinch, perhaps one more.
Yet, some, if they felt weak or strong,
As soon as they walked thru the door,
Stretched out on it, right or wrong.
Took all of the room as they'd done before.

Oblivious that others may care,
If they napped on the sofa, unaware,
That others would like to sit there,
When there was no empty chair.

The old sofa saw much of this.
For many, to stretch out is bliss.
Manners have gone out the door.
Etiquette, we seldom see anymore.
Now it's first come gets best place,
Regardless of age, capability or race.
Few realize it's a disgrace.

—September 11, 2001

SOME CAN'T HELP IT

People can be rude,
Especially, when they're in a bad mood.
The cold shoulder of ice
They give others, is not very nice.

How does one remain sane,
When it's obvious, very plain,
That the treatment they ofttimes get
Is mean, unjust, and they can never forget?

Perhaps if one cracks a smile,
It would ease the tension, at least for a while.
It may even cause them to smile, too,
Make them forget to act like a shrew.

Maybe a gentle "hello"
Might make a mean one, "mellow."
Goodness might "rub off" or, at least,
Change someone's attitude that is like a beast.

Kind words and a gentle touch,
Usually is not asking very much.
Yet, for some, it's hard to give.
'Tis how they grew up and how they live.

—April 9, 2000

SOME SENIOR YEARS

Who among us doesn't yearn,
For some better times to return?
Who doesn't, sometime, lie awake,
Wondering why we have a certain ache?

Who doesn't awake in the morn,
As though having been in a fight,
All tired, aching, feeling worn and forlorn,
From tossing and turning all night?

Who after a few steps they take,
Feel pain in the hips, and knees?
Then it starts, a terrible ache.
The feet swell, as though stung by bees.

Suddenly, there's an urgent need to rest.
Breathing becomes difficult, at best.
Panic sets in, is it the final test,
Severe pain is felt inside the chest?

Lo and behold, 'twas only gas.
Shortly, the chest pain did pass.
But the pain in the joints,
Still persists, at all points.

Some say, "You're as young as you feel.
Getting old is really no big deal."
I look about and the suffering I see,
Makes me ask, "What's ahead for me?"

—May 18, 2000

SOUTHERN BEAUTY

She was southern born and southern bred.
Her striking beauty, turned his head.
After stuffing his stomach, he went to bed.
An intelligent, talented young lady,
She wouldn't dream of doing anything shady.

In her own words, by her own admission,
Certain things she wouldn't do under any condition.
Though it may pay a very high commission,
Without her approval, without her permission,
That was her final answer, her decision.

She is delighted to hear a true love story,
As long as it's funny and not gory nor amatory.
Few men does she really feel she can trust,
Especially ones who continually stare at her bust.
Are their hearts just filled with lust?

But then, women may "invest in their breast,"
For medical reasons and to look their best.
For her, total independence is a must.
In the business world, she is ready to compete.

Socially, she is prudent and discreet,
Pleasant and amiable with all people she does meet.
Congenial, upbeat, very nice and very sweet.
On "Facebook" she deserves a "Special Tweet."

—April 1, 2008

SOUTHERN BELLE

Picture, picture, in the frame,
Who is that lovely dame?
Is she someone's "old flame"?
Does anyone know her name?

What's the history of her past?
Who knew her best, spoke to her last?
Perhaps in a movie she was cast.
Perhaps, she was "fancy free and fast."

Was she a loving, dutiful wife?
Did she lead a life full of strife?
She may have been a doting mother,
Who loved her children like no other.

It's sad when nothing is written,
About families that are now all gone.
Were any, by the "love bug" bitten?
Were any, early in live, left all alone?

The case of the beautiful lady,
Whose picture hangs on the wall,
Was she famous, renowned or shady?
A dancer or singer, was she short or tall?

We may wonder and never really know.
Was she in a carnival or a traveling show?
But, from her picture we can tell,
She was beautiful, perhaps a Southern Belle.

—December 19, 2001

SPEEDSTERS

The speed limit they deliberately exceed,
Through a "red light" they oft proceed.
We must assume that they can read,
So, it's the law that they don't obey.
What more can anyone say?

If you drive the "speed limit" or under,
They come behind you like "rolling thunder."
The eighteen-wheeler, the fearsome semi,
Can and often do, tailgate then whiz by.

Everyone, it does seem, today,
Drive as though they're really late.
"Hurry, hurry, get out of my way,"
Me think, they really do say,
Especially when traveling the Interstate.

In cities, driving can be a bit scary,
For oldsters, tho they be alert and wary.
Drivers that are belligerent and rude,
Try to avoid, they're in a bad mood?
When riled they exhibit violent behavior.
Ignoring them may be your savior.

Traffic lights, too many people do ignore.
"Caution lights" to them mean naught.
To "run a light" many seem to adore.
They have no fear of ever being caught.

—November 27, 2001

SPELLBINDERS

Without a license they preach,
Tho not all truth, do they teach.
It's amazing, the audience they reach,
As far away as a lonely beach.

Articulate, spellbinders can easily persuade,
The gullible, the miserable, with promises made.
Some questions they can easily evade.
Some promises they may keep, others simply fade.

A glib tongue, they surely do possess,
Telling followers, "You, I can bless."
They say, "I speak with the Lord,"
Knowing that the innocent, "eat every word."

They brainwash, prey on people's innocence,
Using any means and any pretense.
Soon, every word followers do believe,
So the "mind benders" continue to deceive.

Some "innocent" looking for relief,
May wind up with much more grief.
Confused, strong becomes their "belief."
Their life is shattered, once truth is revealed.
They're more confused, feel cheated and deceived.

—September 6, 1999

SPENDER

For one so young and tender,
She was also a great spender.
Competing in sales, with the opposite gender,
She was elated, wherever they would send her.

The urge to splurge, you see,
Perhaps is really gender free.
Both love to "flash the cash,"
To impress, others with their stash.

Big tippers, they want servers to know.
They expect lots of attention before they go.
They're saying, "I am really somebody.
I expect service that is not shoddy."

Impression, to them, means a lot.
They're ready to spend all they've got.
Smiles and gestures they freely give.
In the spotlight, they love to live.

They travel with the "in-crowd,"
Voice their opinions out loud.
They spend as tho they're on a quest.
A perfect host, they are to their guest.

—September 24, 1999

SPRING HAS SPRUNG

It's early in the morn and from the window I gaze,
At something I see in the very misty haze.
Who is meandering around at the crack of dawn?
Why, it's a doe and her lovely newborn fawn.

Now I'm certain that spring has really sprung,
When animals begin having their young.
The many tunes that birds have sung.
Are they announcing that new life has begun?

Beautiful sunny days are probably ahead.
Is it time to plant in a prepared bed?
Be aware that if a late frost does appear,
All tender plants may be lost. Oh dear.

It's a gamble that many may take.
They are anxious and fresh produce is at stake.
Yes, 'tis true, it does seem that spring has sprung.
Anticipation of better days is not too far-flung.

But lo, the grass too, is growing very fast.
Mowing is necessary until summer is past.
Then we'll worry about a cold arctic blast.
How cold will it be and how long will it last?

—April 7, 2016

SPRINGTIME IS BEST

All along the wide, green avenue,
Beautiful flowering pear trees grew.
It's a lovely sight, when they're in bloom,
Tends to make one forget about doom and gloom.

I can hardly wait for spring to arrive,
When trees and flowers bloom, are really alive.
Not only do things come alive, they seem to thrive.
People are happy that the winter they did survive.
Sunshine and flowers makes many seem to revive.

After the harsh times of winter are in the past,
People look forward for good times that last.
Lately, after a beautiful and very pleasant spring,
Very hot weather, summertime surely did bring.

Records for hot weather were broken day after day,
Into the fall, seems some hot weather did stay.
What will it take for it to go away?
But then, freezing weather will soon come along,
Staying indoors quite a while won't seem wrong.
Springtime, I do prefer best,
But, I can tolerate the rest.

—Saturday, October 18, 2019, midnight

STORM

The fast-moving, raging storm,
Scared everyone but did little harm.
So suddenly it came and went,
Leaving tree branches scattered and bent.

Treetops broke in many cases.
Had a tornado dipped in those places?
The rain was heavy for a while,
Causing debris to float in a pile.

The ditches are overflowing,
But the sun is now glowing.
Saturated is the ground, water is everywhere.
There's a mess, but no need for despair.

Without loss of limb or life,
Clean up seems to be little strife.
We count our blessings, feel spared.
It's a feeling we all shared,
For the worse, some were prepared.

Storms occur, 'tis nothing new.
Most people here know what to do.
People help each other, lend a helping hand,
Whenever disaster strikes, in our Southland.

—December 14, 2000

STRANGE WEATHER

Today is Sunday November 1st, 2019,
The second day of cold weather we've seen.
September and October, how fast they went.
It was a very hot summer, that we spent.

From summer to winter, we've already gone.
What happened to autumn? No fall at all.
I find this weather strange and I'm not alone.
The leaves on trees will soon be falling.
Pretty soon, Jack Frost will come calling.

I just hope this winter is not too cold.
For severe weather, I'm just too darn old.
Some problem is certain to come up and unfold.
Unlike my younger days, I'm not as bold.
Now I pay close attention to what I am told.

Usually I heed what weather people have to say,
Then prepare and hope to survive another day.
If I'm told to evacuate, I do go somewhere out the way.
And as long as necessary, there I plan to stay.

—Sunday, November 1, 2019, noon

STRANGE...PERHAPS

During their misery and grief,
Some find solace and relief,
In their faith and their belief.
Happy thoughts, of good times past,
Feel good, but too short they last.

Incidents long ago forgotten,
Even some considered "verboten,"
They may suddenly, vividly recall,
Events that happened, big and small.
They describe explicitly, in detail.
Yet, remembering what happened yesterday,
Eludes them, they just cannot say.
What part of the brain did fail?

During their youth, scheme after scheme,
So realistic they, at times, did seem.
Did they really happen or was it a dream?
Will their memory switch off like a light beam?

—December 18, 2008

STRANGER

As she listened to the tick, tock, tick, tock,
Of her big Grandfather clock,
She heard, was startled, by a knock, knock.
Looking thru the "peephole" almost in shock,
There in a bedraggled smock frock,
Appeared a seemingly worn-out jock,
Near her doorstep, sitting on a rock.
Had he come from a nearby dock?
Was he hurt, perhaps in shock?
Did he live in the next block?
Was he destitute and had everything in hock?
Had he strayed from his flock?
Had he just crawled out from beneath a rock?
From nowhere he did appear,
Suddenly, without any luggage or gear.
Instinctively, she had a sense of fear,
For herself and others she held dear.
A quick decision she needed to make,
Allow him inside or leave him out.
For her family and her sake,
Allow him in was a chance she couldn't take.
Holiday Spirit, no longer has she got?
After a slight hesitation, a little delay,
She inquired about his needs this day.
Though very little he did say,

She asked him to "be on his way."
'Tis sad, really a shame,
But then, whom can we blame?
People want to help, render aid,
But are skittish or are really afraid.

—December 20, 2000

STRAY DOG

Was he lost, perhaps a stray,
The young dog, that came by yesterday?
Hungry, he was looking for a meal.
My cat's food, he did steal.

Cowering, he did approach me.
Begging, he wanted to see,
An act of kindness or such.
He was not asking for much.

With his tail between his legs,
He crouches, begs and begs and begs.
Looking, he searches, seeks to find,
Someone, that to him, will be kind.

Later in the day, I noticed he was gone.
He had just "up and left."
Had he lucked up, found a bone,
Or tired of where, last night, he'd slept?

Such poor creatures must
Be under duress and much stress.
It seems so unfair, so unjust,
To see an animal in such distress.

—February 10, 1999

STRESSED TEACHER

The teacher completely lost his cool,
One fateful day at the High School,
When his class treated him like a fool.
The pupils he'd tried and tried to teach,
He just simply could not reach.
He'd taken way too much abuse,
So finally he decided 'twas no use.
The principal said he'd disobeyed the rule,
Even accused him of being a bit cruel.
Yet, no one did he ever hurt.
He never even touched anyone's shirt.
He was known to be honest and fair.
Some students said he was a square.
For his teaching methods they never cared.
They never studied and came unprepared.
Though no one did he ever neglect,
From no one did he gain any respect.
His pupils were a really bad bunch.
Some didn't report in 'til after lunch.
Some of their parents were a sorry lot.
Respect at home, nobody ever got.
Some students never participated in class,
But were crude, rude, and full of sass.
They failed, he would not allow them to pass.
Not eligible to play on the football team,
Some students and faculty members did scream.
Dedicated, the teacher tried and tried,
To teach the class the meaning of "pride,"

By not allowing "slackers" to slide,
Nor athletes with failing grades to "ride."
The "system" he really tried to buck.
They were wrong and to his guns he stuck.
For that he ran completely out of luck.
Except for the few friends he had,
Teachers and students thought he was bad.
Because he didn't see it "their way,"
No longer was he allowed to stay.
"His services were no longer needed.
His teachings were no longer heeded."
It was what the "board" had to say,
When he went to collect his severance pay.

—November 6, 2001

STRIVE TO STAY ALIVE

Days seem so short, I get little done,
But then, I don't get up with the rising sun.
I linger in the bed, in the early morn.
Uncovered is my head, but my body is warm.

Comfortable am I, I do enjoy the rest.
I may sigh and shut an eye, doze until I plan to rise.
Toss and turn, dream and yearn, Until I get dressed.
Unless the phone rings and I get a surprise.

By the time I get going, it's near midday,
All the while I'm knowing, I'm doing it my way.
Alone and retired, am I not now at ease?
Since my wife died, I do or don't do as I please.

But sad to say, not much can I do.
Day after day after day, very little is new.
Doing it my way, the routine is much the same.
Life, at times, does seem to be a game.

I take a pill for every ill, hoping to be pain free.
Yet, inflammation persists still in my joints, back and knee.
This game of life, between Mother Nature and me,
Is full of strife, that continues, you see.
Give up, I cannot do, else the game ends.
Like a deep-sea diver, come up slow, or "get the bends."

—June 7, 2015

SUCCESS

She seemed transfixed, mesmerized,
As if she may have been hypnotized,
As she gazed into the stream.
Was she just having a dream?
Perhaps she was reflecting, with pride,
About her undeniable, deserved success.
Had she driven to this peaceful countryside,
After working under much duress and stress?
Was she now contemplating suicide?
He noticed her beautiful, wavy, black hair,
Shining, all aglow, in the morning air.
He admired her round, rosy cheek,
Her entire profile, reflecting in the creek.
Nearby, near the edge of the creek,
Was parked, her expensive Rolls Royce.
It was, as always, shiny and sleek.
She had, it seemed, a lot to rejoice.
She had climbed the corporate ladder,
Achieving the goals she'd set for success.
Ability, honesty and fairness, did matter,
She'd learned during her rapid progress.
Challenges she'd met head on.
Problems she'd solved before too far gone.
She exhibited much strength and foresight,
As she often worked all or part of the night.
Now something didn't seem right.

SUN OR RAIN

Sunshine, then rain, sunshine, then rain,
Over and over, again and again,
Four times today it's come about.
Every day, 'tis like a sad refrain.
From cursing, I will abstain,
But, I may just let out a shout,
Proclaiming the rain, better than the drought.

How long before I'm able to cut grass?
How long must I sit on my…rear?
Cooler weather's approaching; it's near.
Soon I'll put the mower in gear,
Mow all the grass, make a last pass,
Then with cheer, grin from ear to ear,
As I stow the gear for the rest of the year.

In the fall, there is little to do,
Rake leaves, pine straw, trim trees,
And chop a stump or two.
Enjoy the view and the cool breeze.

In the winter we do much less.
We keep the fireplace burning when cold.
A dreary time of year, for some, I guess,
Especially, for the feeble and the very old.
Yet, mild winters can be a delight.
For sportsmen, hunting and fishing is right.

My favorite time is early spring,
When the weather is cool, balmy and mild.
New life, new growth, spring does bring.
Scenery becomes beautiful in the wild.

Occasionally gentle spring showers,
Awaken dormant wildflowers.
New shoots sprout from plants that earlier dies.
Their blooms attract birds, bees and butterflies.

—September 14, 2000

SWEET TOOTH

Yes, I have a sweet tooth,
No matter how loath I am to admit it.
Sadly, 'tis the awful truth.
This craving, how can I get rid of it?

Cookies, I have a passion for.
Very few are there that I abhor?
Cakes, I enjoy every now and then,
On certain occasions, not too often.

Candy, I can hardly deny.
That I like, no matter how hard I try.
Without it, it seems I can't get by.
I even sneak some, on the sly.
Why then, do I have this crave,
For candy, am I not brave?
Am I like a small child,
When deprived of candy, go wild?

Jellies, preserves and jams,
On toast or biscuits I love to eat.
Yet candied sweet potatoes, yams,
To me, is less than a treat.

Fresh fruits and vegetables are best,
If sweets we desire to ingest.
Peach, pears, apples and sugar beet,
Are many of the things I already eat.

The sugar in my coffee is an imitation.
The drinks I drink are sugar-free.
Sugar-free, fat-free, my ice cream is apt to be.
Many live like this, an entire generation.

—July 15, 2001

TALK SHOWS

People on TV Talk Shows today,
Get very rough, many act wild.
The things they do and say,
May be crude, vulgar or mild.
People take out and show,
Their anger and frustration,
On those who decided to go,
On the show, because they know,
Much pain, and desolation.
Arguments may readily ignite
A hot temper, so they fight,
With their fists or a chair.
Often they pull each other's hair.
A fight may oft erupt,
Between friends, and a lover.
Accusing each other of being corrupt,
May also be a daughter or mother.
People tell all, on TV.
They expose more than need be.
Many complain more than they should,
Would harm each other, if they could.
Mothers come on the show,
Who say they don't really know,
Who is their child's dad.
Now isn't that really sad?
The antics of many,
Is it only done for "shock"?
Like those who expose their "fanny,"

519

Now, isn't that a crock?
Some "Hosts" seem to lose control.
Their "Guests" won't stop when told.
The cruder and nastier, people appear,
The greater the raves, and the cheer.
The shouts begin from the crowd.
The tempo gets high and very loud.
Are the many people we see,
As "trashy" as they seem to be?
IT's sad, yet, it does appear so,
But why, on TV, do they go?
We, the public, do have much to say.
We could stop watching "trash" today.
Quickly, the Networks would react.
They'd cut them off, now that's a fact.

—March 10, 1999

TAXES

When I retired in 1982,
A $800 million tax package, a bleeder,
With the "suave Edwards" the leader,
Was proposed and sailed on through.

Tax, tax, tax,
When is it ever fair?
When the "watchdogs" are too lax,
Do we pay more than our share?

Cigarettes, beer, liquor and wine,
Are heavily, heavily taxed every time.
Legislators say, "Yea, OK, that's all fine."
'Tis a "sin tax" they chime.

Did Monsieur Faucheux really say,
"Laissez les bon temps rouler"?
Mes, je suis bien fache,
Enfin, presque comme le chien enrage.

Though I neither smoke nor drink,
I know how some legislators think,
And in my opinion, it does stink.
"Sin taxes will fly, they do well.
Are not the product users, going to hell?"

Churches pay no tax at all.
Even the "nonreligious" property they own.
Lawmakers stay clear of this, no matter who does moan,
Yet, they constantly soak "the sinner," what gall.

State Excise Tax Increases
On Tobacco and Alcoholic Beverages.
This issue never, ever ceases.
Please vote, no, use your leverage.

—May 8, 2000

TAYLOR DANIELLE JONES

'Twas just a year ago,
That at the hospital you did show.
The event was more than "so-so."
Your elders will have you know.

To no one's big surprise,
You have beautiful dark eyes.
Long eyelashes, like a beauty queen,
The most precious baby they'd ever seen.

With your lovely round face,
A head with dark hair,
You're a joy to embrace,
To hug, and to kiss, just because you're there.

A few curls you have, I hear.
Two teeth have emerged from your lower jaw.
They say, "She looks like her Dad, the dear,
Perhaps, a bit also, like her Grandpaw."

Your future will surely be bright.
You may find that you enjoy the limelight.
Already, I hear, you do love to pose.
That's a beginning, don't you suppose?

Tho I haven't met you, yet,
You are a great charmer, I bet.
Much joy you bring to the family, every day.
Much love is there, I must say.

Happy birthday, you dear, sweet child.
Don't let Granny or Grams, spoil you at all.
Spirited children, to some, may seem wild,
When all the while, they're just "having a ball."

Happy, happy, birthday.
We love you. Aunt Phyllis and Uncle Ray.
(Great-great, that is.)

—August 15, 2000

TELEPHONE

When my cordless phones go dead,
I usually buy a brand-new set.
I've never replaced the batteries yet.
I may save money if I just use my head,
And buy new batteries, when needed, instead.
I keep one phone in the office, one in the den,
Another one in my bedroom, near my bed.
Cordless phones are the only phones that I've got.
A cell phone may be useful when I get out.
When the cable goes dead, so does my phone.
Then, without power, cable, and phone, I'm really alone.
Most families today only have cell phones.
Phone booths and pay phones, too, are gone.
Many people talk less, but text and text and text.
Technology is amazing, what's coming next?
Robots may take over many a chore.
Leisure time, people will have much more.
For better or worse, it's the coming thing.
No telling what the future will bring.

—Monday, October 21, 2019

TESH AND BESH

What if the pianist, John Tesh,
Asked the chef, John Besh,
To cook a dinner that's organic and fresh,
With ingredients that are grown by Mr. Lec Leche.
Dessert may be "creme avec peche."

I'm sure the meal would be a hit.
On the veranda, John Tesh and his wife may sit,
And enjoy the moon in a sky well lit.

The wife may wear a veil of light mesh,
If they decide to stroll along the "Teche,"
The lovely, wide, southern bayou.
In case mosquitoes want to dine, too,
They can easily spoil the evening for two.
The idea sounds great to me, how about you?

Dinner and a long moonlight walk,
May be better than sitting to talk and talk.
Unless one is "muleheaded" and does balk.
Just as bad and sad, is a lad who will always squawk,
Or give everyone the "evil eye" like a hawk.

—January 14, 2017

THAD, THE MUSICAL LAD

On a very remote farm, early one morn, he was born,
Then was given the Christian name, Thad Horne.
While in diapers, he played with a little toy horn.
As a young lad, Thad was given a used French Horn.

He practiced playing this horn every morn,
Even after many sheep, at times, he had shorn.
When older, he plowed the field and planted corn.
But he got tired of looking at the rear end of the horse, a roan.

Many days, after working until he was tired and worn,
No matter, it didn't help to groan and moan.
Resting peacefully on a bale of hay in the barn,
He attempted to play the trombone and saxophone.

Many hours he did spend, while spent, and all alone.
An only, homely lad, he stayed home, was seldom gone,
Worked and toiled until he was just skin and bone.
Tho the work on the farm, caused him no physical harm,
His life was not one, you might say, "full of charm."

From the farm, Thad, could hardly wait to be gone.
He was shown and knew contempt and felt the scorn.
His patience and tenacity eventually did pay off.
Now at him, no one dares to laugh, sneer or scoff.

An accomplished musician, he at last became.
Playing several instruments bought him much fame.
Now known as "Thad, the Musical Lad," he's proud and glad.
He's having the best time of his life, that he ever had.

—Tuesday, November 12, 2019, midnight

THANK YOU,
THANK YOU

To all "first responders and caretakers" today,
I have much praise for all of you, I dare say.
For your aptitude, hard work and fortitude,
I say, "Thank you, you have my gratitude.
I also admire your tenacity and attitude."

You perform your duties well, wearing a mask.
Long hours y'all work, whatever the task.
That's as much as anybody can ask.
Your jobs re risky, but with good PPE,
You won't get COVID-19, hopefully.

CORONAVIRUS is a terrible, terrible foe,
It's pandemic, causing much havoc and woe.
There's so much about it that we don't know.
Many in the medical field, from what I've seen,
Are racking their brain to come up with a vaccine.

In the meantime, staying at home appears to work.
Many at home have fears and sadly some do shirk.
Again, all you guys, medical, police, and cleanup crew,
You are to be praised for all that you do.
Thank you, Thank you!

—April 8, 2020, 1:30 a.m.

THAT TOT

She likes to draw,
A smiling, round and happy face.
Biting her tongue, I saw,
Her struggling to put lines in place.

She prefers a "ballpoint pen,"
Asks for one, again and again.
Circles and lines she makes,
E'en tho her little hand shakes.

Three months older than two,
I'm amazed at what she can say and do.
The fridge, she can open wide,
Snoops around, select items from inside.

Her favorite saying, "I do it myself,"
Be it getting on and off a swing.
Reaching for something on a lower shelf,
Or helping her with a song to sing.

For a couple of hours, she takes a nap,
Usually from about one to three.
She may go from lap to lap,
'Til she gets as drowsy as can be.

Alone with her one day,
Something I'll remember to my end.
At the computer, I stopped when I heard her say,
"Paw Paw, play with me, you're my best friend."

—October 16, 1999

THE BOOR WAS A BORE

His attire is often seen as an eyesore.
Some bet that he's rotten to the core.
Minutes after he came thru the door,
The owner of the very classy store,
Realized that they had met once before.

Remembering him to be a very rude boor,
He later found him to also be a bore.
He told and retold, tales and tales of "folklore,"
Craving attention, hogging and hogging the floor.

Believing him was very hard to do,
As he retold and retold all that he'd been through.
His age would be three scores or maybe more,
For such "experiences" instead of only thirty-two.

His favorite haunts were London and Singapore,
But Paris, Rome, and Venice when he was blue.
A world traveler, to many cities he flew,
North, South, East and West, as the wind blew.

He'd sailed the waters of the oceans he knew.
Paddled piroques, kayaks, a raft and a canoe.
He hunted lions, tigers, eland and gnu,
Bear, deer, moose, cougar and caribou.

"Been there, done that," he'd always say,
No matter the subject, near or how far away.
He was the best, compared to the rest.
If you haven't met him yet, you will someday, I bet.

—October 28, 2007

THE BUFFET

He sat back and stared at every plate.
They were clean, everything he ate.
With both hands on his belly,
He moved it, it shook like jelly.
Three plates had been full,
With all the food they could hold.
He'd said he could eat a bull.
By golly, a truth had been told.

He certainly enjoyed the buffet.
He tasted nearly everything on display.
He tried four different kinds of meat,
Plus all the veggies he could eat.
A salad he had on the side.
Soup and gumbo, he also tried.
Shrimp, both boiled and fried,
Catfish fillet, he was not denied.

He washed it all down with three teas.
Gulping them was a breeze.
For dessert he slowed down a bit,
E'en tho the dessert bar was a hit.
Pie and ice cream was all he had.

"He said, I enjoyed it all, I'm glad,
But I don't want to overdo it, feel bad."
A small man, about five-foot-five,
It seems to take a lot for him to survive.

—September 9, 2001

THE BUG

The very elusive bug,
Hid under the "throw rug."
Sometimes it flew across the room,
Evading the fly swatter and broom.

It walks across the ceiling fine,
Tho erratic, never in a straight line.
If it suddenly lands in your hair,
You'll immediately know it's there.

When you least expect it'll bite,
I'm sure it does with all its might.
Does it bite out of hunger, fear or fright?
Or simply out of pure delight?

If it happens to get inside your ear,
The noise becomes unbearable, I fear.
If it bites, at the least, you'll twitch,
Or get a rash that'll make you itch.

The bug is determined to survive,
And so far, it's still very much alive.
It has dodged every single swat,
And has taken about all we've got.

As a last resort I'll have to spray,
If I'm to get rid of this bug today.
I'll spray and spray the room well.
I'll get it if my room he plans to dwell.

—August 29, 2001

THE CAJUN

The burly, husky, Cajun,
Had been irked, was raging.
Who had stolen his bateau?
He was furious, wanted to know.
He was sullen, in his piroque,
Mad as a big wild hog.
Suddenly, he spotted "T-Lou,"
Paddling his brand-new canoe.
They met on the banks of the bayou,
"Chewed the fat," as they say.
No help tho, so far today,
For the Cajun, from anyone he knew.
Down the bayou, he paddled some more,
Looking, searching, along the shore.
Somewhere near the bayou, it must be,
His ole bateau, most did agree.
He finally came upon an old shack,
That was built way out back.
Used by trappers, always on the go,
But of the bateau, nothing did they know.
Far from home, he arrived at a camp,
Slid his piroque, onto the ramp.
Calling out, with no answer in return,
He started to gather wood to burn.
Scrounging around, he noticed a shed.
Upon entering, he nearly dropped dead.
In plain view, was his bateau.
Beware, he knew, must leave, must go.

Straight for the Sheriff, he made haste.
There was no time to waste.
The "posse" sped to the site at night,
Caught the thieves, already in flight.
The Cajun said, "Merci beaucoup,"
Pointing to each, "you, you and you."
He drove his bateau, home on the bayou,
Glad 'twas over, the ordeal he'd been through!

—January 17, 1999

THE CORONAVIRUS, A NEW FOE

Here I sit, at home in self-isolation.
I don't leave the house to visit friend or relation.
My son goes to the grocery store for us,
Runs errands, etc., does chores without a fuss.

At my age and condition, I must stay at home.
There's no reason for me to roam and roam.
This coronavirus doesn't fool around.
Every day it claims more victims in town after town.

As more people are tested, the numbers really rise.
That many more test positive, is really no surprise.
More "self-isolation" people need to do.
Why take unnecessary changes when you don't need to?

We all need to "work together" to see this thing through.
Avoiding a crowd is definitely wise, it's really a must,
Even the ones that you dearly love, miss and trust.
The coronavirus is a new foe that is not biased at all.
If you have a poor immune system, you may take a fall.

More vulnerable are the very young and the very old.
It matters not if you're timid or very brave and bold.
Heed the advice of the wise and do what you're told.
You may get to live a long life with the fold.

—March 18, 2020, 6:00 p.m.

THE CRAWFISH

The crawfish is a feisty and tenacious creature,
Whose tasty tail is its great feature.
Found in a pond, stream, river, and bayou,
It can be a delicious dish for you.

In an etouffee, a bisque, gumbo, boiled or fried,
That all are delectable can't be denied.
Cousin to the lobster that many savor,
You be the judge after each dish is tried,
Then decide which one you favor.

An invite to a "crawfish boil,"
Is great, especially since "others" toil.
Everybody enjoys such an informal treat,
Where you're told, "Just come to eat."
'Tis an occasion for kith and kin to greet and meet,
Enjoy a magnificent feast that's hard to beat.

—March 2, 2008

THE FERAL CAT

The Feral Cat and her kittens are a joy to see,
But very skittish are they of thee and others, even me.
On my patio they now snooze near my door.
Years she's been around, never this close before.

When I go out, nearby she will remain.
When visitors come, swiftly she'll leave the scene.
For many years she's hunted in my nearby field.
We feed her and for her, many rodents the field does yield.

During those longs years, many kittens were born,
Usually three per litter, on my patio or my barn.
Some were adopted, others once full grown,
Stayed around a while, then they were gone.
Did they want to be alone and out on their own?

Here, like their mother, they hunted and were well-fed.
Did they fight and die, were captured or simply fled?
Of this litter of three, two kittens remain.
The mother is so old, she may never have kittens again.

Tho old she is still bold and a sight to behold.
Go near her kittens and she'll show her teeth and hiss.
At a distance eyeing her kittens, nothing does she miss.
Adopted were her kittens by my neighbor and her friend.
Hopefully, they'll live happily to the very end.

—May 31, 2018

THE FLIRT

Always, always he did flirt,
With anyone wearing a skirt.
Female in pants, that didn't hurt,
Especially with a partially open shirt.
Flirting, to him, had always been a game.
As such, 'twas never any shame.
'Twas only to see if it would open a door,
For conversation, not really to score.
A female with a cute face,
Caused him to pick up his pace.
For him 'twas never a disgrace,
As long as all was kept in its place.
If a gal had a cute face and great shape,
Awed, he may just stare and gape.
Perhaps the courage to just say "hello,"
Was as far as he, just then, could go.

Once he got to know her name,
He would likely forget it was a game.
Forgetting a dame's name was a shame.
Next he'd try to get a date,
But too often, he was too late.
That always seemed to be his fate.
Something he, at times, did hate.

He flirted and flirted until he was thirty.
Then he decided to settle down.
Married, he was often tired and dirty,

But lived peacefully in a quaint little town.
Going to work routinely, one day,
He stopped for coffee on his way.
A neighborhood lady, the nosy type,
Watched him flirt, with his hyped-up tripe.
Skipping another bite, she rushed to report,
To his wife, that he truly was a bad sort.
His wife, being a good sport, did retort,
"Tell me exactly what he did do."
The biddy stretched the truth, the shrew.
The wife, about his flirting, already knew,
Told her, "Surely you misconstrue,
But, I have a dog that chases cars, too."

—September 7, 2001

THE GANG

The punk and his rowdy pals,
Was really a sorry lot.
They harassed mostly the gals,
Every chance they got.
They walked fast, at almost a trot,
Moving about from spot to spot.
Huddled, they seemed to scheme and plot,
"Up to no good," some said, "that's what."
Trouble befell the group,
Early in their life, many times.
As teens, they were like a troop,
Were involved in many crimes.
When they became young men,
Gentlemanly they definitely were not.
Big troubles really did begin,
When they started using "pot."
With little reluctance and no chagrin,
Even realizing that it was a sin,
Their criminal activities increased.
Following the "wrong path" they couldn't win,
They would surely become deceased.
Their "path" would lead them to jail.
Sure enough, an attempted robbery did fail.
Very little money they got.
But a night cashier was fatally shot.
They were easily tracked and caught.
The judge could not be bought.
No one would come to post bail.

They were denied the clemency they sought.
They wailed, to no avail, remained in jail.
For mercy, they did plead.
They cried, asked forgiveness for their deed.
Admitted it was all about greed.
Hinted that they were on "speed."
"Counseling," they cried, we need.
"No, 'tis jail," the judge decreed.
A "long sentence" they all got,
Resulting from that dastardly plot.
How will life be inside that jail?
How often will they receive mail?
They will remain there, like it or not,
Getting "three hots and a cot."

—July 13, 2001

THE GP

Long ago, in the times of yore,
The Doctor came to your door.
He would make a "house call,"
Treated the family, one and all.

Doctors were more personal then,
Especially, in the small town.
They were often everybody's friend,
Every child, teenager, and adult around.

"House calls" Doctors no longer do make.
If sick, a trip you must take.
No matter how bad you are, or feel,
They no longer come to you to heal.

More Doctors are "specialists" today,
Treating a "specific problem" their way.
GPs still treat many ills and pain.
To specialize, longer they must train.

Through the years we've seen,
Many changes, in the medical scene.
But, overall we do get good care.
Now Hospitals and HMOs are everywhere.

—March 6, 1999

THE GUM TREE

The hazardous gum tree is gone today.
It cost $1,450 to cut and haul it away.
In the midst of an azalea bush it stood.
It and the azaleas did look very good,
But the tree leaned too close to the house,
And too much too often it did sway.
I was afraid it might crush us one day.
In doing so, it could fall on my bed.
'Twas better to chop the tree down instead.
This may prevent me from losing my head.
Other trees may also be in harm's way.
During a storm, they sway and sway.
If they crash and fall the wrong way,
It'll be bad luck for me that day.
Hopefully, luck will be with me during a storm.
No trees will crash causing any harm.
Time will come and go as in the past.
Life will be good and we will last.
I feel better now and I must say,
"Nervous was I, every time a storm came our way."

—Wednesday, October 23, 2019, 9:45 a.m.

THE INVESTOR

He owns stocks, many company shares,
In companies that sell trucks, cars, and vans,
In those that sell kitchen and other wares,
In some that make steel and tin cans.

He buys and sells shares almost every week.
Bargains, great deals, he always does seek.
Because the stock markets has its "ups and downs,"
Some days he smiles, other days he frowns.
It all depends when and if, he's buying or selling.
If he makes a profit or loss, he's not telling.

A Company once sent him "sample" paper tissue,
After he'd purchased a number of shares.
Tho free tissue was not really the issue,
He bought more, "he admires Companies who cares."
His extensive holdings are very diversified.
So many ventures he has tried.
He's been successful with land, oil and cattle,
Though he's lost and won, many a battle.

Anywhere he pleases now, he can come and go,
Fancy restaurant, stage or Broadway show.
Always real butter now, forget about the oleo.
He can travel, take a cruise, and visit Rome,
Go to the Far East, China, Japan or Borneo.
But alas, all is not well at home.

Success came at a very high price.
Some thought he was not very nice.
Consequently, eventually, he lost his mate.
Incompatibility, too oft, he was, too late.
Inconsiderate, seldom did he keep a date.
Divorce, was his ultimate fate.
Sadly, tho many times he'd make "a killing."
Somehow, now, his life is not very fulfilling.

—September 11, 2000

THE ISLAND

In a dingy, he struggled with the oar,
Trying to reach an island he'd seen before,
That he opt to hike on and explore,
Though it was a bit beyond the shore.

The people there he did adore,
Were friendly and good to the core.
Was it about the truth or folklore?
He wanted to learn much more.

Sun and waves left him tired and sore.
It was the skimpy clothes he wore,
Like the natives did in days of yore,
When it was all fun and games galore.

Living in the huts without a door,
Nothing but mats on a dirt floor.
On the beach, here everyone,
Run and have lots of fun in the sun.

Some lie down and bury their buns,
Mother, daughter, father and sons,
Sisters, brothers and many others.

On the beach are activities for each.
Lucky are the ones that the beach,
Is nearby, well within easy reach.

THE KITE

Out in the pasture with his kite,
The lad ran will all his might.
Desperately trying to make it fly,
It wouldn't stay up, he wondered why.

Too long, perhaps was the tail.
He tried again, but it did fail.
He made it a bit shorter still,
Then ran longer towards the hill.

Deciding to wait for a breeze,
He went inside, got an orange to squeeze.
May as well, he thought, eat a bite,
Wait 'till the wind appeared on the site.

Before long, a breeze did blow.
From where, he didn't really know.
'Twas breezy now, just about right,
To get his kite up for a long flight.

The kite went up with little ease,
Thanks to the soft, gentle breeze.
Up, Up, towards the sky,
It went 'till it was real high.

The lad was elated, very glad.
'Twas fun today, that he had had.
The kite flew 'till out of string,
Finally coming down in a distant spring.

—January 27, 2000

THE LADY

He offered to buy her favorite drink.
She replied, "Let me think.
Brandy is dandy and handy.
It's so, 'liquor is quicker' some find,
But I won't pine, wine will be fine.
It's divine and I won't mind,
Provided you take me out to dine."
Was it just a ploy,
She was using on this lovelorn boy?
Playing with him like a toy,
Was it what she really did enjoy?
Perhaps she was just being nice.
For the meal, he'd pay the price.
Or would she lure and entice
Him, using some charming device?
She was shrewd, tho not lewd,
Informed, endowed, well adorned.
Well-mannered, not crude,
Not naïve, rude or a prude.
After dinner, he took her to her door,
Kissed her hand, not her cheek.
Politely, as he'd done before,
Trying not to appear meek,
He asked for a date the next week.
She said yes, without any protest,
Agreed to another date.
He could then discuss and debate,
Without any fuss, what she may detest.

On their scheduled date,
They did freely communicate.
He found her to be truly, a lady,
Detecting nothing about her shady.
Now would they date again,
Would a romance begin?
Of this he had no doubt.
Elated, he did shout, would never again pout.
"While whiskey makes me frisky, 'tis risky."

—August 19, 1999

THE MASK

Today, when in public you do appear,
"Face Covering" is now proper gear.
Because of COVID-19, a "Face Mask,"
'Tis not much to ask, a small task.

It's recommended to be carried and used.
Without one, admittance may be refused,
In many places, no one is excused.
Few, if any, are amused and some may be confused.

The Mask must cover the mouth and nose.
A shield for the eyes, some also propose.
All this makes good sense, I suppose,
But where are they obtained, who knows?

People are still dying, every, every day,
No matter what they try the Virus won't go away.
Some hope and pray that the summer heat,
Will do wonders and the CORONAVIRUS beat.

To develop vaccines, people are hard at work.
Anxious to save lives, they do not shirk.
Meantime, be smart and do your part.
Try your best and strive to stay healthy and alive.
Working together, more people may survive.

—May 13, 2020

THE MOLE

The lone, energetic mole,
Burrowed hole after hole after hole.
Tunnels he made between each,
So that them, he could easily reach.

Underground he stayed most all the day,
Eating insects he met along the way.
Well adapted to the dark,
He comes and goes, leaving his mark.

Was this mole, young or old,
Very energetic, or simply very bold?
Was he tirelessly looking for a mate,
Or seeking more insects, like the ones he ate?

Seldom does he venture above ground,
Tho his tunnels, are at times, easily found.
Do cats mistake him for a mouse,
Who somehow, got out of the house?

He must be wary of the cat, this date,
Who may detect, where he's at, and wait.
If he's not careful, he'll meet his fate.
An agile cat, is a threat, at any rate.

—October 29, 1999

THE NEOPHYTE

Sobbing and sobbing, again and again,
Like a perpetual crying machine.
Why she couldn't refrain.
Desperately, she tried to explain.
Some time ago, on an airplane,
While on a trip to tour parts of Spain,
She met a handsome, blue-eyed, young swain.
He was sharply dressed, very neat and very clean.
As they deplaned in a torrential rain,
She got wet, was embarrassed, but suffered no pain.
She introduced herself as "Elaine,"
Daughter of Ian McBain and his wife Lorraine,
Farmers, who cultivated lots of sugarcane.
He helped her and with her boarded a train,
Which took them over plain after plain,
To her destination with a strange terrain.
Tho reared in Spain, he did profess and proclaim,
That he was an Irishman, named Shayne McCain.
She admitted she'd never been to "lover's lane."
Like a swan on her very first flight,
Who then spread her wings with much delight,
For this neophyte, it was love at first sight.
She loved him with delight, night after night.
She did so knowing that it was not right.
Not because of his might nor her fright,
But because of love, she described her plight.
After he had his fun, the son of a gun,
Went "on the run" and her he did shun.

Now he looked at her with disgust and disdain.
Again the train took him over plain after plain.
Now she wished she had used her brain.
She saw him no more, never again.
A mystery, his whereabouts to this day, remain.

—June 7, 2015

THE NOSE

There are, I do suppose,
Things we can do about our nose.
Some opt for a "nose job,"
To look better than "a slob."

If it's too long, with a crook,
Surgery can change this unwanted look.
Being too big and much too flat,
Surgery again, can change all that.

Women may want a nose that is petite,
To look more, like the chic elite.
A nose that's small, nice and slim,
On a face, that's cute, petite and trim.

Too long a nose, with a slight bump,
Makes one feel down in the dump.
But, as you may already know,
If you lie, it will continue to grow.

A scar across my nose, came to be,
By an accident, that happened at sea.
For nearly fifty years, it's been with me,
And I'll take it to my grave, you see.

This, though, bothers me not,
For it's the only nose that I've got.
There are other things I'd prefer to correct,
But then, at my age, what the heck.

—October 15, 1999

THE NURSE

The dedicated, helpful nurse,
Makes the patient feel better, not worse.
Many things, they need not rehearse.
They don't see their job as being a curse.

A very special person, indeed,
Who places first, their patients need.
Tho perhaps tired and very weary,
Performs a job that may be sad and dreary.

A nurse, be they female or male,
Must be smart and overcome distraction.
They do better if they're hearty and hale,
Caring for the sick with compassion.

The patient may see the nurse more,
Than the doctor they may adore.
Daily care, a nurse may give,
When one is hospitalized, to live.

Years ago, perhaps a nurse did less.
They were more of an assistant, I guess.
Today it is definitely not so.
A highly skilled medical professional,
Is the highly educated nurse we know.

Admired is the nurse,
That puts the patient's need first.
Dedicated to give the best of care,
Not going to work "just to be there."
Not regarding the job only as "fare,"
To simply "fatten their purse."

—March 4, 1999

THE OLE INDIAN

It was a pitiful sight to see,
This Ole Indian, inside his tepee,
Lying down on his "bear rug,"
Barely able to sigh and shrug.

His pipe of wood, he could barely smoke.
Evidently, he'd had a stroke.
He was awfully frail and weak.
No longer was he able to speak.

Having recently lost his mate,
It was now surely sealed, his fate.
Her body was still on the rack,
Out in the snow.
Yet to see her, he was flat on his back,
Impossible for him to go.

His pony was untied, turned loose.
For it, he no longer had any use.
He was such a pretty pony, a paint.
But no longer could he ride, too faint.

Unable to arise, though he does try,
Soon he'd be left in the snow to die.
'Tis the way it's been done for years.
They go willingly, without fear or tears.

—February 2, 1999

THE PAIR

They are such a lovely pair.
He's so manly and she's so fair.
He's nearly bald, she has silver hair,
But they don't mind, don't really care.

They met a short time ago,
Have since then, been a steady duo,
He takes her where she wants to go,
As long as it's near and he feels oh, so, so.

They take strolls into the park,
During the day, but not after dark.
They may dine out, go to a show,
Occasionally, taking things slow.

Is it love, or are they just pals?
Is it different for guys than gals?
Each other's company they now keep.
But just what is it that they both seek?

For many years, each had a mate,
So they felt a bit strange, on their first date.
Now, what is to be their fate?
Happiness they hope, at any rate.

Youngsters, they surely are not.
How much time, have they really got?
They ask themselves this, day after day.
Still, how long can they go on, this way?

He is eighty-six, she's eighty-five.
They both feel very much alive.
Children, neither have, they are alone,
So they'll do "the best of it" before they're gone.

—November 8, 1999

THE PARK

Lights light up the park.
Now people don't stumble in the dark.
Some people who jog at night,
Say that with lights they have less fright.

Many just sit on a park bench,
To enjoy the peace and quiet.
A lone spot without any stench,
Serves them well, in fact, just right.

People will stroll with their dog.
Let them "use" any ole log.
Dogs usually stay near their master.
On a leash, they can't go much faster.

People who accompany a pet pig,
Are careful not to let them dig.
Small "potbellied pigs" that people tame,
Enjoy the park where they play a game.

Horses, at the park, people ride,
Usually by twos, side by side,
They trot along with pride.
Bikers may challenge them,
For the "right of way,"
A very foolish thought, I'd say.

Always on the lookout for sneaky freaks,
People jump when they hear creaky squeaks.
They're aware that danger lurks there.
They heed the animals who sniff the air.

—September 8, 2001

THE ROUTINE

Every morning, the more I linger,
The more I hate to prick my finger.
A diabetic, I must check my glucose.
I know that I must, but often I'm a bit morose.

Even though very sharp is my lancet.
After many years, I still cringe, you bet.
It really doesn't hurt that bad,
Yet, when it's over, I'm very glad.

I check my blood glucose, very close, every day.
It's a daily routine, I must say.
I just need to know that number,
Good or bad, whether I'm glad or sad,
Especially after a long night of slumber.

Carbohydrates and sweets, I eat sparingly.
Occasionally though, I splurge daringly.
The next day, if things go awry,
I compensate, try my best not to cry.

My kidneys, because of diabetes, are affected.
It just happened, apparently 'tis nothing I neglected.
Now the "numbers" are dangerously low.
What to do? I just don't really know.
I'll just follow my doctor's advice and take it slow.

—July 19, 2016, 2:39 a.m.

THE TREK WEST

Many Pioneers, after the great Civil War,
Decided to go west, although it was very far.
Most were veterans starting a new life, no matter the strife.
Traveling in covered wagons, struggling at best,
Every family on the wagon train, was on a quest.
The journey would prove to be quite a test.

Crossing prairies, plains, desert, rivers and streams,
Oxen, mules and horses pulled wagons, many teams.
Over mountains and valleys, even when the weather was extreme.
Blizzard with snow, lightning, thunder and rain,
Strained every nerve, for the people on the wagon train.
From starvation some died, never to roam again.

Always pressed for time, forever they were hurried.
When people perished, immediately they were buried.
Wagons were repaired and couples paired and married.
Indians too, were fought along the way.
Many walked longer than they rode, many a day.

Babies were born, people got tired and worn.
If someone on the train committed a crime,
The Wagon Master swiftly presided at the trial, every time.
After all, it's a long trek, by heck.
Everyone who signed up, risked their neck.
Because of Pioneer's wit and grit, our nation is greater today.
You might even say that "they led the way."

—Saturday, November 2, 2019, midnight

THEY ARE GONE

She was my true love,
The one that I always did adore.
Now she's gone to Heaven above.
I love and miss her, more and more.

Sixty-three years, eight months and eleven days,
We were married and four children she bore.
Our life was normal in many ways.
It's hard to believe that she's not here anymore.

Her parents and siblings, she did outlive.
A beautiful family, parents and children four.
So much love and talents they had to give.
The good times with them are no more.

Here I am and all my in-laws are gone.
I was older than my wife and her siblings.
That they're gone hurts to the core.
Sometimes, in a crowd, I feel all alone.
I'm usually the oldest and don't "fit in" anymore.

At times it's hard to endure.
The painful memories, and there is no cure.
I wonder every day "what's in store."
But I know it won't be the same anymore.

Mother Nature is fair and very wise.
Death will eventually knock on my door.
Therefore, it comes as no surprise.
I love them and mourn them, but I'm not sore.
They will remain in my heart forevermore.

—September 19, 2017

THINGS I MISS

'Tis the "female touch" that I really miss,
Especially the old "hug and kiss."
Someone to scratch my itching back,
Is another thing that I also lack.

Clipping my toenails, I can no longer do.
A Mate would be very handy for that, too.
On the patio in a chair to trim my hair,
Would prove to me that a partner did care.
For many years, to help me, my wife was there.

Besides cleaning the house and doing the cooking,
She was always "well-dressed and good-looking."
Handling the money, she bought nice clothes and shoes.
I think that helped her from having the blues.

It's been over six years now without a mate,
Yet, I've not tried or considered trying to date.
I think that now I'm too old and it's too late,
I would be too much of a burden for any woman to take.

Pills for this, capsules for that, all I can do is chat.
Cream for pain while I'm in my chair I got,
For my knees where the pain is usually at.
Special tablets I take daily for the gout.
This I do, without fail, every day,
Yet, some of the pain, never goes away.

—April 9, 2020, 2:30 a.m.

THRILLS FROM WILL

It's pure folly to think that Holly,
Would deem it jolly to ride the trolley.
Up the steep hill, just to visit Will.
He cared more for Jill from the mill.

Yet, Will's greatest thrill was once Lil.
Of course, Lil always paid the bill.
For this, would Holly just stand still?
Did she give Will a cold shoulder, the chill?

Is Will in for a fall, from a boulder, a bad spill?
Perhaps Will gives Jill the biggest thrill.
Wooing women is Will's greatest skill,
That he remains very good at still.
He really, really knows the drill.

When he has the time to kill,
Will loves to grill without any frills,
Plenty of good food that fits the bill,
Where one and all can eat and drink their fill.

—June 2016

TINY SPIDER

About an inch above my bathroom floor,
A tiny, tiny spider, seems suspended in air.
It's maybe half a foot from the door.
I can't see the web, but I know it's there.

Only with my glasses on, it's legs I can see.
It seems smaller than a grain of rice, to me.
What does it eat to live, perhaps a mite,
Or any really minute insect that comes in sight?
The web may snare wee ones in flight.

So small, just to survive is quite a feat.
The nearly invisible web on site, is very neat.
To snare prey, its method must be unique.
Very still it stays, until it snares what it did seek.

Being so small, danger must be all around.
Surely, how it survives must be profound.
So fascinating is it, I hate to be the cause of its demise.
But it chose my bathroom to live in and that was unwise.
Other people using my bathroom may not like a surprise,
Even though it may be more beneficial than they realize.

—Monday, November 4, 2019, 11:00 p.m.

TOO LONG I SIT

Too long I sit in my Lounge Chair.
It's very tough on my poor derriere.
Day in, day out, I just sit and sit,
Because I can walk or stand, just a bit.

It's hard to get comfortable these days,
Even though I've tried many, many ways.
My butt gets sore from sitting down.
I try hard to smile instead of frown.

Lying in bed, I just cannot move around.
When I do go to sleep, it is not very sound.
It's been a while since I've walked on the ground.
Now "self-quarantined" I stay indoors at home.
Because of COVID-19, we're told not to roam.

To contain CORONAVIRUS, precautions we must take.
Disobeying orders could be a grave mistake.
No longer can we hug and kiss or handshake.
A distance of six feet from others we must keep.
We follow the crowd, not unlike some sheep.

Wearing a mask while shopping or trips we make.
To protect others is good advice that we should take.
Yes, too long I sit in my Lounge Chair.
Now too long also, on my head, is my hair.

—April 11, 2020, 1:40 a.m.

TRAPPERS WITH GUTS

Can we really imagine how they felt,
Trapping beavers for their pelt?
With a musket on their shoulder,
And an ax and knife on their belt,
They feared no foe, no falling boulder,
Braved the frigid weather that nature dealt.

In the mountains, mostly living alone,
They had their way, answered to no one.
Days into weeks into months they were gone,
Surviving by their grit and brawn.
Up and about often before dawn,
Every day they made their rounds,
Checking their traps in streams and ponds.
Facing adversities, they stood their ground.

These grizzly adventurers were a breed,
Who trapped to survive, not for the greed.
Depending on the land for their needs,
They used pack animals more than fancy steeds.
They hunted for meat and foraged for berries and nuts.
Their crude shelters were merely huts.
Yes, these "loners" had plenty of "guts."

—January 26, 2007

TWO DOGS

Two dogs appeared on Christmas Day.
One was short and long-eared,
The other very tall and very gray.
Had they come to visit or to stay?
They were not menacing, no reason to be feared.

That they were hungry, we understood.
After eating turkey, they devoured the cat's food.
Both seemed a bit skittish and shy.
We were strange to them, perhaps that's why.

All the food they ate, they ate real quick,
We hoped it was OK, they wouldn't get sick.
We tried our best to be a good friend,
But failed the test, to our chagrin.

After the feast, they simply went away,
No thanks from the beasts.
They had their way, decided not to stay.
To them it was just another lucky day.

—Rudolph Ray and Kayla Porche, December 1996

TWO IN THE MORN

My mind is alert, 'tis two in the morn.
Though wide awake, my body is tired and worn.
Woe is me, I'm in a pickle, I'm torn,
Between watching TV or going to bed.
But then, why worry, I'll just rest my head.

My body, too, in a recliner chair,
Watch TV while I read or write and snooze there…
Then, when truly sleepy, hit the hay,
Whether three, four or five a.m., it's okay.

Then if I choose to sleep most of the day,
Who's to argue, who's to say
If it's right or wrong, especially on a rainy day?
Retirement is not the same for all.
Some enjoy a game, some dancing at a ball.

Many like to plant a garden, work with the soil.
A few see "work" only as a struggle, toil.
Several time a week, some go out to eat.
Occasionally dining out, for others is a treat.
For me, home-cooked meals are hard to beat.

Cruises, sightseeing, camping and travel,
Some embrace, to enjoy, relax and unravel.
A leisurely, comfortable and happy long life,
Is the goal for which we toil and overcome strife.

—January 2008

TWO OF EACH

My two ears served me well for years,
But now, be it very far or very near,
Whether out of curiosity or fear,
I find that I can hardly hear.

Two eyes as blue as the blue skies,
Enable me to read day and night.
Glasses now help my weary eyes.
I'd be lost without my eyesight.

Hands and arms, oh yes, two of each,
To grab and hold anything within my reach.
The loss of one or the other,
Would so change my life, oh brother!

Two legs, two knees and two feet,
Enable me to walk on the road or street.
My hips, knees, and ankles you see,
Are joints, that at my age, could well be,
The cause of very much pain for me.

Forty years I smoked cigarettes and don't know,
If nicotine scarred my two lungs severely.
I quit smoking thirty-two years ago.
Will I suffer with COPD yearly?

My two kidneys are gradually failing.
If the numbers suddenly decreased,
I may feel like crying or even wailing,
Because, by then, I'd soon be deceased.

—2017

WATCHING TV

In my Recliner, I sit and I doze.
Occasionally I rub my eyes and nose.
The news is on and it's the same old, same old.
Every channel, they repeat what they were told.

Commercials take as much time as the news.
Boring it gets, therefore sometimes I just snooze.
Politics seem to dominate the airwaves.
I can't distinguish the "knights from the knaves."

People are killing people here and there.
Violence occurs daily everywhere.
Nowhere are people safe from harm today,
Sad to say, not even in the good ole USA.

Unstable and mentally ill, some killers must be.
Apparently 'tis so, from what I see.
What can be done? What will be done?
Many would like to know, including me.
I guess I'll just have to watch more TV.

—May 10, 2016

WEDDING VOWS

"It's just a piece of paper," some people may say.
About their marriage license, today this may hold sway.
To too many, "until death do us part,"
Means just until I've had a change of heart.
Who is to blame when married couples split?
Is it money or honey, was one bit or hit?
Did love and passion just fade away?
Who insisted on having their way?
Many hearts are broken, day after day.
Especially children who have no say.
Vows to some mean nothing, they just don't care.
Some, though married, dare to have an affair.
Then it's very difficult to clear the air.
Be it husband or wife, the other may lead a sad life.
A cheater or beater causes a spouse much strife.
Some will wait until their children are grown to divorce.
Others moan and grown then very early change course.
A few forget about "to love and to hold."
They don't argue or shout, are bold and leave their spouse cold,
Gone without a "goodbye," never to return.
With a sigh, the spouse thinks, "What a
louse" and does a slow burn.
Not knowing the fate of the mate, love may turn to hate.
What could I have done, they debate, but it's now too late.
All of us that "death did us part," dearly miss our "sweetheart."

—May 30, 2018

WHAT A PAST

With a sudden blast from the past,
She recalled the "good life" that didn't last.
It was in Paris, France on a Grand Tour,
That she met her Swain, on the train.
When he whispered "Ma Cherie, c'est lamour."
She fell hard, that's for sure.

Promising her good fortune and fame,
He encouraged her to follow her dream.
"In the crowd," she used heroin and cocaine.
Life seemed beautiful, although a bit insane.

Remembering how easily she was impressed,
Then for him, how often she had undressed.
For a while, she admired how well she progressed.
When he lost interest in her she became distressed.

All her love and joyous feelings were suppressed.
Suddenly, she felt all alone and very depressed.
Realizing that she must act and act fast,
Lest for long, she wouldn't last.

She turned her life around 360 degrees.
From then on, living the good life was a breeze.
Now she can enjoy the forest and the trees.

—July 7, 2016

WHAT DO YOU THINK?

Many think of the "high cost of living" and sigh.
Me thinks the problem is the "cost of living high."
In many households today, both husband and wife,
Have a vehicle, a cell phone, a job and strife.

Few do save, live from payday to payday.
With car notes, house notes, rent and utilities to pay,
Little money is left for food, clothing and health care.
Yet, many go to ball games, fests, concerts and a fair.

They entertain themselves and try to enjoy life.
Today, many husbands cook more than their wife.
Life is tough and struggle many do.
Others fall apart, sadly it's more than just a few.

Some may falter and turn to drink,
Trying to drown their troubles and sorrow.
But what happens, I do think,
They irrigate them and deeper their troubles get.
Debts increase and loans they can no longer borrow.

Some turn to drugs and their obligations are no longer met.
With the haze they can see no tomorrow.
It's the beginning of the end.
Some may lose it all, even very friend.

—April 12, 2017

WHAT TO DO FOR FUN

When I need a "walker" just to walk,
It's certain that I cannot run.
No matter how much I wish to squawk,
Most of the time alone, I seldom talk.
Sitting too long is definitely not fun.
Vitamin D, I get less from the sun.

Medication limits my time in the sunshine,
But I don't want to sit around all day and pine.
Occasionally, with relatives, going out to dine,
I enjoy, if I'm feeling okay, that's well and fine.

Going to a concert, I won't exert myself, that's out.
I don't like the music and too many fans scream and shout.
Fancy dancing, seems to me, is just jumping and prancing.
To have fun, I need to seek where it only takes one,
Before I get too weak, since I'm going on ninety-one.

Going to a theater, a movie to see,
I don't care for, It's just not for me.
I'll wait until the movie is shown on TV.

As for me, it's still fun to read and write.
I do one or both, almost every night.
And now I'll just say, "Good night,
Sleep right and hope that tomorrow is bright."

—October 29, 2019, 11:00 p.m.

WHAT, WHAT

It's sad, the things that I forget.
Just as bad, is how clumsy I get.
My coordination, at times, is lacking.
Are these signals that my brain isn't tracking?
Does it get worse as I age? You bet.

Ofttimes it's difficult to think.
Does my brain, like my bones, shrink?
Me thinks it's so, it's really so.
Also gone is my "get up and go."
Too, my eyes just blink instead of wink.

Some say that age is just a frame of mind.
Perhaps, they are just nice, being kind.
They may be naive or just do not know,
That physical disabilities makes us slow.
Other distractions they may find.

Aches and pains seem to never go away.
They remain with me, day after day after day.
With them I try and try and try to abide.
I continue to hope and pray they'll subside.
Even with medication, pains have their way.
They are stubborn and determined to stay.

With certainty, we'll live until we die.
Meanwhile, will we laugh more or cry?
Will our years be "golden or like iron, rust"?

Who will remain that we can really trust,
Until we expire and return to dust?
We all wish for a happy end in the "by and by."
As for now, the necessities of life are a must.

—February 24, 2010

WHEN IT RAINS

The house seems smaller, when it rains.
The grass grows taller, as soon as the water drains.
Cooped inside, children may play.
Small ones hide, when not in the way.

Mom must abide, with them all day,
Even as older ones, have their say.
Colors and a coloring book, for some, all it took.
Content, to "just do their thing,"
Some are just happy to read or sing.

All day, many want to just watch TV,
No matter what's aired for them to see.
Sesame street, Futurama and cartoons,
Power Puff Girls, Teen Titans and Looney Tunes.

Teens play music very, very loud,
As much at home as in any crowd.
Recognizing Artist and song makes them proud.
The loudness makes Mom yell out loud.

Yes, when it rains, the household may change.
More peace of mind, Mom surely gains,
When children are safe at home, out of range.
Later in life the house gets roomier,
But for some alone it's also a lot gloomier.

—April 25, 2004

WHY CRY?

A Talk Show Host, sobbing and sobbing on TV,
For her audience and all the world to see.
Controversial, surely it must be.
Uncontrollably, she shed more than a tear,
Over a dog that she had once held dear.

It was not over what she did fear,
But over a "ruling" that she did hear.
Although she broke an agreement, they say,
By insisting on "having her own way,"
When she decided to "give the dog away."

But what about the "tearful display"?
Was it staged and if so, why?
Why let the nation, see her cry?
It was taped, so why not edit out the crying?

By crying, for sympathy was she really trying?
That must be it, there is no denying.
A big question does remain.
By crying, what did she hope to gain?
To me, things on TV don't always appear sane.
Many things appear worthless or vain.

—October 28, 2007

WHY WORRY?

We're often told "worry not,"
No matter the ills or ails you've got.
Don't worry, but 'tis OK to concern,
Worry or concern, how do you discern?
Trials and tribulations, we ofttimes face.
It's common occurrences in the Human Race.
The trick is solving them without disgrace.
Considerations taken must be time and place.
Circumstances and events are considerations, too,
But then, most people do what they must do.
Worry does seem to be a waste of time,
Especially when there's no reason or rhyme.
Helplessness is an uncomfortable feeling.
Disillusionment may cause some reeling.
Some "worry warts" worry about every little thing.
No matter how big or small, it matters not at all.
They can't help themselves, perhaps 'tis their downfall.
In a state of anxiety they seem to cling to something,
Even though they offer no solution, nothing.
It hurts my pride when the glide in my stride,
Diminished 'till it was no more, it was too sore.
It was no joke, that I had become a "slowpoke."
No longer agile, every once in a while,
I'm put to the test and must stop to rest.
My mind is aware that my bones can't bear,
The strain of stress when under much duress.

—2019

590

WIDE AWAKE

Many nights I lie in bed wide awake.
Why can't I sleep, for "Pete's sake"?
I count sheep after sheep, until I tire.
It's difficult to sleep, no matter when I retire.

When I finally fall asleep and snore,
I may sleep 7 to 10 hours or maybe more.
Then, when I awake, my joints are achy and sore.
Two or three hours later, I'm drowsy encore.

Some of my medicine may be to blame.
So many I take, it's a darn shame.
If they keep me alive, I shouldn't complain.
Quit the medicine, and I may become lame.

To bed late, up late, eat, read and watch TV,
Write poetry when there is nothing I care to see.
Read "trash mail," "good mail," and a magazine or two.
Everything is routine, is it that way with you?

It's better to do something when able, to do,
Than to just sit around, mope and be blue.
So when I feel the urge to complain and gripe,
I write a poem, then get on the computer and type.

—March 2017

WILDLIFE

A little wild bunny rabbit one day,
Was near my driveway at midday.
Was he lonely, did he want to play?
He looked happy, did not run away.

Slowly he hopped across my yard,
To hide, he wasn't trying very hard.
Perhaps he was lost, was not a stray.
Around my place, he knew his way.

Into the field, he eventually did go.
Taking his time, he went there slow.
He certainly was putting on a show.
Was his nest in there? I don't know.

Soon I spied a neighbor's cat.
Had he mistaken the bunny for a rat?
The cat knew where the bunny was at.
My field is full of rabbits, mice and rats.
More so, since I no longer see feral cats.

Squirrels, I see scampering from tree to tree.
Without cats and dogs, they enjoy being free.
There's lots of acorns under the oaks, I see.
Next spring, how many squirrels will there be?

—Sunday, October 20, 2019

YARD WORK

Yard work, a pleasure or hard work?
That it can be laborious, no one denies.
One may be considered a fool or a jerk.
Yet, it can be healthy and enjoyable, if one tries.
But, if it becomes a chore, one may shirk.

Invigorating, gardening can also be,
Rewarding and pleasant, too, you'll see.
Fresh vegetables, healthy, and tasty,
Are best eaten ripe, don't be hasty.
It feels great to grow your own.
'Tis one of great pleasures known.
Many fruits and vegetables can be "homegrown."
Tomatoes, potatoes, beans, peppers, and peas,
Can be grown and harvested with relative ease.
Okra, corn, cucumbers, melons, and greens, too,
Are equally as satisfying and good for you.

Grow your own, if you have the space.
Spend less time grocery shopping, in the rat race.
You'll save money and when at the table,
Be grateful for the "bounty" when saying "grace."
'Tis true, of course, if you're willing and able.

—RRP, July 2008

YEAR OUT, YEAR IN

Another year came and went.
Much the same, our time was spent.
Every fete was a special event.
Next month, Mardi Gras, then lent.

Higher prices, much to our lament,
Takes all we earn, every dollar, every cent.
Gas now cost more than ever.
When will it drop again? Perhaps never.

That the cost of much, will continue to rise,
Is expected, comes as no surprise.
A college degree is harder to get.
As tuition keeps rising, students get deeper in debt.

Many hospital beds are not in use,
Because the need for medical personnel is not met.
A shortage of nurses, etc., is the excuse.
Many government programs seem to flop.
Some get worse, when will it stop?

Too many politicos play the "blame game,"
Yet, in office they remain, what a shame.
"Change, a change" is an often heard refrain,
From "lawmakers" that are much to blame.
If they win to lead, what will the people gain?

Tourism brings millions to some city.
Elation is seen in every restaurant, bar and hotel.
The infusion of money spent, not out of pity,
Help some coffers, but which coffers, does anyone tell?

This New Year, what will it bring?
Will there be "Peace on Earth," like we sing?
It would be a change, a wonderful thing.

—January 5, 2008

YELLING

Yelling in front of children is an awful act!
Children are told to behave or else get a whack.
The kids are in awe, they are taken aback.
Surely most of us are sane, not rabid.
Then yelling must only be a very bad habit.

Is that what we do to the ones we love most?
Some are so scared you would think they saw a ghost.
This is not right, our ways at times are too mean.
Let's amend our thoughts, our acts we must clean.

Yelling at parents, a thing once unheard,
Now is too common, this is absurd.
"Honor thy Father and Mother," we are told.
Yelling at them, can you imagine some being so bold?

Sibling rivalry we say, yelling by Sister or Brother,
But it's terribly wrong, yelling at each other.
Some children are unruly, truly that's obvious to all.
Some are mischievous, just want to have a ball.

Who sets the example, is where some disagree.
Should it be school or home? You or me?
I think all of the above, and don't forget the church.
Too many children feel abandoned, left in the lurch.
A good example to set, is not to yell.
Instead be a good listener, hear what they have to tell.

—May 18, 2020

ABOUT THE AUTHOR

Ray was a ninety-one-year-old Cajun who spoke French before he spoke English, the third of twelve children, army veteran, widowed father of four children, grandfather of seven children, great-grandfather of ten children, and great-great-grandfather of one child. He had the kindest heart and always had a joke for everyone and everything! Ray enjoyed writing poems for family and friends for every occasion. He was lucid, of great intelligence (finished high school at sixteen years old), had a warm smile, a jolly laugh, and was loved by all who knew him. This book is his legacy for loved ones.

CPSIA information can be obtained
at www.ICGtesting.com
Printed in the USA
LVHW030354121121
702953LV00001B/8